UNFORGOTTEN YEARS

by

Samuel Hosain Lamarti

British Library Cataloguing in Publication Data:
a catalogue record for this publication
is available from the British Library

ISBN   978-1-871828-95-5

Typeset in 11pt Minion Pro at Haddington, Scotland

Printing and cover design by
West Port Print and Design, St Andrews

Published with assistance from
the Drummond Trust,
3 Pitt Terrace, Stirling

CONTENTS

PREFACE

Horace, the Roman poet, once advised all authors to keep what they had written for nine years before they published it. It is advice which prolific writers can hardly welcome. It took me nearly twelve years to complete my autobiography. Had I followed Horace's advice, it might easily have taken over two decades to publish it. Obviously, that would not have been reasonably possible.

The reason for taking such a long time was that I had kept no diary or journal of any kind. Had I done so this book may well have been published much earlier. In this case, I had no choice but to embarked on writing my story with complete reliance on memory. Such an adventure by one in his three score years and ten "might be a miracle second only to that of the crossing of the Red Sea!", as a colleague jokingly suggested. Fortunately, ever since my childhood I have gratefully been noted for strength of memory. I recall noticing a statement somewhere which read, "Memory is history recorded in our brains". So, in the absence of a diary the alternative was the use of memory. After all, as Oscar Wilde put it, "Memory is the diary that we all carry with us".

The focus in this book is on those relevant milestones in my journey to the fold of Christ and subsequent events. That journey and its aftermath was full of many battles and many victories, as exemplified in our Lord's word to His disciples, *"In this world you will have trouble. But take heart! I have overcome the world"* (Jn. 16:33 NIV). Moreover, this book is not cast into a polemical mould. Neither my former faith is disparaged nor its founder deprecated. I have been careful *"to speak evil of no one"* (Tit. 3:2 RSV). Rather, I remain appreciative of certain aspects of Islamic theology that have helped to clarify some grey issues, and finally facilitate my path to Christ.

Samuel Hosain Lamarti
April 2017

INTRODUCTION

Sam Hosain Lamarti and I were students at Trinity College in the mid-1970s, but the journeys that took us there could not have been more different. Mine was as conventional and as ordinary as it gets, but Sam's was a road rarely travelled and his extraordinary journey is articulated with both innocence and affection in the first half of this autobiography.

In the words of a Moroccan proverb he describes the memory of his home town of Larache in Spanish Morocco as, "two places one would hardly ever forget – the place of his greatest enjoyment, and the place of his greatest hardship". The reader will not take long to discover how this proverb describes Sam's early life.

I wish I had known Sam better in those early Trinity College days; reading his story now, I have gained insights into how lives are shaped by Islamic teaching and culture which would have been good for me to have understood four decades ago. I might draw down some different lessons and conclusions from those which overlay this book, but I would have been better equipped to live in today's multi-cultural society, better able to welcome the stranger and less judgemental of those whose background and experience are very different from mine.

Sam's mother was only 24 when she died. He describes a distant relationship with his father and, perhaps most poignantly of all, he describes the influence of the missionary doctor responsible for his recovery from the depression and anxiety he suffered as a small boy following his mother's death. No doubt Dr Rigby prescribed love and care alongside any medicine that he might have used; Sam describes a vivid memory of being held in the Doctor's arms and feeling "some sort of peace"; remarkably this was the first stop on the journey that would lead him to a ministry in the Church of Scotland. One way or another there are always significant early life experiences which shape and form young minds – in Sam's case it would be impossible to underestimate the influence of the Mission House and the missionary doctor. In contrast with his splintered family life, and with the stern influence of his grandfather, the Mission House was safe, secure and loving. Throughout his school and seminary days he continued to be a regular visitor there.

At Qur'anic high school Sam learned by heart the 114 Suras of the Qur'an and a natural progression was to take his place in the Islamic Seminary where the meaning of the Qur'an would be overlaid on the words that he had learned by rote. This is where Sam's rigorous and enquiring mind leads him to take issue with the lessons being taught. He brings his close reason to bear on the Qur'anic idea of 'Tahrif' wherein the scriptures of the Jewish and Christian faiths are regarded as having been subject to falsification. This stretch of the book is not only biographical; it is also academic and apologetic. Sam's forensic examination of 'Tahrif' is one part of his journey from the faith of his birth to his embrace of the Christian faith. This is one strand in Sam's journey; the other is his discovery of the "glorious personality of Jesus and the unfathomable love of God revealed in Him". This is a description of the foundation upon which Sam's new found faith was built and upon which that faith has been sustained through hardship and testing, joy and sorrow.

It is deeply disconcerting to read what follows. He is expelled from the seminary, rejected by his family and is left living homeless. These are but a sketch of the issues which test the faith of a young man in his late teens. Now living in a strange city he seeks out a Christian congregation and is perplexed to find that their interest in his well-being stops short of asking whether he had a roof over his head.

Fast forward to the American Bible College in Beirut and then to Emmanuel College in the north of England: Sam discovers what folk like me could only describe as deeply patronising and anachronistic approaches to the teaching of theology and ministry. In Beirut, almost without question, he accepts that his given name (Mohammad) must change to give him a Christian identity; from now on he is Samuel. His early introduction to life in the United Kingdom was infused with imperial and racist attitudes which others would have challenged head-on. Sam, however, with characteristic graciousness shrugs these off, holding instead to his deep sense of belonging in the will and purpose of God. From time to time the reader might be forgiven for thinking how naïve it is to see the hand of God in every good thing that happens while making excuses for the human frailties which lead to offence and disappointment, but such is the overall optimism of the writer who stretches at every turn to see the good in others and even the funny side of trial.

One area, however, in which Sam does not lie down and roll over is in his understanding of the plight of the Palestinian people. Here again I wish I had had his insight when we were together at Trinity College. From deep within his own cultural identity he sees the weakness of Christian Zionism and, contrary to the evangelical tradition which formed his Christian faith, he articulates the paucity of understanding the modern day State of Israel as some key player in the end game of history, rather than as a place where peace with justice for Palestinian and Jew alike have to be hammered out.

Sam's remarkable journey eventually brings him to the place where we first met. At Trinity College he was a diligent student and throughout his ministry his studies have never stopped. His love of language and his knowledge of the Bible made him into a Church of Scotland minister who self-identifies as a preacher and teacher. His story will take you to his three parishes, it will describe his failures as well as his successes and it will describe a faith that sustained him through many highs and lows. For me a distinguishing mark is in the early lesson learned from the tragic story in which he recalls conducting the funeral of a baby whom, a week earlier, he had refused to baptise. The memory of this marks Sam to this very day. He never again refused a baptism and he ministered on the dictum that "people will remember a minister's kindness in time of trouble when they have forgotten every sermon that they ever preached".

In the years following Trinity College our ministries took on a different shape and developed along different paths. On just a few occasions our paths met and we shared a little of our respective journeys. From those moments I can vouch for the ways in which Sam's close relationships shaped him and how his passion for the faith and love for his Lord shaped his ministry. You will be touched by the way that Sam reveals some of his innermost feelings, and whatever your understanding of divine providence, no one could fail to be intrigued and inspired by his story.

The reader will enjoy pithy wisdom and sayings collected from all over the literary world; but, mainly they will be rewarded with an insight into what is like to have come from another culture, and perhaps come to appreciate the need to be more generous and more gracious in accepting of the stranger in our midst.

John Chalmers

Unforgotten Years

Chapter 1

UNFADING EARLY MEMORIES

I have a room whereinto no one enters
Save me myself alone:
There sits a blessed memory on a throne,
There my life centers.

(Christina Georgina Rossetti, *Memory II*)

Miguel de Cervantes, the 16th century Spanish writer, begins his famous *Don Quijote de la Mancha* with the phrase, "In a certain corner of La Mancha, the name of which I choose not to remember . . ."[1] I find this expression rather touching. I am not sure I can explain the reason for this particular feeling. Obviously, not every feeling can have a reason, and not every reason one gives explains adequately the way one feels about one particular thing or another. But one thing is sure, unlike Cervantes I do not wish to leave my native city unnamed or speak of it in the abstract. Its name is Larache. It is a seaport city, famous for its charming blue and white houses. Geographically, it is located in northwest Morocco – the area formerly known as Spanish Morocco. After a period of over five decades, its memory still gives me a sense of nostalgia, for it is by no means the least among the cities of that North African country.

Larache is famous as being the site of Lixus, the ancient Roman city, and is included in its urban perimeter. The site is located in the north of the modern seaport of Larache, and is approximately 3 kilometres from the Ocean and the entrance of river Locus into it. The view of that awesome scenery from the rooftop of my own home will always remain indelibly stamped upon my mind. Lixus is perched on the hilltop overlooking the sea and the serpentine meanders of the river Locus. The site, as I vividly recalls, is so beautiful that it can best be appreciated with a picnic. There is much to fascinate the visitor in

---

[1] Miguel de Cervantes, *Don Quijote de la Mancha*, trans. by Tobias Smollett (New York, 2001), p. 1.

1

this ancient city of Lixus. Baths, unknown temples, 4th century AD walls, a mosaic floor of the intricate and confusing ruins of the Capitol Hill are all there to be explored.

As an ancient city of what was known as 'West Mauritania', Lixus was originally settled by Phoenicians during the 7th century BC and gradually grew in importance as confirmed by archaeological discoveries. Later it came under Carthaginian domination. But, after the destruction of Carthage, Lixus came under Roman control and was made an imperial colony, reaching its highest point of success and power during the reign of the emperor Claudius (41–54 AD). A number of ancient Greek writers believed that Lixus was the mythological garden of the Hesperidia – the keepers of the golden apples. Also, according to legend, it was the sanctuary of Hercules and the place where he gathered the golden apples, which was his eleventh task. The historical importance of the city of Lixus continued until the Islamic conquest in the 7th century AD, which was marked by the establishment of a mosque. The Islamic presence there was soon extended to the southern bank of the river Locus, which eventually led to the founding of the city of Larache, probably about the end of that century.

From then little or nothing is mentioned about Larache until about the 12th century when it suffered a devastating attack, probably by Norseman pirates. However, the city did not come to its full strength until the 15th century. Equally interesting is the fact that the city of Larache was used as stopover by the Algerian and Turkish pirate ships. In 1471 the Portuguese occupied it and then lost it to Morocco in the famous battle of *Wadi al-Makhazin* on Aug. 4, 1578, in which three kings met their fate. But the city had to undergo external attacks from the Portuguese and the Spanish until 1610 when Muhammad al-Sheikh, the Sa'dian King of Morocco, offered it to Spain as a gift. Larache was again restored to Moroccan sovereignty in 1691 under the Sultan Mulay Ismail, whose father, Mulay Ali Cherif, was the founder of the Allawi dynasty.[2] After that it took 221 years for the Spaniards to return and remain in control of it for 45 years until its Independence in November 18th, 1956.

---

[2] See Giles Milton, *White Gold: The Extraordinary Story of Thomas Pellow & North Africa's One Million European Slaves* (Hodder & Stoughton, 2004), pp. 88-89.

Marked by the successive Arab and Spanish invasions, the structure of the city differs from one district to another. The configuration of the old part of the city is certainly an Arab type, whilst the modern part adopts the Andalucian style. But even in the old town there are houses with arcades which point to the Andalucian past. There are however a number of interesting things to see in this historic city. For example, there is the famous 'Castle of the Stork', which was built in the 16th century by King Ahmad al-Mansour of the Sa'dyian dynasty. In addition to this, the visitor will find the city's interesting archaeological museum where the currencies of the site of Lixus are displayed.

Larache was under Spanish influence during the Protectorate (1910–1956), which was by no means smooth sailing. It witnessed, and in some ways, played a part in the brutal Spanish civil war and the emergence of dictatorship under Francisco Franco. My own paternal uncle, who partly being drunk and partly out of sheer bravado enlisted in the military, met his fate a week later at the infamous battle of Terwel, in eastern Spain. Franco's dictatorship when it came applied as much to Spain as to its entire Protectorate in northern Morocco. But, according to my recollection, it was in some ways a benevolent dictatorship in comparison with that which exists in almost all Arab and Islamic countries today. There are a number of incidents I could mention as an example, but this remains outside the scope of this book. Suffice it to say that despite some alterations that were introduced after the Independence, Spain has left its indelible mark on this city as on the entire northern Morocco, its former Protectorate. To this day, the city of Larache has a number of interesting sights and features. The former *Plaza de Espana*, now called in French *Place de la Liberation*, marks the transition from the Spanish new town to the old town (*al-Medina al qadima*).

In the centre of the plaza, there is a beautiful garden surrounded by a number of sidewalk cafes and restaurants. In the summer of every year this area used to be the scene of a highly colourful Spanish fiesta, which lasted a week. The countless flamboyant parades during the day and the din of various parties of flamenco singers and dancers in the evening that went on until the small hours of the morning are still some of the fondest memories of my youth. Adjacent to the plaza is the splendid gate of the old town (*Bab al-Medina*), which, through many years, must have undergone a good number of renovations.

Passing through this gate, one arrives at the fascinating old town and its old small market (*Souk as-Saghir*). It is one of the country's most popular and beautiful places. I still recall how, in my early youth, this old market of ceaseless hustle and bustle used to turn almost every late afternoon into a pandemonium. There were all sorts of entertainment – storytellers, musicians with their singers and dancers, magicians, palm readers, snake charmers acrobats etc. The poor who could not afford to go to the cinema in those days had an open and free entertainment with a big range of varieties to choose from!

How can I forget it? I cannot be like the man who said to another, "I remember your name perfectly, but I just can't think of your face!" I certainly remember both its name and its face. After all, as a Moroccan proverb has it, "The memory of two places one would hardly ever forget – the place of his greatest enjoyment, and the place of his greatest hardship." My hometown afforded me both of these, as I well remember.

Early Childhood

I was born in that beautiful city of Larache on the 15th of April 1941. Two years later my brother, Mustapha, was born. The aftermath of the Spanish civil war at this time was having its unpleasant economic impact on Spain as well as on its Protectorate. Food supplies were very scarce and strict rationing was in motion, which lasted well over a decade. Evaporated milk, for example, which was fed to babies, albeit watered-down, was so scarce that many of them had to be weaned prematurely. Yet, there was no shortage of tins of evaporated milk that decorated the kitcken shelves of my home; and my maternal uncles, who were officers in Franco's army, made full use of their rank to keep that area of the kitchen well stacked!

The family atmosphere in which I was born and brought up was comfortable, secure and stable. Moreover, in such a strongly patriarchal culture where women were marginalized and where divorce and polygamy ruined many a family, my family was certainly one of a few exceptions. Divorce was simply unknown in the marital history of my father's family and also of my mother's family.

My father was a businessman in the shoe and leather trade, which seemed to take the greater part of his time. The other part was taken by the pleasures of partying and drinking sessions with his friends. He must have known that such conduct was unbecoming of one belonging to a respectable Muslim family. Therefore, whether out of fear or reverence for his venerable father, he kept this part of his life a tight secret from everybody, or at least so he thought! As a result, his appearance at home was almost like a ship that passes in the night. But all that changed soon after mother (his wife) died. He never married again. He lived in a separate house from the rest of the family. He remained that way until he passed away in 1990 at the age of 77.

It must be said however that he was not a man whose memory many would cherish. Much of his attitude had left a very bad taste in many a mouth. This plus his reckless living did much to bring his business to a sad end. It is not exactly sure how people would remember him, but in my memory, as the older son, he would always be the father who lavished all his love, cuddles and kisses on my younger brother but not on me. As a matter of fact, I never once felt his hand except when he stretched it out to hurt me. To this day I still wrestle with the question as to why he never once called me by my own name.

In short, my father was for no apparent reason the embodiment of the worst nightmare in my childhood life, which was also the cause of much of my illness during that period. The harsh and abusive treatment I suffered at his hand shortly before and indeed some years after my mother's death is now buried in the past. Interestingly, it is one of the grimmest commentaries on fatherhood that Martin Luther himself could hardly bring himself to pray the Lord's Prayer and to say, "*Our Father*", because of the sternness, the strictness and even the cruelty of his own father.

"An exaggeration," said Khalil Gibran, "is a truth that has lost its temper." With no axe to grind, many who knew my mother spoke highly of her. Without hesitation, they described her as one of those few young ladies of the city who were a byword of all that is beautiful, prudent and above reproach. But, fortune did not smile on my younger brother and me for long. She died when I was approximately four years old. My memory of her at times is understandably dim, but at other times, the mist of the past lifts and her image becomes slightly clearer. It was the image of a pleasantly white faced and jet-black haired lady dressing me in a traditionally immaculate Moorish dress. The occasion was most probably 'al-Mawlid al-Nabawi' day (i.e. the feast of the prophet Muhammad's birthday). She was getting me ready to accompany her father (my grandfather), who led the *Hamdushya* Sufi party in a huge religious procession that day.[3] My eyes were fixed upon her as she carefully and elaborately dressed me. It was as if my little mind had turned into a recording video camera. That recording has since been worn out by the ravages of years. It looks today like one of those silent, hazy and constantly interrupted movies of the earliest part of the 20th century. I can still see her in a fit of laughter as she dressed me and talked to me excitedly. I cannot remember what was amusing her or what she was talking about, for I was captivated by something else. Something fascinated me as I looked at her. It was her golden tooth! O how I wished I had a golden tooth like that! To this day, anyone with the tiniest piece of gold in his/her teeth would bring back that memory.

Sadly, my entire childhood memory of her remains hazy and fragmentary. She passed away at the early age of 24, and a tiny detail of her funeral has remained indelibly stamped on my mind. Apparently, after she had been ritually washed and shrouded, I recall how a tall man, probably one of my maternal uncles, took me up in his arms and walked into the incense-filled room where her body lay. He stood by her corpse and lowered me slowly towards her face. Then he quietly placed his finger on her forehead and said in a trembling whisper, "Kiss mummy here bye bye."

At that age, it is hard to imagine how I felt or what went through my mind. More likely I was in a maze. My childhood mind must have been confused, and as Will Rogers once put it, "When you are confused, it's when you don't know enough about a thing to be worried." The impact of that incident was not felt until some years later, and has remained with me ever since. Death is certainly a terrible experience, not for those who leave this world but for those who are left behind. For the dead, all sickness and pain are ended, and even death itself is passed. But for those left behind it is hard to tell how long their deep sense of grief and desolation will last. Perhaps their worst part is when they come to pick up the pieces, and some of them can be terribly hard and thorny to handle.

---

[3] The *Hamdushya* Sufi party bears the name of its 18th century founder, Sidi Ali Ibn Hamdush, a native of the city of Zarhun, near the Atlas Mountains.

A Bumpy Start

According to the Islamic Sunni schools of jurisprudence, when the mother dies, the custody of her children goes to her mother (i.e. their maternal grandmother). But if she is no longer alive, the custody goes to their mother's sister (i.e. their maternal aunt). The father is legally obliged to pay maintenance, which, after taking into consideration his income, the judge will determine how much the monthly or weekly payment should be. Interestingly, the Maliki School of jurisprudence (to which the inhabitants of Morocco belong) even forbids the father to ask the custodian to allow the child – if he takes him or her out for a day – to be fed while the child is with the father, who in any case must return the child to the custodian before nightfall.[4] This was in fact a precautionary measure, so that the father may not try in the process to reduce the maintenance payment or stop it altogether. But laws are made for man, and man can make use of them in a manner that suits his own end. And as a Spanish proverb puts it, "Laws, like the spider's web, catch the fly and let the hawk go free". It would be fair to describe my paternal grandfather as the hawk in the aftermath of my mother's death. He was a man of strong character, a self-made man, shrewd and with a strange combination of religiosity and ruthlessness.

Knowing that his son, following the death of his wife, was becoming incapable of paying for the custody of his children, he embarked on a sinister action. The best way to get around this article of law was through the use of monetary muscles. The use of bribery in Muslim courts in those days was by no means rare, and this was encouraged by the fact that the Spaniards were not allowed, according to Protectorate Treaty, to interfere in Islamic court matters. Consequently, an unjust verdict was given. The judge ruled that the children spend the day in their father's family home, and in the evening go to spend the night in their mother's family home. In this case, the maintenance payment was reduced almost to nothing, and was shortly thereafter dropped completely. The ruling had incensed a considerable number of people in the city, among them the venerable and retired grand-judge, Abd as-Salam Aztut. But there was nothing that anybody could do. As Spanish citizens, my mother's family appealed to the Spanish government to intervene, but all to no avail. Apparently, for Franco's

---

[4] See Abd ar-Rahman al-Jaziri, *Kitab al-Fiqh ala al-Madahib al-Arba'a* (Cairo n.d.), Vol. 4, pp. 534-542.

fascist government it was politically expedient not to touch this issue with a barge pole. And as Aesop in the 4th century BC put it, "Any excuse will serve a tyrant."

For my younger brother and me, life became intolerable as we shuttled day after day between the two bitterly opposing families. However, having achieved their goal, a few years later my father's family saw no need to stick to the terms of the judge's verdict. It was now up to the children to suit themselves. Consequently, my younger brother decided to stay permanently with my father's family, but I preferred the status quo instead. The reason for this was not because I was resigned to my father' family, but because I was simply trying to tread carefully. At this very early age, I was aware that something bad had happened, and this family must have been responsible for it. This seemed to be re-enforced by the hard and unscrupulous attitude of my paternal grandfather, the head of the family. I was careful not to do the opposite of what my younger brother had done and confine myself permanently to my mother's family. That could upset my father's family, who obviously played second fiddle to no one. I therefore decided to continue shuttling between the two families. In this way I thought the road might be smoothed over after those hard bumps of court disputes. I was unaware that some other bumpy roads still lay ahead.

A 'Sickness Not Unto Death'

The death of my mother, the simmering tension between the two families following the court ruling and the unsettling impact that these had upon me, were bound to have their repercussions. For a child of seven or eight years of age to walk a very tight rope in the current atmosphere could only result in nervousness, stress and depression. At play I took no part in the games with other children. I simply sat and watched pensively, and on occasions I would withdraw and sit somewhere else alone far from the clamours and the noises of the playgrounds. Then, both families began to notice with grave concern my unusual long periods of silence, my disinclination to eat and my extraordinary long sleeps. But, the alarm bell sounded when they noticed the gradual swelling of my stomach. The possibility that I could follow my mother into the grave within a short time had thrown the two families into panic. They soon buried the hatchet and resolved to spare no effort to save my life. Over a period of time, I was rushed from one private Spanish doctor to another, but all to no avail.

The last doctor to see me was reported to have said privately that my chance of recovery was very slim. Now, quite often when medical efforts fail, the possibility is that people could turn to the supernatural or to superstition, or to both. Prayers were offered for me in local Mosques and visits to local shines of renowned saints were frequent. Amulets of Qur'anic verses were also put round my neck and tucked under my pillow in the hope of bringing me a swift recovery.[5] The result was that my condition remained unchangeably the same.

One day, a distant relative who happened to be visiting me asked the grandfather if he had thought of taking me to what was known in the city as 'dar al-tabib al-Inglizi' (the English doctor's clinic). He looked away pretending he had not heard him. Did he do so out of pride? For a man who always paid for his and his family's medical treatment, it looked as though he was rejecting the idea of accepting charity. The 'English doctor's clinic' offered free treatment. As a matter of fact, neither pride nor money had anything to do with it. The so-called 'English doctor's clinic' was basically a Mission House, and respectable Muslim families of the city would simply not go near it. The head of the Mission House at that time was Mr Henry Isaac, a highly energetic and zealous missionary figure.

Unexpectedly, a few days later, the grandfather reluctantly took me up in his arms and made his way to the 'English doctor's clinic'. Tired and hardly able to open my eyes, I still recall my glimpse of a white and dark-haired young English doctor. He spoke Moroccan Arabic in a soft and gentle voice and had a very pleasant smile. If my memory serves me well, that first encounter somehow seemed to instil some sort of peace into me. In fact, that was extraordinary because until then, I had developed a combined sense of fear and dislike for doctors, but for this one, I had no such feelings at all. There was obviously something unique about him. His name was Dr Philip Rigby, the man who later on became instrumental in leading me to the saving grace of the Lord Jesus Christ.

---

[5] The Qur'anic chapters generally selected for such amulets are Suras 1, 6, 18, 36, 44, 55, 67, 78. Five verses known as 'Ayatu al-Hifz' i.e. 'verses of protection', are also frequently inscribed on amulets. They are Suras 2:256; 12:64; 13:12; 15:17; & 37:7.

For the time being, the doctor began to take serious medical (and most probably prayerful) care of me. And within a few weeks, there were clear indications that recovery had begun, to the joyful surprise, and indeed relief of my people. Years later, they would often jokingly say to me, "you've cast a stone into your grave and returned home!" – a Moroccan idiom meaning, 'your illness was not terminal'. This recalls Jesus' response to Mary and Martha regarding their brother Lazarus, *"This sickness is not unto death"* (Jn. 11:3-4). But the sentence that follows is of supreme significance, *"This has happened"*, Jesus continued, *"in order to bring glory to God, and it will be the means by which the Son of God will receive glory."*

What Jesus meant probably was that whether Lazarus was in the throes of death or in its grip, death would not have the last word. By bringing him back to life or bringing life back to him, the Father and the Son would ultimately be glorified. Looking back, I can confidently say that my grave condition as a little boy was something through which God was glorified. My serious illness and my contact with Dr Rigby had brought life back to me, and in due course brought to me the gift of life abundant through Jesus Christ.

Light That Passed Unnoticed

As my home was not far from the clinic, I could make my way to the doctor without my grandfather, who had so far taken me twice or three times. For him, this probably came as a double relief – the relief that I was now on my way to recovery, and the relief of not having to be seen going to the Mission House! However, my frequent visits to Dr Rigby in the Mission House soon found me playing with Mr & Mrs Isaac's children, John and Catherine, including an adopted Moroccan boy called Sellam. The real attraction here was not only the fun of playing with the missionaries' children, but the real attraction was the British toys that the missionaries' children had! With the passing of time, I became one of the kids of the Mission House, and as such, I was present at the wedding of Dr Rigby, which was celebrated there. Although I was ten or eleven years of age, I cannot remember precisely most of what took place at that wedding, but I can certainly remember it as that occasion when my little belly became my god! I can vividly recall gorging myself with those exotic sandwiches and cakes of the best that efficiency and imagination could produce. Now, if gluttony is sin, then retribution was swift to follow! I remember being violently sick at home, which made some of my family members think that the cause of the sickness could either be pork or some kind of food cooked in wine! They did not know that those English missionaries shunned both pork and alcoholic beverages. At any rate, what happened did not stop me from returning to the Mission House. And as time went on, I came to be regarded by those missionaries as one of their children, in spite of being at times the leading mischief-maker among them! Presumably, they believed that through much love and prayer the grace of God would be able to transform my life and behaviour one day.

Once a week the Isaacs and their missionary colleagues used to hold a children's meeting and teach them Christian choruses and stories from the Bible, after which they would hand them sweeties on their way out. And as a little mischief-maker I was among them, and was a recipient of those sweeties, which I enjoyed so much. To maintain a good number of kids, excellent Christmas prizes were promised to all who attended faithfully and learnt a reasonable number of choruses and Biblical verses. And in this, I showed a keenness that was rare among the rest of the children, and was not disappointed when Christmas came.

The question is, did I understand the meaning of those choruses and Biblical texts then or was I simply indifferent to them? Looking back, I am not sure if I really understood them. What is sure however is that I went to the Mission House mainly for the 'loaves and the fishes', including of course those attractive foreign toys that the missionaries' children had! But the time came when I was given, not an understanding, but a blunt and negative verdict about what I was being taught at the Mission House. It happened one day as I was playing with my brother and cousins at home. By way of showing off, I started singing a couple of Christian choruses to them. The female members of the family who heard me were immediately shocked and horrified at what they described as 'kalam al-kufr' (i.e. blasphemous words). They screamed at me to stop at once. I was frightened and began to cry. I did not know what I had said or done to deserve that terrifying kind of rebuke.

On his return home, the grandfather was fully informed. Strangely enough, he kept calm. In fact, he was so calm that when I came home for lunch from the local Qur'anic school, I was pretty sure the old man had heard nothing. But, as this was a serious matter, grandfather was not going to play ostrich. After lunch, he beckoned me to come and sit beside him. I did so nervously thinking that after all he might well have been informed and that I was in for it. The grandfather then calmly asked me how I was doing at 'al Masid' (the Qur'anic school).[6] I replied that I was now writing on my 'lauh' (tablet) without much help and that I was also starting to learn some Qur'anic Suras by heart. And to head off what I thought might be coming to me, I recited loudly 'al-Fatihah'[7] followed by the last three shortest Suras of the Qur'an – 'al-Nas' (Men or People), 'al-Falaq' (Daybreak) and 'al-Ikhlas' (God's Unity). This last one reads: "*Say: He is God alone: God the eternal! He begetteth not, and He is not begotten; and there is none like unto Him.*"[8]

The old man paused for a while as though pondering the words of this last Sura or thinking of the next question. Instead he looked at me with a faint smile and said, "You are a clever boy, and one day we want you to be a great man. But, that will never happen if you continue to visit those bad English folks whose aim is to corrupt our Muslim people with their false teaching, especially the good and clever children like you." In the silence of my little innocent heart, I was astonished to hear grandfather talking in those terms about a people in whom I saw nothing but love, care and goodness of the highest sort. He continued, and this time in a sharper tone of voice, "I do not want you to go near their house ever again. But if you do, then you will get to know the other side of me, and you won't like it." He then looked me straight in the eye and asked me softly, "Do you promise to do as you are told?" I nodded my head in agreement, and received a pat on the back together with a special benediction, "May Allah smile in approval upon you, my boy!"

---

[6] In Morocco, the Qur'anic school is called 'al-Masid', whilst in Egypt and the Middle East it is known as 'al-Kuttab'.

[7] al-Fatihah is the name of the opening chapter or Sura of the Qur'an. As the reader will notice this chapter is a prayer. It is held in great veneration by Muslims. They regard it as the quintessence of the whole Qur'an, and often repeat it in their devotions, both public and private as the Christians do the Lord's Prayer.

[8] Interestingly, this Sura was not a response to the Trinitarian doctrine of the Christian faith. Rather it was a response to the polytheists of Quraysh who asked Muhammad concerning the distinguishing attributes of the God he invited them to worship. See George Sale, *alkoran of Mohammed* (New York 1883), p. 459.

Knowing how severe grandfather could be, I was relieved that I had been treated leniently. But the Mission House and its good people were not easily forgotten. Looking back after more than five decades later, I realise how present the Light of Christ was in that Mission House where I used to spend some of my time. Yet, sadly, it was a Light that had passed completely unnoticed. I had neither the mind nor the will to realise it at the time. But today it remains a part of my early memory. And as Richard B. Sheridan once put it, "Our memories are independent of our wills. It is not so easy to forget."

Chapter 2

FROM LEARNING TO EDUCATION

"Education is not the filling of a pail,
but the . . . lighting of a fire."

(William Butler Yeats)

Finley P. Dunne once wrote, "You can lead a man up to the University, but you can't make him think." Professor Robert Davidson of Glasgow University used to remind us as students that if we were there just to get a degree and no more, the course would actually fail. In the University, one's duty is not so much to learn what to think as to learn how to think. In other words, one must indeed study in order to pass, but more so one ought to cultivate his study and bring it to a fruitful harvest. The focus must not only be on the seed, which eventually disappears in the soil, but also on the fruit produced where the real profit lies. Such is the difference between learning and education. As B.F. Skinner briefly put it, "Education is what survives when what has been learnt has been forgotten."

A few weeks after that hearty lecture from my grandfather, I was taken to what might be described as a paid Qur'anic high school. It was here that the children of comfortable and religious families were taken to learn the Qur'an by heart. In terms of style, method and even atmosphere, it was almost a medieval throw back. The discipline under which the pupil lived daily was highly intense. Chunks of Suras from the Qur'an were memorized and recited to the teacher at the end of about every twenty-four hours. Here the pupil could not afford to be complacent as the sword of Damocles was constantly hanging over his head. The stern teacher walked up and down among his pupils brandishing his birch as they nervously swung back and forth noisily memorizing their assigned portions of the Qur'an. Any sluggishness or drowsiness on the part of any pupil, especially during the summer heat, was met with a swipe of the birch across his back. Failure to live up to the rules of this Qur'anic high school inevitably led to the dreaded bastinado – a punishment by beating the soles of the feet with a stick. The same could apply in the case of grave misbehaviour committed outside the school. At about the age of twelve, I remember receiving my portion of the bastinado a few times. Once for giggling during the Friday prayer at the local mosque, and once for joining a bunch of ragamuffins to steal figs from a nearby garden! Needless to say, on another occasion I was bastinadoed together with another couple of children for dancing in the local mosque, imitating a Sufi group in their Thursday night sessions!

At the Qur'anic high school I was noted for having what might be termed today 'a computer-like memory'. As the Qur'an consists of 114 Suras (about two thirds of the New Testament), I managed to commit it to memory within two years and a half. The teacher had already recommended to grandfather that when I had finished the Qur'an, I should go on to memorize the well known *Alfiya* of Ibn Malik.[1] He further suggested that I might also get to memorize the poetic manuals of Ibn 'Ashir and Sidi Khalil on Shari'a. It must be understood at this point that in such a school, the Muslim pupil is not being educated in the meaning of the Qur'an and other related subjects. He is there simply to commit them to memory and learn to recite them with the best possible diction. These things are studied in depth in the next phase when the pupil moves to that educational institution, known as 'al-Ma 'had ad-Dini' – the Islamic Seminary. Here some modern sciences like mathematics, geography, geometry and physics were taught, albeit on a smaller scale. The main focus was on 'tafsir' (exegesis) both of the Qur'an and the Hadith, usually based on the works of classical orthodox expositors.[2] The curriculum also included 'al-mantiq' (logic), and 'al-fiqh al islami' (Islamic jurisprudence), which covered all aspects of religious and temporal life of the Muslim community.

At the age of sixteen, I was taken to the Seminary to be enrolled as a student. The atmosphere there was not as stifling and draconian

---

[1] *Alfiya* means 'thousand liner' i.e a poem of a thousand verses, which serves as a rhymed manual and deals with the grammatical rules of classical Arabic. The poem is then subjected to a lengthy and thorough exposition. Books by many old and modern scholars on this issue abound, and the *Alfiya* of Ibn Malik are found throughout the Arab world.

[2] Ignoring these early expositors was considered '*dalal*' (deviation), and '*batil*' (falsehood), leading ultimately to '*kufr*' (unbelief), as Farid Esack has rightly observed. See his *The Qur'an: A User's Guide* (Oxford, 2005), p. 23.

as in the previous school. At the Qur'anic high school one could learn in the manner previously described, but the Seminary was the place where I was being educated in all that I had learnt by heart. The Seminary was renowned for its discipline, and its method of education was exemplary. Students derived tremendous academic incentive both from competition, which the Seminary indirectly encouraged, and to a great extent from their religious zeal. All religious subjects were studied along traditional and fundamental lines. For example, the use of historical or literary criticism in studying the Qur'an was unheard of. Today in parts of the Muslim world where some form of literary criticism is known (even if not yet used), it is perceived as a potential danger to the authority of the Qur'an.[3]

In common with all who were newly enrolled, I was admitted to a one-year probationary study to qualify for a full time degree course at the Seminary. As there had been no trace of a scholar in the history of either of my families, I was driven with a burning ambition to be the first. And what could be better than a scholar in Islamic jurisprudence? I was determined to be a jewel in their crown one day. Years later, I came to realise the significance of that spiritual dictum which says, "Man proposes but God disposes".

Back to the Mission House

Schools usually took three months summer vacation. My period of probationary study was coming to an end, and the final exam was scheduled to take place in autumn. It was a long hot mid-summer day, and for those like me who were not given to siestas, nothing could be worse than boredom on a day like that. The day itself was grey but stiflingly humid. I decided to take a walk to a nearby pine forest called in Spanish *El Vivero*, a fine picnic area. The road leading to that forest passed by the Mission House. A passing glance at it reminded me of the days when I used to visit it. I toyed with the idea of popping in one day to say hello to the people I had not seen for a long time. I had no fear of being seen going into the Mission House. After all, I was no longer a child and grandfather's threatening measures a few years before were now no longer valid. On my way back home about sunset, I had an extraordinary feeling as I neared the Mission House.

---

[3] *Ibid.* p. 111; see also Ahmad (Jallandari) Akhtar, 'Qur'anic Exegesis and Classical Tafsir', *IQR*, 1968, 12: 1, 17-119.

I felt strongly drawn to that house, and before I could think what to do next, I was knocking at its door. The man who opened the door was none other than Dr Philip Rigby, the very man who had treated me successfully years before. His smile, his gentleness and his amiable demeanour remained unchangeably the same. He recognised me immediately and was pleased to see me. As a matter of fact, I had expected to see Mr H. Isaac, for he was always the first to rush to open the door. I was told that he had gone to work among the Tuaregs of southern Algeria. After a brief conversation, I asked if their religious meetings were still being held, and was informed that one of them was going to begin shortly and that I was more than welcome to attend it. I reluctantly accepted and was led to a small room, which I recalled was used as a dining room. As soon as a few more people joined, the service began.

I soon discovered that everything in that service was totally unpalatable to me. I disliked the hymns that were being sung in what I thought was a slow and dreary western music. Next I listened to the New Testament reading, which was in the vernacular, and I did so with nothing less than a derisive grin. My attitude was by no means unique. In doing so, I was simply reflecting the popular mentality of my Muslim environment. Muslims, who are used to the Qur'an written and recited in the finest classical Arabic, would expect any other sacred book to be written or at least translated in similar style. Aware of this view, the Christian Arabs of the Middle East who lived in a sea of Islam have always had the Bible in classical Arabic. I still think that missionaries in Morocco and Algeria might have been gravely mistaken when they translated the Bible into the vernacular. Muslims do not usually think much of Jewish and Christian scriptures, and their translation into the vernacular was evidently unhelpful. In spite of that their motive must have been sincere.

As I sat listening, I was by no means indifferent to what was being said or done. My reaction was one of negative criticism and contempt for what was happening. But soon all that turned into a simmering anger and fury as Dr Rigby began preaching about Jesus whom I knew as the prophet 'Isa'.[4] What he said about him was nothing short of blasphemy. He frequently referred to Jesus as *the Son of God*. For me, the Qur'an's response to this claim was clear, "*This is Jesus, the son*

---

[4] For full discussion on this name, see Geoffrey Parrinder, *Jesus in the Qur'an* (Oxford, 1966), pp. 16-21.

*of Mary; a statement of the truth concerning which they are in doubt. It is not for God to beget a son. Glory be to Him! When He decides a thing, He simply says, 'be!' and it is."*⁵ Then he went on to claim that God sent His Son, Jesus, to the world to die on the cross for the sins of mankind. In the silence of my own mind, I could cite the Qur'anic counter claim, *". . . Yet they slew him not, and they crucified him not, but had only his likeness. And they who differed about him were in doubt concerning him: No sure knowledge had they about him, but followed only an opinion, and they did not really slay him, but God took him up to Himself. And God is Mighty, Wise!"*⁶ Then Dr Rigby went further and told his small audience that God's eagerness for the salvation of the world was such that He emptied Himself of all His eternal glory and became a man in order to redeem man by His death on the cross.

This was the height of blasphemy. In a sense, I was not surprised to hear the deity of Christ being proclaimed. I was aware that the infidel Christians did not only associate Jesus with God and classified him as His son, but they also believed that he was God Himself. At this point I recalled the Qur'anic refutation, which declares, *"They are infidels, who say, 'verily God is the Messiah the son of Mary'. Say: 'who could obtain anything from God to the contrary, if He chose to destroy the Messiah the son of Mary, and his mother, and all who are on the earth?'"*⁷ I wondered how clever and highly educated westerners, like this gentleman, could bring themselves to believe such ridiculous blasphemies. His claim about the deity of Jesus, I thought, simply defied logic. For example, let us assume that Jesus was God, and died on the cross and was buried for three days and three nights. During this period in which God was dead and buried, who was sustaining this universe? I decided to put that question to the Doctor after the meeting, and put it to him I did, albeit with a touch of confidence and arrogance.

After the meeting, there was a brief conversation in which the Doctor expressed his delight to have seen me after a long time and hoped to see me again soon. I made no response to this, but instead I

---

⁵ *Sura Mariam* [19]:34-35, 91-92. For other Qur'anic verses that disputes the Sonship of Christ see *Al-'Imran* [3]:59; *Sura Yunan* [10]:68; *Sura al-Furqan* [25]:2; *Sura at-Tawba* [9]:30.

⁶ *Sura an-Nisa'*[4]:157-158. This passage seems to be contradicted by *Sura Al-'Imran* [3]:55 See J. M. Rodwell, The *Koran* (London, 1994), p. 36.

⁷ *Sura al-Ma'idah* [5]:19, and 75.

felt hesitant and indeed embarrassed by this spontaneous attitude of profound kindness and friendship. Should I now ask him that intricate question and risk returning evil for good? A gentle look and a smile from the Doctor seemed to suggest that he guessed I was wanting to say something, and stood there as if ready to listen. Reluctantly and in a polite tone of voice I told him that I had enormous difficulties with his suggestion that Jesus was God. The Doctor nodded still with a smile. I went on, "Now here is my question," I said with a touch of confidence and arrogance; "when God (Jesus) was dead for a period of three days and three nights, who was in charge of this vast universe?" The Doctor's response was most astonishing. He calmly but unhesitatingly replied that he could not answer that question. He went on to acknowledge that the question was clever and indeed very reasonable coming from a young Muslim student like me.

He repeated this twice or three times, and each time I felt my ego was being well massaged! What I failed to notice was the remarkable humility and meekness of that foreigner. I was not upset, agitated or baffled in any way. Prior to saying goodbye, he said that he would try to think of that question, but promised no correct answer to it. Now, partly because of my sense of triumph, and partly because I was somehow touched by the sincere honesty and friendship of the Englishman, I promised to come back and see him again. After all, I felt I owed him something for what he had done for me once as a sick child.

As I made my way home, it occurred to me, that there was nothing wrong with Dr Rigby and his colleagues in the Mission House. They were extremely good, highly benevolent and sacrificial in their service to the sick and the needy. To some charity is a duty, to others it is a joy, but to them it was apparently both. It was however their belief that was wrong and indeed appallingly blasphemous. The fault did not lie with them personally, but with their sacred scripture, which I passionately believed was 'muharrafa' – distorted or falsified, according to Islamic teaching. I therefore resolved to make a comparative study of the Bible and the Qur'an, so that in due course I would be able to contend for the truth of Islam and expose the falsehood of their Christianity. Meanwhile, true to my word, I frequently visited the missionaries and attended their meetings, but all the time keeping a low profile. I was learning about the tenets of their faith and their Biblical literature as much as I could. Outside the Mission House I was scouring the

Qur'an and other Islamic literature for every ounce of evidence that would rubbish their scripture.

Within a short period, however, things began to change. In what some might call a twist of fate, those missionaries began to grow on me. But, far from being a twist of history or a twist of fate, the hand of providence was beginning to work. So, partly because of my happy childhood memories of the Mission House, and partly because of the unquestionable love and trust I had seen in those foreigners, I unconsciously began to develop a sense of attachment to them. Strangely enough, this attachment was being strengthened by meals to which they had often invited me to share with them. According to my culture and tradition, sharing in a meal is (and has been since time immemorial) a significant means of strengthening the bond of friendship – it is a sort of covenant meal between those who partake of it. Incidentally, this concept did exist in Biblical times.[8] There is a sense in which Holy Communion is an echo of this custom and tradition.[9] In addition to all this, those missionaries' moral and spiritual high ground, which I knew was rooted in their scripture, was for me an object of great admiration. But, their Christology and Trinitarian doctrine, which form the central core of their 'Injil' (New Testament) and their theology, I quietly viewed with utmost scorn and ridicule.

A Glimpse Of Christ

Summer vacation was coming to an end, and no effort was being spared in studying and revising for the exam, which was set to take place at the end of October 1958. I was now at the age of seventeen and my most important aim was to qualify for a full time degree course at the Seminary. Everything else was put on the back burner, including my comparative study of the Bible and the Qur'an, which I had already embarked upon. The level of tension and anxiety was rising higher with each passing day, and each passing day brought me nearer to that day of reckoning. Oddly enough, I did not stop going to the Mission House to attend the meetings. Apparently, this was not one of the things I had dropped to prepare myself for the forthcoming exam. The reason for doing so has become clear to me only years later.

---

[8] See Gen. 31:43-46, 54; Ex. 24:9-11.

[9] Read carefully Mk. 14:17-25.

The hand of providence must obviously have been at work. But, at the time, I simply went for reasons already mentioned. A few days before the exam, I happened to be in one of those meetings in the Mission House. The strain of studying and worry about the exam seemed to be wearing me out. In that particular service, Dr Rigby preached basing his sermon on Mt. 7:7-11. It contained the words of Jesus in His sermon on the mount, and it read as follows:

> Ask, and it will be given you; seek, and you will find;
> knock, and it shall be opened to you.
> For everyone who asks receives, and he who seeks finds,
> and to him who knocks it will be opened.
> Or what man of you, if his son asks him for bread, will give him
> a stone? Or if he asks for a fish, will give him a serpent?
> If you then, who are evil,
> know how to give good gifts to your children,
> how much more will your heavenly Father who is in heaven
> give good things to those who ask Him.

Usually, I hardly ever paid serious attention to the reading from the Bible let alone to the sermon, and when I did, it was only to respond with silent criticism and ridicule. But on this occasion, and for the first time, these words of Jesus seemed to touch me for their beauty and tenderness. I could not help but reach out to one of the copies of the Bible and see these words for myself, and I even marked that passage in my mind. After the meeting, I had a little conversation with Dr Rigby over a glass of Moroccan mint-tea. After that I went home with those words of Jesus still echoing in my mind. During the next couple of days I would open my copy of the classical Arabic New Testament and read that passage, with some sense of wonder and fascination.

On the evening before the exam, I decided to go to bed early so that I could get up in the morning refreshed and ready. But, unfortunately, I could not sleep. All sort of things were pouring into my mind. Primarily the fear of failing in the exam did not only rob me of my sleep, but also caused me to shiver in my bed at the very thought of that awful prospect. Unexpectedly, among all the troubling thoughts that were bombarding my mind, the words of Jesus in Mt. 7:7-11 stood out to me, but this time not as an object of fascination, but as a challenge. In spite of my fascination with this passage, I began to wonder if the words of this passage were really those of Jesus or mere fabrication. The concept of the Bible being falsified was deeply rooted in my mind. How could I know that these were the authentic words of Jesus?

In the turmoil of my mind, I came upon a simple, and some would say, a very naïve idea. I decided to put this Jesus to the test by asking for His help to pass the exam the following day. I still recall that short prayer, which I offered in the silence of my own heart that night. I said, "Lord Jesus, tomorrow is the exam. I have studied hard enough for it, but I am scared and worried in case I fail. If you are indeed what those missionaries say you are, and if those beautiful words of promise in Mt. 7:7-11 are truly yours, then I desperately ask you to help me pass. If you help me, then my entire attitude towards you will be different, and I might even become one of your followers." After I had said this, a sense of calm came upon me, and within a short time I was fast asleep.

Next day in the morning, I reported to the Seminary where about two hundred students or more gathered to sit the exam. It was to be a written and oral examination in five subjects: Islamic History, Moroccan History, Grammar, Pre and Post Arabic Literature, and General Knowledge of the Qur'an and the Hadith. The exam commenced at 9:00 a.m. and apart from a one-hour break for lunch, it continued until 4:00 p.m. The exam continued and ended the following day. The most fascinating thing for me was the fact that the sense of calm that came upon me after that short prayer, seemed to continue with me throughout those two days exam. It was an extraordinary experience, which I could not understand at the time. But today I can look back and realise how graciously active was the hand of Divine Providence in my life then. Indeed, William Cowper, the great hymn writer was correct when he wrote, "God moves in a mysterious way His wonders to perform." In this context, Don Orione once wrote, "God wishes each of us to work as hard as we can, holding nothing back but giving ourselves to the utmost, and when we can do no more, then is the moment when the hand of Divine Providence is stretched out to us and takes over."[10]

Four days later, I met a student who told me briefly and in a hurry that the exam results were out, and did not make good reading. A massive number of students had failed the exam, and that only eight had passed. I turned ashen as I listened to the bad news, concluding

---

[10] Quoted in *Westminster Collection of Christian Quotations*, Compiled by M.H. Manser (Westminster John Knox Press, Louisville, 2001), p. 304.

that I would be among those who failed. Despite the chance given to all who failed to re-sit the exam in a few months' time, my sense of devastation was enormous, to say the least. Should I go to the Seminary and have a look at the list personally? No, I had neither the heart nor the mind to see my name among those who had failed. Instead, I decided to go home.

I had not gone a few yards when I heard a shout behind me, "Congratulations!" It was the voice of the Seminary janitor, who lived just a couple of doors from me. At first, I thought the janitor was either joking or being sarcastic. But, the old fellow was serious, and told me to go and see for myself. I ran to the Seminary as fast as my legs could carry me. I looked at the list of those who had passed. They were indeed eight as I was previously told. I read the first name, the second and the third, which I knew only too well. When I came to the fourth, it was my own name. I looked at it so intensely until I could see it no more for tears – tears of joy. I was so overwhelmed by the fact that this was an answer to my prayer that I immediately fell in love with Jesus, or at least I felt so.

On reflection, it was not real love, for real love for Jesus is submissive, and that is the hallmark of being a Christian. In fact, I was not thinking of becoming a Christian, because that would mean embarking on something, which was going to take my entire heart, mind and all. And I was not ready for that yet. My feeling at the time could best be described as one of a 'profoundly sincere fondness for Jesus'. He was my champion! Nevertheless, this was to be a step in the right direction. Meanwhile, my journey from learning to real education had led me to a greater and more sublime education – a real glimpse of Jesus.

Chapter 3

A FIRST STEP TOWARDS CHRIST

"The beginning is the most important part of the work."
(Plato, The Republic)

Long journeys are anything but comfortable. I had passed my exam, an event, which I passionately believed was an answer to the prayer I had offered to Jesus that night. That was the time when I had a glimpse of Him. It was a foretaste of undreamed of things to come. Although I was unaware that I had taken a step in the right direction, the journey to the real knowledge of Jesus Christ as Lord and personal saviour was by no means easy. In any case, the Chinese proverb was correct, "A journey of one thousand steps begins with the first step." I was a pretty determined young man, and I could fully agree with the saying, "A good start makes for a good ending only if you don't start something you can't finish."

Apart from telling Dr Rigby and his missionary colleagues, who were pleased to hear the news of my remarkable experience, I kept this matter secret from everybody else outside the Mission House. I was aware that this piece of news might have serious repercussions if the outsiders got wind of it. However, as a result of what had happened, my friendship with the missionaries was strengthened, and my attitude at the meetings was now transformed beyond belief. I was no longer the quietly censorious and disdainful young guest of the past. Rather this time I was interested and attentive to what was being preached, and often even received it with a sense of quiet enthusiasm and full approval.

Looking back, I could see myself at that moment in time like the man who was enthusiastically casting out demons in the name of Jesus although he did not belong to His circle. The disciples who reported this to Jesus had forbidden him to do so. Jesus replied, *"Do not forbid him; for no one who does a mighty work in my name will be able soon*

after to speak evil of me. For he that is not against us is for us."[1] At this
stage therefore I was for Jesus, but not yet in the circle of Jesus. For the
time being, I was somehow conscious of the smile of Christ's approval
upon me, and in His own good time He was going to love me into His
goodness and grace.

The Study Days

My entry into the Seminary was a prize I cherished enormously,
and the days of my study there were among the happiest days
of my life. In 1959 I was about eighteen years of age and about to
enter my second Seminary year. Throughout this period, my study
record could stand the closest possible survey. And apart from being
the pride and joy of my own folk, at the Seminary I was regarded
among the best. In the subject of literature particularly, I was viewed
as a sort of authority on Ibn Wannan, a famous eighteenth century
Moroccan poet, otherwise known as Abu al-Shamaqmaq. In terms
of its linguistic beauty, this long poem could match the best that the
wealth of classical Arabic poetry has ever produced. One must have
a good grasp of pre-Islamic and post-Islamic history and literature to
understand and appreciate its contents. It also reflects a good deal of
the cultural life of the eighteenth century Morocco.

In addition to this and other subjects in the curriculum, I took
immense interest in the study of Qur'anic exegesis, and was able to
distinguish myself both in the knowledge and in the debating skill of
this subject in Seminary conferences. To reach this level one had to be
steeped in the works of classical orthodox expositors like al-Tabari,
al-Baidawi, al-Fakhr al-Razi, al-Qurtubi, al-Zamakhshari, Ibn Kathir,
not to mention others. But the exposition I prized most was that
of Shaykh Muhammad Rida (1865–1935).[2] He was the pupil of the
famous Muslim scholar and reformist, Shaykh Muhammad Abduh
(1849–1905).

Far from being a liberal, one can perhaps detect the influence of
some contemporary European Orientalists in his treatment of at least a
few Qur'anic texts. It should come as no surprise that Orientalists were

---

[1] Mk. 9:38-40; see also Mt. 12:30.

[2] His famous Commentary is titled *Tafsir and Manar* in 12 vols. Sadly, the
author died before its completion. The Commentary stops at Sura Yufus
[12]:52.

quite active and their works widespread in the days of Muhammad Rida both in Egypt and throughout the Middle East. However, I once mentioned this point to some of my fellow Seminarians, who seemed to take it with a pinch of salt. They could go so far as to agree that what the European Orientalists had introduced might have been of some benefit to the Muslim world, but most decidedly not in matters relating to the study of the Qur'an and other Islamic subjects.

In saying this, they left me with the impression that these things are the exclusive monopoly of the Islamic 'Ummah' i.e. the Muslim community. In fact, on one occasion they suggested that my friendship with the English missionaries and my frequent visits to their house might be of some use to me like learning English or receiving medication. But when they start delving into Islamic matters, they ought to be ignored. At this point I could only respond with a smile!

For the first time, it dawned upon me that my frequent visits to the English missionaries were being noticed. I became worried and wondered if the experience I shared with Dr Rigby and his colleagues had leaked out. After finding out that nothing of the sort had occurred, I realised that my fellow Seminarians knew nothing of this. Indeed, I imagined that they were positive that for a youth so rooted in Islam like me, nothing that those missionaries said or did could ever sway me from my faith. I decided that from then on I ought to be a little more cautious and careful in my conversation with them. However, this did not prevent me from continuing to visit the Mission House and spending time with Dr Rigby and his co-workers whom I had by now taken into my confidence.

The God of Surprises

Not long after this incident, a very interesting book fell into my hand titled *al-Bakurat al-Shahiyya fi al-Riwaya al-Diniyya*.[3] Written by an anonymous Syrian author, the book relates a strange story, which made a lasting impact upon me. In August 1861, a distinguished Muslim scholar from Damascus named Ahmad Abd al-Hadi received a letter from a Christian friend in Aleppo. The letter drew the attention of the Muslim scholar to the fact that the Bible, contrary to the popular Islamic notion, could not have been distorted or falsified, since the

---

[3] This remarkable book is known in English by the title '*Sweet First Fruit*'.

Qur'an itself confirmed its teaching and commended its reading. This challenging letter led Abd al-Hadi to invite some of his learned Muslim colleagues to discuss its contents and formulate a response. They spent several months re-studying the relevant passages of the Qur'an to find out the real meaning of what was said about the Jewish and Christian scriptures. The Qur'anic texts about these two sacred books are by no means few. Among the texts under discussion, for example, was one relating to Jewish scripture, which states:

> *Verily, we sent down the Law (the Torah) wherein are guidance and light. By it the Prophets, who bowed (to God in submission), judge the Jews; and the Rabbis and the Doctors judged by that portion of the Book of God, of which they were the keepers and the witnesses.*[4]

As for the Christian scripture, in the same sura the testimony of the Qur'an leaves the reader in no doubt about its authenticity:

> *. . . And we gave him (Jesus) the Gospel wherein is to be found guidance and light, and confirmation of the Law that had come before him: a guidance and an admonition to those who fear God.*
> *Let the People of the Gospel judge by what God has revealed therein." (v.49)*

The intensive studies and discussions of important Qur'anic texts such as these brought those eminent Muslim scholars to the conclusion that the scriptures of the Old and New Testament could not possibly have been falsified. They concluded that the most ancient manuscripts of the Bible pre-date the Qur'an by centuries, so that these Qur'anic verses could not refer to a text of the Bible that was different from the one, which exists today.

The scholars soon turned to the study of the Bible in obedience to these texts of the Qur'an, which they believed and studied from their youth. Different reactions appeared among them. Some felt that the safer way was to cling to Islam as they had always done. But others discovered in the Bible the message of the coming of Jesus as the Saviour of mankind, and, gradually, the divinity of this Saviour, His death and resurrection. At this stage, the reaction from their relatives

---

[4] Sura al-Ma'ida [5]:47.

and neighbours was one of anger and dismay. Consequently, these Muslim scholars were arrested and put in prison.

At this period, Syria was part of the Ottoman Empire. Apparently the local officials would have been happy to drop the case had it not been for the prisoners' opponents who insisted on pursuing it. Eventually, they accused 'Umar al-Harith, the youngest prisoner, of doubting the divine origin of the Qur'an. This was sufficient to convict him of insulting the Qur'an and the prophet Muhammad. He was filled with inexplicable joy as he was sentenced to death and beheaded.

The rest of his companions were deported to Lebanon where they were baptised and confirmed in the faith of Jesus Christ. However, under international pressure, the Sultan of Istanbul ordered that the exiles should be allowed to return to their native land after two years. Shaykh Ahmad Abd al-Hadi, who was responsible for this whole episode was already elderly, and he died five years later. On their return, these noble Christian exiles lost no opportunity for explaining their new faith to other Muslims.

The decision I had once made to undertake a comparative study of the Bible and the Qur'an had been shelved in the light of my remarkable experience of passing the exam. My glimpse of Christ on that particular occasion had brought my research work to a standstill. But this book was indeed a pleasant surprise. It certainly excited my interest in the Islamic notion of 'al-tahrif' i.e. the alleged claim that the Bible has been falsified. I was so impressed by this book that I read it twice and digested all its detailed arguments. As a result, my mind was rekindled with the desire to make a serious assessment of the widely popular Islamic claim that Jewish and Christian scriptures have been falsified. I was also determined that this time such a study assessment should be done in a judicious and objective manner.

However, it would not be far off the mark to point out that until now, I was neither a Christian nor a Muslim. I was in a spiritual limbo in which, strangely enough, I seemed perfectly comfortable! But the time for waking up had to come, and the hand of Providence was there to do it by putting into my hand that remarkable book, which I still have today. That book was indeed a pleasant surprise, and behind it there was the God of all surprises.

A Storm in a Teacup

The Seminary hosted a visiting lecturer who gave a paper on what he called, 'The Erroneous teachings of Early Islamic Heresies and the People of the Book (i.e. Jews & Christians)'. As he spoke, it became obvious that he was saying nothing new or original. He was depending on two early Islamic polemical works. One was *al-Farqu baina al-Firaq* by Abd al-Qahir al-Baghdadi, the 10th century Muslim theologian. It was exclusively targeting the early Islamic heresies. The other was *al-Fasl fi al-Milal wa al-Ahwa' wa al-nihal* by the Muslim theologian and polemicist, Muhammad Ibn Hazm of Cordova (994–1064).[5] In addition to his fierce attack on all kinds of Islamic heresies, Ibn Hazm devotes a considerable part of his attack on Jewish and Christian scriptures. In criticising them, he endeavours to find contradictions and incompatibilities of their writings in order to justify the accusation of falsification of texts. It may be worth pointing out that when he comes to the New Testament, he is not certain whether it is falsified or purely fabricated by man.[6]

During this lecture, I noticed a rather laughable scene. Whist the visiting lecturer was prosing, a number of students were dozing! Some looked keenly interested but others were simply bored. As for me, I could see many holes in what he was saying, and each hole seemed big enough to drive a bus through it! I had many question marks as I listened to that lecture. When the time came for questions, I was careful not to ask any question that might stir up a hornet's nest. This subject was a minefield and the risk of walking into it was high. During question time, I sat quietly wondering if it was wise to ask any question at all in this context. My close friendship with the missionaries, which most students knew, somehow made me feel nervous and vulnerable in this situation. I could easily come under suspicion if my question (or questions) happened to be dismissive of the *'Tahrif'* concept, which is taken by Muslims as more or less an axiomatic article of faith. After much hesitation, I raised my hand to ask my question. At this point the students in the hall fixed their eyes on me, including those who were intermittently dozing!

---

[5] It is important to note that these books are still in circulation today. Ibn Hazm's work in particular is still highly prized by many Muslim polemicists.

[6] See Angel Gonzalez Palencia, *Historia de la Literatura Arabico-Espanola* (Madrid, 1945), pp. 221ff.

"What are the real grounds of evidence for the falsification of Jewish and Christian Scriptures?" I asked rather nervously.

"There are many," answered the guest speaker, "but the greatest of them all is the amount of contradictions which permeate their pages. Yet, in terms of consistency and credibility, the Holy Qur'an stands in glaring contrast to these books." And to bolster his statement he quoted the Qur'anic verse, *"Can they not consider the Qur'an? Had it been from any other than God, they would surely have found in it many contradictions."*[7]

"But can we in all good conscience" I asked, "take contradictions as a proof of corruption or falsification? Do you not agree, for example, that a contradictory document or book may not necessarily suggest that some anonymous hands had tampered with it? May it not belong to one single author, who may even be well known to us?" At this point I was strongly tempted to add that there are contradictions in the Qur'an itself. Hence the Islamic theoretical tool of *'al-Naskh'* (abrogation) was used specifically to resolve such contradictions. But I decided to bite my tongue.

"Yes, what you said is true." he replied. "Human authors," he went on, "are prone to mistakes and contradictions. But, it is impossible for God to contradict Himself, and the Qur'an as His expressed *'bayan'* (i.e. clear declaration) is a perfect example. It is free from any discrepancy or contradiction." He then cited the Qur'anic text: *"No falsehood can approach it (the Qur'an) from before or behind it. It is sent down by one full of wisdom, worthy of all praise."*[8] By this he was implying that any sacred writing that carries contradictions has been falsified.

The atmosphere in the hall was saturated with approval for the lecturer's answer. Some might even have rubbed their hands in glee that I was now firmly put in my place. But, whether out of anger or pride or both, I got up and respectfully invited the attention of the guest speaker to two Qur'anic verses, requesting him to give his learned and judicious opinion on them.

"We have two verses in the holy Qur'an that are a bit difficult to reconcile," I began; "they relate to Pharaoh's hot pursuit after the Israelites and what happened thereafter. In one verse we read, '*So*

---

[7] Sura al-Nisa'[4]:82.

[8] Sura Fussilat [41]:42.

Pharaoh sought to drive them out of the land; but we drowned him and all who were with him.[9]

"The other verse," I continued, "tells us the following: *'And we led the children of Israel through the sea; and Pharaoh and his hosts followed them in eager and hostile sort until, when the drowning overtook them, he said that there is no God but He whom the children of Israel believe, and I am one of the Muslims.' 'Yes, now', said God: 'but thou hast been rebellious hitherto, and wast one of the wicked doers. But this day will we rescue thee with thy body that thou mayest be a sign to those who shall be after thee . . .'*[10]

There was a deadly hush as I paused for a few seconds, with everybody waiting to see what I would come up with next. But to their relief or disappointment, I had only one short polite request for the speaker:

"Can your eminence give us your personal view as to these two rather interesting verses?" I briefly added, and then sat down.

"If you think that these two verses contradict each other", the speaker replied, "then you are mistaken. As a matter of fact, these verses complement each other. Simply put, the second verse is an extension or expansion of the first. After drowning him, God simply brought him out of the water for all the Israelites to see his dead body."

"That may be so," I replied, "but what should be the answer to those who say that the Torah does not mention that Pharaoh had personally been drowned and afterwards God brought his dead body out of the waters for all to see. In the Jewish legend, however, Pharaoh was saved from drowning in order to relate to the Egyptians the great miracle God had shown His people. In their opinion, this is quite agreeable with Sura Yunus [10]:92. The idea that he was drowned and his dead body was later brought out for all to see is a clear attempt by commentators to harmonize Sura Yunus [10]:92 with Sura al-Isra'[17]:103.

"You are now not only suggesting that there are contradictions in the Qur'an, but that it is also infected with Israelyyat (Jewish legends)," declared the speaker in what sounded like a sharp voice veneered over with a forced smile.

---

[9] Sura al-Isra' [17]:103.

[10] Sura Yunus [10]:90-92.

"That is not what I said," I retorted, "I simply asked for your explanation of these two verses as a response to the opinions just mentioned."

The visiting speaker repeated what he had said earlier that the second verse is an extension of the first one. At this point, I held my peace, realising as a proverb has it, 'a still tongue makes a wise head'. Meanwhile, I had the feeling that the atmosphere in the hall was far from relaxed. On the way out of the hall two of my student friends remarked that the speaker did not seem to give a satisfactory answer to my question. They wondered why I went silent when I could have pressed him a bit further. A third student who had just joined them remarked that my silence was as good as victory. "In my opinion," he said, "it does not necessarily mean that one has lost the argument when he goes silent."

In the course of our conversation, however, they gave me an implicit note of warning that a hard core element of students were of the view that my motive was to show that the Qur'an was not free from contradictions. They also warned me that some of them might lodge a complaint with the Principal. It transpired the following day that the Principal was fully informed of the entire episode, probably also by the guest speaker himself, but decided to let sleeping dogs lie. Whether because of his concern for the Seminary's reputation or because he was a friend of my grandfather, the Principal chose to dismiss what happened as of no consequence. He simply regarded the incident as the English cliché has it, 'a storm in a teacup'.

The Allegation of 'Tahrif'

What happened on that occasion had further strengthened my resolve to look into the subject of 'tahrif' (i.e. the alleged concept that Jewish and Christian scriptures have been corrupted or falsified). But there were other incentives as well. One of them goes back to my fondness of Arab history and literature, and I was among those in the Seminary that distinguished themselves in these subjects. Among my favourite historians was Abd-al-Rahman Ibn Khaldun (1332–1406 AD), who was born in Tunisia of Spanish Arab extraction. He is considered as the greatest and most reliable Medieval Arab historian. He developed a consistent philosophy of history, as well as a unique method of writing in the area of political economy and sociology.

In the course of reading his account on ancient Near East history, I was astonished by what this great historian wrote regarding the Jewish scripture. Contrary to Ibn Hazm (the Muslim polemicist), Ibn Khaldun was able to write:

> The claim that their scholars (Jewish Rabbis) had altered many places in the Torah is remote, according to Ibn Abbas as reported by al-Bukhari in his Sahih. He (Ibn Abbas) said, "God forbid that any nation can purposely resort to changing its (sacred) book that was revealed to its prophet. They altered and distorted it only by (their) interpretation. And the Exalted One testifies to this when he says, *'And they (the Jews) possess the torah wherein is the rule (or command) of God'.*[11] Had they literally altered the Torah, they would not have the Torah wherein is the rule (or command) of God." Therefore, when the holy Qur'an speaks of alteration and distortion, it is the interpretation which is intended.[12]

To my surprise also I discovered that the unreasonable claim that the Bible had been literally corrupted or falsified has always been challenged by a number of Muslim scholars since the 9th century. The famous Muslim scholar and reformer, Muhammad 'Abduh, pointed out that the charge that Jewish and Christian scriptures have been falsified –

> makes no sense at all. It would not have been possible for Jews and Christians everywhere to agree on changing the text. Even if those in Arabia had done it, the difference between their book and those of their brothers, let us say, in Syria or Europe, would have been obvious.[13]

It was these and many more factors that led me to examine the Qur'an and the Hadith seriously regarding the issue of *'Tahrif'*. The result of my detailed examination of these and other Islamic sources, which will shortly be presented to the reader, led me to the conclusion

[11] Sura al-Ma'idah [5]:46.

[12] See Ibn Khaldun, *Tarikh Ibn Khaldun: Kitab al-'ibar fi diwan al-Mubtada wa al-Kahbar* (Beirut 1992), Vol. 2, p. 9. It is worth noting that here Ibn Khaldun was undoubtedly influenced by the 9th century scholar & polemicist, al-Qasim Ibn Ibrahim al-Zaidi. He was the earliest representative of the view that the Bible was free from any distortion or falsification.

[13] See Muhammad Rida, *Tafsir al-Manar* (Beirut n.d.), Vol. 2, p. 49.

that the claim of falsification was obviously a later invention. As a matter of fact, the idea of *'tahrif'* (falsification of sacred documents) is not foreign to Muslims themselves. For centuries Shi'a and Sunni Muslims have mutually charged each other with falsifying the Qur'an.[14] In any case, the question that kept coming to my mind was this: if according to the Qur'an and the Hadith, the texts of Jewish and Christian scriptures were intact, then how and when was the charge of falsification made, which became a principal part in Muslim polemics against Judaism and Christianity?

It has been suggested that Ibn Hazm was the first Muslim to charge that the Bible was corrupted. There is even the suggestion that the charge of falsification originated at the time of the Crusades. But it is more likely that the attack on the integrity of the Bible began only when Muslim scholars became conversant with the Bible. On realising that its teaching could not be reconciled with that of the Qur'an they had no option but to claim that the Bible was corrupted. As long as it was concealed from them, they believed firmly in its authenticity as the Qur'an clearly states.

Attention can be drawn to the fact that Muhammad himself (and his followers) had very little knowledge of the contents of Jewish and Christian scriptures, and what he knew was apparently through hearsay. From the beginning he had appealed to the evidence of the *'Peoples of the Book'* (i.e. the Jews and the Christians), as he was convinced that the contents of the Old and New Testaments coincided perfectly with what he preached on the basis of his revelations. The outcome of this is obvious in the Qur'an itself. "As a matter of fact," wrote J. W. Sweetman, "even after taking all the similarities between the Bible and the Qur'an into account, the Qur'an manifests a clearly inadequate and incomplete knowledge of the contents of the Bible."[15] So then, opinions may differ as to the origin of the *'tahrif'* allegation, but it is almost certain that the origin of the idea in Islam goes back to the time when Muslim scholars became aware that the contents of Jewish and Christian scriptures did not mostly accord with those of the Qur'an. And in order to protect the integrity of the Qur'an that was now at stake, they resorted to the bold assertion that the Bible was falsified.

---

[14] On this point see Ignaz Goldziher, *Mohammedanische Studien* (Halle, 1890), Vol. 1, pp. 272, 281.

[15] J. Windrow Sweetman, *Islam and Christian Theology* (Lutterworth Press, London 1945), Part 1, Vol. 2, p. 139.

The Quest for the Truth

It has just been stated that from the beginning, Muhammad knew precious little of Jewish and Christian scriptures. And what he knew was through hearsay and most of it inaccurate. Meanwhile, he passionately believed that what he preached on the basis of his revelations was in full agreement with the scriptures of the 'People of the Book'. The term frequently used is 'musadiq' (from 'tasdiq'), which means confirming or affirming the authenticity of these Scriptures. This word is mentioned no fewer than eighteen times, and almost always in connection with the Scriptures of the Old and New Testaments. The following few passages may be cited as an example:

> O Children of Israel! Remember the favour, which I bestowed upon you, and fulfil your covenant with me as I fulfil my covenant with you, and fear none but me. And believe in what I have revealed <u>confirming</u> the revelation which is with you . . .[16]

When the 'People of the Book' (particularly the Jews) declined his invitation, Muhammad still continued to emphasize that his message was confirmatory of their Scriptures.

> And when it is said to them (the Jews), "Believe in what God has sent down", they say, "We believe in what was sent down to us": yet they reject all besides, although it be the truth <u>confirmatory</u> of their Scripture . . .[17]

The term 'confirmation' in the following verse applies both to Jewish and Christian Scriptures, as Tabari, the famous expositor, clearly declares.

> This Qur'an . . . A <u>confirmation</u> of (revelation) that went before it, and a fuller explanation of the Book – wherein there is no doubt – from the Lord of the worlds.[18]

In the beginning of my research, I had thus discovered that after all the Qur'an affirms the authenticity of the Bible in the clearest possible

---

[16] Sura al-Baqara [2]:40-41, see also v.89.

[17] Sura al-Baqara [2]:91.

[18] Sura Yunus [10]:37; also Sura Yusuf [12]:111; see Tabari, *Tafsir* (Beirut 1995), Vol. 7, p. 153.

terms. I had indeed learned the Qur'an by heart and later learned its exposition under the best teachers of exegesis in the Seminary. My knowledge of the Qur'an and the Hadith was further enriched by the works of classical orthodox expositors, which were in abundance at the Seminary's library. But there were many things in these Islamic sources, which I either took for granted or simply glanced over, and among them a good number of passages pertaining to the Bible. I also recall that these passages did not seem to detain the lecturers long enough. But during that summer period when I started my in-depth research study into this subject, I was astonished by what I discovered. There are highly remarkable titles, which the Qur'an uses to describe the Scriptures of the Old and New Testaments. It would be sufficient at this point to draw attention to two of them:

1 The Book of God

The Qur'an clearly acknowledges and indeed describes the Torah as the 'Book of God'. It is worth noting that the term 'Book of God' is substituted often by the words 'al-Towrat' (the Torah), or 'al-Injil' (the Gospel), or simply by the word 'the Book':

> Surely we sent down the Torah, wherein is guidance and light. By its standard, the Prophets who surrendered themselves (to God), judged the Jews, as (also) did the Rabbis and the Doctors of the Law. For to them was entrusted the protection of God's Book and they were witnesses thereto . . .[19]

The Qur'anic recognition of the Torah as 'God's Book' remained consistent, apparently even during the period when the relationship between Muhammad and the Jewish community of Medina was at an all-time low:

> And when there came to them a Messenger from God, confirming to them the previous revelations made to them, some of those to whom the Scriptures were given, threw the Book of God behind their backs as if they did not know . . .[20]

The Gospel (or the Evangel) that Jesus proclaimed is also clearly affirmed as a message from God:

---

[19] Sura al-Ma'idah [5]:47.

[20] Sura al-Baqara [2]:101.

And in their steps (the Prophets), we sent Jesus the son of Mary, confirming the Torah that had come before him: We sent him the Gospel: wherein was Guidance and light . . .[21]

Interestingly, the Qur'an does not overlook the distinctly characteristic impact of the Gospel upon the followers of Jesus:

We sent after them (the Prophets) Jesus the son of Mary, and bestowed upon him the Gospel; and we ordained in the hearts of those who followed him compassion and mercy.[22]

2 al-Dhikr

The word is derived from the verb *'dhakar'* or *'dhakkir'* (i.e. to remind or to bring to remembrance). As Hebrew and Arabic are Semitic languages, the equivalent of the verb *'dhakar'* can be found in Jeremiah 2:2 *"Zakirti . . . hesed n'urayk"* i.e. *"I remember (or I bring to remembrance) the devotion of your youth."* Hence, *'al-dhikr'* in the Qur'an is descriptive of the divine oracle as a reminder to mankind. The Qur'an frequently describes itself as *"dhikrun li al-'alamin"* i.e. a divine message of reminder and admonition to all creatures.[23] But there are Qur'anic passages in which the word *'al-dhikr'* applies also to the Bible:

. . . Before this, we wrote in the Psalms, after 'al-dhikr' (the Torah given to Moses): *"My righteous servants shall inherit the earth".*[24]

The worship of other gods was contrary to the unity of God. Monotheism was not only the message (*al-dhikr*) of Islam, but also of the Prophets who came before. In other words, there was no difference between the divine message of the Qur'an and that of the Prophets before:

---

[21] Sura al-Ma'idah [5]:49.

[22] Sura al-Hadid [57]:27.

[23] See for example the following verses Sura Yusuf [12]:104; Sura Sad [38]:87; Sura al-Qalam [68]:52.

[24] Sura al-Anbiya' [21]:105. It's worth noting that the quotation *"My righteous servants shall inherit the earth"*, is from Ps. 37:11 where the sentence reads precisely, *"The meek shall inherit the earth"*. It is the only Biblical quotation found in the Qur'an.

*Or have they taken for worship (other) gods besides him? Say,
"Bring your convincing proof: this is the Message (dhikr) of
those with me and the Message (dhikr) of those before me.
But most people know not the Truth, and so turn away."*[25]

When the polytheists disputed Muhammad's prophethood, they were
urged to ask those who possessed (*al-dhikr*) the oracles of God i.e. the
Jews and the Christians:

*And before you (Muhammad) also the messengers we sent
were but men, to whom we granted inspiration: if you realise
this not, ask of those who possess the Message (al-dhikr).*[26]

It follows therefore that the God who sent down His divine oracle,
or message (*al-dhikr*), is fully responsible for guarding it against any
corruption or forgery:

*We have, without doubt, sent down the Message (dhikr); and
we will assuredly guard it* (from corruption).[27]

According to classical orthodox commentators, including modern
ones, the word *'dhikr'* in this particular verse refers specifically to the
Qur'an. Then they proceed to smuggle their theological concept of
'tahrif' into it by suggesting that of all the other Scriptures, God has
accorded the Qur'an His own divine protection. As regards the other
Scriptures (of the Old & New Testaments), and particularly the Torah,
God has assigned its protection to the People of the Book i.e. the Jews,
who later falsified it. This suggestion is based on the phrase in the
last part of Sura al-Ma'idah [5]:47, *"For to them was entrusted the
protection of God's Book . . ."* In fact, in its context, the phrase does not
mean more than: God's Book was committed to them as a true guide
in their spiritual and judicial administration of the people.

If indeed God had taken charge of protecting the Qur'an and let
the Jews get on with the protection of the Torah, then He could be
charged with grave dereliction of his divine responsibility, favouritism
and devaluation of one divine Message against another. As a matter
of fact, this is not what the Qur'an seems to say. Indeed, the Qur'an
gives Jewish and Christian Scriptures such noble titles as *'the Book*

[25] Sura al-Anbiya' [21]:24.

[26] Sura al-Nahl [16]:43; see also Sura al-Anbiya'[21]:7.

[27] Sura al-Hijr [15]:9.

of God' (Sura al-Baqara [2]:101), 'the Word of God' (Sura al-Baqara [2]:75, 'a light and guidance to man' (Sura al-An'am [6]:91, 'a guidance and mercy' (Sura Hud [11]:17), 'an admonition for all matters' (Sura al-A'raf [7]:145, 'a lucid Book' (Sura al-Safat [37]:117), 'al-Furqan' or an illumination (Sura al-Baqara [2]:53; Sura al-Anbiya' [21]:48).

The Qur'an also describes the Christian Gospel as guidance and a light, confirming the Mosaic Law; and the Christians themselves are urged to look into their own Scriptures to find God's revelation to them (Sura al-Ma'idah [5]:49-50).[28] It is also interesting that even Muhammad is exhorted to test the validity of his own message with the contents of the previous divine revelations to the Jews and the Christians (see Sura Yunus [10]:94). Finally, it is worth noting that there is some ambiguity in the phrase *"we will assuredly guard it"*, which some have taken as referring to Muhammad rather than to the Qur'an. Apparently, the reason for this is that the Arabic pronoun in this text *'lahu'* can either be neuter (it) or masculine (him). Moreover, those who see this phrase as referring to Muhammad support their view with Sura al-Ma'idah [5]:67 *"... God will protect you* (Muhammad) *from men".* [29]

I had the entire Qur'an stored in my memory. I knew and could easily recite the above-mentioned passages any time, and if the circumstances permitted I could readily give an orthodox expository talk on them. But the real significance of these passages had not dawned upon me yet. However, when the hand of Providence began to work, it led me to look again into these Qur'anic passages where, for the first time, and indeed as a very important step, I was able to discover a mine of information.

---

[28] Norman L. Geisler & Abdul Saleeb, *Answering Islam: The Crescent in the Light of the Cross* (Grand Rapids, Michigan 1995), p. 207; John Takle, 'Islam and Christianity', in *Studies in Islamic Law, Religion and Society*, ed. E.H.S. Bhatia (New Delhi, India: Deep & Deep Publications, 1989), p. 217.

[29] See Tabari, *Jami ' al-Bayan 'an Ta'wil Ayi al-Qur'an* (Beirut, 1995), Vol. 8, pp. 11-12; Al-Qurtubi, *al-Jami' li Ahkam al-Qur'an al-Karim* Cairo, n.d.), Vol. 6, pp. 3621f.; Ibn Kathir, *Tafsir al-Qur'an al-'Azim* (Cairo, 2001), Vol. 2, 547; al-Zamakhshari, *al- Kashshaf* (Beirut, 1995), Vol. 2, p. 550.

Chapter 4

A FINAL STEP TO CHRIST

"Our father refreshes us on the journey with some pleasant inns. But will not encourage us to mistake them for home."

(C.S. Lewis)

The witness of the Qur'an does indeed establish the authenticity of the Bible in spite of the widespread Muslim assumption that it has been falsified. But I was aware that it would be imprudent to rest my case on this point alone. There remained a serious question that needed to be answered. For example, what of those Qur'anic passages where *'tahrif'* (i.e. falsification or distortion) is clearly mentioned? Do they refer to the Bible? Is it possible that after affirming the veracity of the Bible, the Qur'an then contradicts itself by suggesting that it has after all been falsified? There was certainly some more investigative work to be done.

It was the summer vacation of 1959, in which I had plenty of time to look into this issue. To do this I decided to spend ample time in the national library, which was adjacent to the city gate. Here there was plenty of valuable material that could be of great assistance to me in addressing the above questions. The energy and keenness with which I was being driven to look into this subject was, to say the least, unprecedented in my life as a young Seminarian. Looking back, I cannot but admit that the hand of God was obviously active at that particular point in my life.

Meanwhile, my frequent visits to the Mission House continued as before. All the time, Dr Rigby and his colleagues seemed to inspire me with a remarkable sense of trust and encouragement. Their loving attitude made me feel I was a member of the Mission House family. These wonderful feelings played a vital part in leading me finally to the full experience of the saving grace of the Lord Jesus Christ. To this day, I still recall with a deep sense of appreciation how I had never been treated as an outsider. Herein was the love of God clearly manifest.

It was a love that was free from any trace of partiality. Indeed, Jesus taught that the impartiality of divine love should be the hallmark of the children of God. In describing God's sublime attribute of love, Jesus made it clear that *"He makes his sun rise on the evil and on the good, and sends rain on the just and on the unjust."* It was perhaps this sentence, which led Cervantes to write, "When God sends the dawn He sends it for all." But our Lord does not stop there. He goes on to urge His followers to live in imitation of that perfect divine love: *"You, therefore, must be perfect as your heavenly Father is perfect"*.[1]

The shining life of that medical missionary and his colleagues was constantly challenging me to take seriously the message they were propagating. Their message was very much consistent with their quality of life and work. It is true to say that the message that does not translate itself into action is a dead one, however strong and lovely it may sound. Emerson once said of Seneca, "He says the loveliest things, if only he had the right to say them." Robert L. Stevenson was able to say of a teacher, "I cannot hear what you say, for listening to what you are." In my own life, the hand of Providence was apparently working on two fronts: the remarkable witness of that medical missionary on the one front; and the investigative study I was keenly conducting on the other. There is a sense in which the one was complementing the other, and behind them both the hand of God was actively working towards the fulfilment of His purpose in my life.

The Unchangeable Word of God

In the course of my research, I was greatly surprised to discover how the Qur'an affirms so clearly the veracity of the Bible. Not only that, but there are Qur'anic passages, which equally affirm that it is impossible for the divine message to be changed or tampered with in any way. Muslims may like to apply such passages to the Qur'an alone. But surely the veracity of the Bible, which the Qur'an itself so clearly affirms, must also of necessity rest upon the fact that, being the word of God, it cannot possibly be altered or tampered with in any way. To claim otherwise would be tantamount to calling God's protective power into question.[2] I noted that there are at least two

---

[1] Mt. 5:44-48.

[2] See Sura al-Hijr [15]:9.

Qur'anic passages, which point to the unchangeableness of the Word (or Words) of God in Jewish and Christian scriptures:

> ... *It is not thee (Muhammad) they cry lies to, but it is the signs of God that the evildoers deny. Messengers indeed were cried lies to before thee, yet they endured patiently that they were cried lies to, and were hurt, until our help came to them. <u>No man can change the words of God</u>; and there has already come to thee some tiding of the Envoys."*[3]

The background of this passage was Muhammad's encounter with his sworn enemy, Abu Lahab, and his companions, according to most commentators.[4] Abu Lahab is reported to have said to Muhammad that it was not him that they dismissed as false but the message, which he claimed to bring. The prophet then was encouraged to follow the example of the former prophets, who endured patiently their hardships. Like them, he too will be vindicated in the end; and as in their case, the divine *'words'* (i.e. of warnings, threats and promises) that were once revealed to them, and are now revealed to him, are true and *"no man can change them"*.

In the same Sura, I found another verse, which carries a similar import. Indeed, this verse seems to have a direct reference to Jewish and the Christian scriptures rather than to the Qur'an, as Muslim commentators suggest. This is so especially when one reads it in the context of the verse that precedes it. The two should therefore be read together:

> ... *Shall I seek for judge other than God? When it is He who hath sent unto you the Book* (the Qur'an), *explained in detail. They know full well, to whom we have given the Book* (i.e. the Jews and the Christians), *that it* (i.e. the Qur'an) *hath been sent down from thy Lord in truth. Never be then of those who doubt. The Word of thy Lord doth find its fulfilment in truth and in justice. <u>None can change His Word</u>: for He is the one who heareth and knoweth all.*[5]

---

[3] Sura al-An'am [6]:33-34,115; see also Sura al-Safat [37]:171.

[4] See Tabari, *Jami' al-Bayan*, Vol. 5, p. 40; Ibn Kathir, *al-Qur'an al-'Adhim* (Cairo, 2000), Vol.2, pp. 130-132; al-Qurtubi, *al-Jami' li Ahkam al-Qur'an al-Karim*, Vol. 4, pp. 2413f.

[5] Sura al-An'am [6]:114-115.

The background of this passage appears to be that Muhammad's opponents challenged him to provide a just and trustworthy arbiter who could verify his claim of being the recipient of divine revelation. In response, he could appeal to two arbiters: *"God"*, and those *"to whom we have given the Book"* i.e. those Jews and the Christians who embraced Islam like Salman Suhayb and Abd-Allah Ibn Salam. They could apparently assert that both Jewish and Christian scriptures had predicted the coming of Muhammad as a new prophet with a new revelation. In view of this, he is told never to be one *"of those who doubt. The Word of thy Lord* (in Jewish and Christian scriptures regarding Muhammad) *doth find its fulfilment in truth and in justice. None can change His Word."*

Interestingly, the Arabic verb *'fulfil'* is in the past tense *'tammat'* (fulfilled). The sentence therefore may safely be translated, *"The Word of thy Lord* (in Jewish and Christian scriptures regarding Muhammad) *hath truthfully and justly been fulfilled."* Moreover, his appeal to the scriptures of the people of the Book in this respect may well be an implicit challenge to his opponents to check for themselves, and consult those who possess these scriptures. In their quest, according to him, they will find his divine mission already foretold in those books and fulfilled in their own time.[6] Thus, the Word of God in those scriptures is true and authentic, for *"None can change His Word."* In the words of Tabari on this sentence, "No alteration in what He (God) has announced in His books (i.e. Jewish and Christian scriptures) . . . for the slanderers could neither add to the books of God nor subtract from them."[7]

The references to the authenticity of the Jewish and Christian scriptures are abundantly clear. Both the Old and New Testaments also give stark warning against any attempt to tamper with the Word of God, which they contain. In the Old Testament, the Torah makes it plain: *"You shall not add to the word which I command you, nor take from it, that you may keep the commandments of the Lord your God which I command you"* (Deuteronomy 4:2). *"Everything that I command you, you shall be careful to do; you shall not add to it or take from it"* (12:32). The Book of the Wisdom of Solomon declares: *"Every word of God proves true; He is a shield to those who take refuge*

---

[6] See also Sura al-A'raf [7]:157 where Muhammad is said to have been foretold in the Old & New Testaments.

[7] Tabari, *Jami' al-Bayan*, Vol. 5, p. 13.

in Him. Do not add to His words, lest He rebuke you, and you be found a liar" (Proverbs 30:5-6). The New Testament (*al-Injil*), describes the dire consequences that might befall those who would tamper with the written word of God: *"I warn everyone who hears the words of the prophecy of this book: if any one adds to them, God will add to him the plagues described in this book. And if any one takes away from the words of the book of this prophecy, God will take away his share in the tree of life and in the holy city; which are described in this book"* (Revelation 22:18-19).

The space of this chapter forbids the citations of many other implicit and explicit Qur'anic passages, which hold Jewish and Christian scriptures to be genuine and of divine authority. For me, meanwhile, there was one verse, which stood out to me as the clearest Qur'anic verdict that these scriptures are beyond all reasonable doubt entirely unimpeachable. This Qur'anic verse, which became the focus of my attention, reads as follows:

> *Those to whom we have sent down the Book (Jews and the Christians), study it as it should be studied: they are the ones that believe therein: and those who reject Faith therein, the loss is their own.*[8]

However, it should be pointed out to the English reader of this text that the phrase, *"study it as it should be studied"* in A.Yusuf Ali's English translation, may be the nearest meaning of the Arabic *'yatlunahu haqqa tilawatihi'*. Incidentally, J.M. Rodwell's translation reads, *"who read it as it ought to be read"*, and that of A.J. Arberry, which reads, *"who recite it with true recitation"*.[9] However, commentators are unanimous that in this particular text, the verb *'yatlunahu'* carries the same meaning as the verb *'talaha'* in Sura al-Shams [91]:2 *"By the Moon when she followeth him!"* (*wa al-qamari idha talaha*). Thus, the word *'yatlunahu'* in the above text signifies the practice of following what is being read, recited or studied both in terms of faith and conduct. Moreover, it was uniquely important for me to find out what Muslim commentators' view of this text was.

---

[8] Sura al-Baqara [2]:121.

[9] See A.Yusuf Ali, *THE HOLY QUR'AN: Text, Translation and Commentary* (London, 1975), p. 51; J.M. Rodwell, *THE QUR'AN* (London, 1994), p. 13; A.J. Arberry, *The Koran Interpreted* (Oxford University Press, 1998), p. 15.

The first to be consulted were the works of classical Muslim expositors. The commentary of al-Jalalayn is a brief but popular work. For the latter, the text clearly refers to the People of the Book "who study it exactly as it was sent down", (i.e. with no attempt to tamper with it in any way).[10] The highly distinguished Tabari cites a host of early commentators who take the verse as meaning those "who follow it as it should be followed", or "who act upon it". He then goes on to cite Ibn Mas'ud, a noted companion of the prophet, who was much consulted on account of his knowledge of the Qur'an. Commenting on this verse, Tabari reports Ibn Mas'ud as saying, " 'As it should be studied' (Ar. *haqqa tilawatihi*), means to permit what it permits and forbid what it forbids, and to read it as God has sent it down, and do not displace words from their right places."[11] For al-Zamakhshari, the text refers to "the faithful among the People of the Book . . . They neither distort it nor change the sign of the messenger of God . . . in it". On the contrary, those who deny this are the ones who distort it. (i.e. alluding to the distortion of the meaning of the text rather than the text itself).[12]

It is outside the scope of this chapter to cite many more Muslim commentators like al-Qurtubi, Ibn Kathir, al-Razi, al-Baidawi and others. One may add to the list of such notable expositors the name of the more recent scholar, Muhammad Rida, the pupil of Muhammad Abdu.[13] In all my careful study of these and other commentaries, I was astonished that in their treatment of this text, the commentators are entirely unanimous that the word of God in Jewish and Christian scriptures has remained unchangeably the same.

The Qur'anic Idea of '*Tahrif*'

So far the above-mentioned findings were a source of great enlightenment to me. No doubt, these things had not been foreign to me as a Seminarian. But there is a sense in which a rediscovery

---

[10] *Tafsir al-Jalalayn* (Beirut, n.d.), p. 26.

[11] Tabari, *Jami ' al-Bayan*, Vol. 1, pp. 726f.

[12] al-Zamakhshari, *al-Kashshaf*, Vol. 1, p. 182. The idea that Muhammad was predicted in the Jewish & Christian scriptures was quite prevalent among early Muslims, according to Sura al-A'raf [7]:158.

[13] See Muhammad Rashid Rida, *Tafsir al-Manar* (Beirut, n.d.), Vol. 1, pp. 446f.

can be most refreshing. In my case, it was a surprise and indeed an illumination of a unique sort. But what of those passages where *'tahrif'* (falsification) is mentioned in relation to the word of God? With the Qur'an stored in my memory, I could easily and carefully summon those verses where *'tahrif'* is mentioned. Consequently, I was able to find no more than four verses that seemed to refer to it. With the amount of exegetical literature at my disposal, the significance of my findings marked a final and decisive step towards my coming to the Lord Jesus Christ. The first of those passages reads as follows:

> 1 *Can ye (O men of faith) entertain the hope that they (the People of the Book) will believe in you? Seeing that a party of them heard the word of God, and perverted it knowingly after they understood it.*[14]

The background of this text is uncertain. A couple of apocryphal stories are told to provide a background to it. But it is certain that the antagonists here are the Jews of Medina. There are also differences of opinions about it, none of them points to the literal falsification or distortion of the sacred text. Tabari reminds his readers first of all "the distortion came from *'a party of them'* who were listening to the word of God", and not from all the Jews. He explains that this distortion was in regard to the meaning of the word of God: "They change its meaning and alter its (right) interpretation." According to him, "If the written word of the Torah had been intended, He (God) would not have said, '(They) *heard the word of God, and perverted it.*' Hence, what is intended here is not the written but the verbal distortion of the word of God."

Interestingly, Muhammad Rida is in full agreement with Tabari, and does not hesitate to quote him on this point.[15] Ibn Kathir takes the phrase *'and perverted it'* as meaning "they interpreted it contrary to its (proper) meaning".[16] As for al-Baidawi, the phrase *'and perverted it'* may refer to "the description of Muhammad, or the verse of stoning; or the explanation thereof, and they interpret the same accordingly as they desire".[17] In brief, all the commentators I had consulted are

[14] Sura al-Baqara [2]:75.

[15] See Tabari, *Jami' al-Bayan*, Vol. 1, pp. 518-522; see also M. Rashid Rida, *Tafsir al-Manar*, Vol. 1, pp. 354f.

[16] Ibn Kathir, *al-Qur'an al-'Adhim*, Vol. 1, 117.

[17] Abdullah Ibn 'Umar al-Baidawi, *Tafsir* (Cairo n.d.), Vol. 1, p. 91.

unanimous that what is clearly intended in this verse is not the written but the verbal distortion of the word of God.

Other passages read:

> 2   *Then woe to those who write the Book with their own hands, and then say: "This is from God", to traffic with it for miserable price! Woe to them for what their hands write, and for the gain they make.*[18]

Many of his contemporaries, and even to this day many Muslims quote this verse as a proof that Jewish (and perhaps also Christian) scriptures have been tampered with or even fabricated. They overlook the fact that those who undertook to *"write the Book with their own hands"* in Muhammad's time were *some* of the Jews of Medina and not *all* of the Jewish people. Such a blanket indictment is hermeneutically unfounded, and stands in glaring contrast to the views of Muslim commentators. For example, Muhammad Rashid Rida, the distinguished Muslim expositor, gives a comprehensive summary of their comments on this text. The preceding context (v.78) refers to some ignorant Jewish individuals who were acquainted only with rabbinical glosses or foolish traditions. They seem to have written out such glosses or traditions, and brought them to Muhammad claiming that they had divine authority. They were probably saying that they were just as binding as the scriptures themselves. Now, 'al-kitab', usually translated "the Book", can also literally mean 'the writing' and not necessarily the sacred scriptures. However, it may be taken here as 'the Book' i.e. that which this Jewish group may have believed to have similar authority as the scripture. This is highly probable, especially as it is well known that Talmudic Judaism does acknowledge the Oral Law (or Tradition) as divinely authoritative as the scriptures of the Old Testament.

Such rabbinic materials, for example, may well have included the cancellation of stoning for adultery. Another may have been the interpretation of passages of the Old Testament, which had been used by Muhammad's followers as bearing out his claims to be a prophet that should arise. Consequently, Muhammad pronounced woes on them for writing that which was originally human and devoid of divine authority.[19]

---

[18] Sura al-Baqara [2]:79.

[19] M. Rashid Rida, *Tafsir al-Manar*, Vol. 1, pp. 360ff; see also Sir W. Muir, *The Coran & the Testimony it bears to the Holy Scriptures* (Brighton, 1903), pp. 141f.

> **3** *There is among them a section who distort the Book with their tongues; (as they read) you would think it is a part from the Book, but it is no part of the Book; and they say, "That is from God". But it is not from God: It is they who tell a lie against God, and (well) they know it.*[20]

It is extremely hard to know the background of this particular text. Indeed, none of the Muslim scholars on this field, like al-Suyuti and al-Wahidi, provide a background to it. The important issue here is that the distortion took place by way of tongue twisting by some Jews as they read the sacred text, with the aim of concealing its real meaning. And this is precisely the view of all Muslim commentators.[21]

The verse seems to indicate an incident in which a group of Medinan Jews were being reproached for trying to deceive Muhammad and his followers. They were pretending that certain passages, which they were reading to Muhammad and his followers, were from the scriptures when in fact they were not. In other words, they were reading out the traditions, the commentaries or some other rabbinical material. And they were doing it in such a way as to make it sound as though they were quoting the scriptures. In fact, they did so by 'twisting their tongues', that is, by a fraudulent or equivocal manner of speech. Such a deceitful mode of speaking is also found in Sura al-Nisa'[4]:46. The text has evidently no allusion whatsoever to tampering with the scriptures themselves. The Jews could not possibly venture to commit any such sacrilege as the alteration or falsification of their sacred scriptures. In every age, the Jews have been extremely scrupulous regarding the letter and text of their scriptures however unscrupulous they might be in other respects.

> **4** *But because of their (the Jews') breach of their covenant, we cursed them, and made their hearts grow hard. They change the words from their places and forget a good part of the Message that was sent them . . .*[22]

As a matter of fact, this verse is by no means clear. As a result, Muslim commentators differ as to its real implication. For example, some

---

[20] Sura Al-'Imran [3]:78.

[21] See al-Fakhr al-Razi, *Tafsir* (Cairo, nd), Vol. 2, p. 72 also p. 721; al-Qurtubi, *al-Jami' li-Ahkam al-Qur'an al-Karim*, Vol. 3, pp. 1362f.; al-Zamakhshari, *al Kashshaf*, Vol. 1, p. 369; Tabari, *Jami' al-Bayan*, Vol. 3, pp. 438-440.

[22] Sura al-Ma'idah [5]:14.

like al-Qurtubi, seem to take the phrase *"They change the words from their* (right) *palaces"* as an indictment of some Medinan Jews who were distorting or misinterpreting the signs of the prophet Muhammad in their scriptures.[23] Others like Ibn Kathir and Tabari see it simply as a reference to those who misinterpreted their scriptures probably to suit their own unworthy ends.[24] It is hard to determine the nature of those unworthy ends. It is possible, but not probable, that the misinterpretation had to do with the Talmudic cancellation of stoning for adultery. Tabari, for example, takes the phrase, *"They change the words from their* (right) *places"*, to imply the verbal distortion of "the ordinances set by God. They (the Jews) used to say, 'If Muhammad orders what you already practice accept it. But if he disagrees with it, then beware'".[25]

One must find a little more clarification of this elsewhere. Taking vv.15-16 as a context, Suyuti seeks to provide a background by telling the following story: "The Jews came to the prophet of God (may God bless him and give him peace), and asked him about stoning. He answered, 'Who is among you more (religiously) knowledgeable?' They pointed to Ibn Surayya (a scholarly Rabbi). Wherefore, he (Muhammad) adjured him by Him who sent down the Torah on Moses, and raised Mount Sinai (over the heads of the Israelites),[26] and by the covenants, which were committed to them (the Israelites), until he (Ibn Surayya) trembled with anxiety. Then he replied, 'When it (i.e. adultery) increased amongst us, we punished with one hundred lashes and shaved heads (i.e. contrary to the Pentateuch).[27] But, he (the prophet) could not but pass the sentence of stoning on them (i.e. the adulterers)'."[28]

This story, if at all true, suggests that the Jews in Muhammad's time no longer carried out the sentence of death for adultery.[29] Indeed, for

---

[23] See al-Qurtubi, *al-Jami' li Ahkam al Qur'an*, Vol. 4, pp. 2112f; al-Zamakh-shari, *al-Kashshaf*, Vol. p. 603; see also *Tafsir al-Jalalayn*, p. 139.

[24] Ibn Kathir, *Tafsir al-Qur'an al-'Adhim*, Vol. 2, p. 35.

[25] Tabari, *Jami' al-Bayan*, Vol. 4, p. 212.

[26] Sura al-A'raf [7]:171. God's threat to let Mount Sinai fall upon the rebellious Israelites is not recorded in the Pentateuch, but in the Talmud. See *Abodah Zarah* ii. 2.

[27] For the punishment of adultery in the Torah, see Lev.20:10; Deut. 22:23-24.

[28] Suyuti, Bab al-Nuqul fi Asbab al-Nuzul (Cairo, nd), pp. 164f.

[29] In fact, historically, the death penalty for adultery had ceased to apply in 30 AD according to the Jerusalem Talmud Sanh. 18a & the Babylonian Talmud 41a.

centuries capital punishment for adultery was mitigated into divorce, according to the Talmud.[30] For Muhammad, the cancellation of God's law by a Talmudic tradition in this case was tantamount to altering the divine word in the Torah.

The Outcome of the Findings

One would venture to say that what I had discovered proved beyond astonishment to me. In fact, what is mentioned above is only part of the whole discovery I made regarding the subject of 'Tahrif' (falsification) in the Qur'an. The subject is certainly vast, and would need an entire book to deal with it in full. Nevertheless, what has been presented above is the sum and substance of the Qur'anic perspective of it.

As a result of my research, I observed that the Qur'anic charge of (verbal) falsification is levelled only against the Jews, but never against the Christians. Meanwhile, both Jews and Christians are described as a people who *"forgot a good part of the Message that was sent to them"*.[31] Looking at the spiritual state of the Christian Church in Muhammad's time, and even today in the West, the accusation may be well deserved. But by the same token, this charge can also be levelled against Muslims today who have *"forgot a good part of the Message that was sent to them"* in the Qur'an. In any case, there is neither in this text nor elsewhere any charge against the Christians of any sort of distortion of falsification of their scriptures. As for the Jews, whatever liberties they might have been inclined to take with their own scriptures, such attempts could never extend to the sacred text carefully preserved both by them and by the Church throughout the world.

To sum up: my careful study of the Qur'an in relation to this claim convinced me that the charge of falsification is totally unjustifiable. Indeed, it is entirely inconsistent with the sentiments expressed in many Qur'anic passages; and the claim made by Muslims that the Bible has been falsified is untenable. This was my major discovery and final step towards the Lord Jesus Christ.

---

[30] The Babylonian Talmud, Sota v.1.

[31] Sura al-Ma'idah [5]:15.

Chapter 5

COMING TO KNOW JESUS

"There are as many paths to Christ as there are feet to tread them, but there is only one way to God."

(A. Lindsay Glegg)

Free from any sense of inhibition, the amazing discovery gave me a new incentive to study the Bible. Uncomfortable with the then current New Testament in the vernacular, I obtained a copy of the Bible in the classical Arabic currently used throughout the Arab world. Beginning with the book of Genesis, I poured over that sacred book with a remarkable interest, being convinced that I was now reading a holy book that was entirely free from any kind of so-called *'tahrif'* (falsification).

Meanwhile, my study of the Bible continued simultaneously with my visits to the Mission House, which had now entered a different phase. I could now, for example, ask questions of Dr Rigby or one of his colleagues, with no intention of laying any theological trap for them as before. Rather I could ask questions and behind those questions I had every sincere desire to learn and be enlightened in certain Biblical matters. Moreover, my interest in the preaching of the gospel by Dr Rigby had increased much more in intensity than before. The same could be said of the prayers that were being offered during the services. I still recall how much I valued those prayers in which I was often mentioned by name. I was so submerged in all these things that had any one asked me whether I could define myself as a Christian my answer might have been more likely in the affirmative.

The truth of the matter is that though I was *"not far from the kingdom"*, I was certainly not in it yet. I was hardly aware at this stage that the hand of God was busy taking away *"the little foxes that spoil the vines"*.[1] Although I was enjoying reading my Bible, I could not say that I understood everything in it. For example, from

---

[1] Song of Songs 2:15.

a theological and cultural point of view, I was quite at home with the Old Testament, for much of it is reflected in the Qur'an, Hadiths and Muslim commentaries.[2] Therefore, it should come as no surprise that Islam bears greater resemblance to Judaism than to Christianity. But in reading the New Testament, there were a number of things I either could not understand, or if I did, they certainly caused me some degree of apprehension.

Addressing the Problem

There is no doubt that for Muslims, the Christian doctrine of the Trinity is a highly objectionable issue. For them, it is unquestionably a blasphemous concept according to the Qur'anic statement, *"They do blaspheme who say, 'God is the third of three', there is no god except one God"*.[3] All commentators have taken these words as a proof that Christians believe in three gods. But, at the same time I was becoming aware, with Dr Rigby's help, that Christians did not believe in three gods. The notion of three gods is as objectionable to Christianity as it is to Islam. In fact, Christianity is a monotheistic faith. The Nicene Creed begins, "I believe in one God". I was also able to read for myself (in Arabic) the Articles of the Church of England, which begin with the affirmation: "There is but one living and true God, everlasting, without body, parts, or passions; of infinite power, wisdom and goodness; the Maker and Preserver of all things both visible and invisible". My careful reading of the New Testament seemed to confirm this.

Yet, Muslims continue to charge Christians with believing and worshipping three gods. During that time, I was at a loss to know the basis on which Islam and Muslims were making this claim. As a result, I felt a bit uneasy. Yet, this uneasiness was due more to my frustration than to anything else. I was in no doubt that the scriptures of the Old and New Testaments were free from any kind of forgery or distortion. I was also certain that there was an answer to the above-mentioned accusation, and I wanted to know it immediately. At last I decided that for the time being I should not be in a hurry for the answer. Time is a great teacher. I was confident that with patience I

---

[2] For a study on this subject, see Abraham I. Katsh, *JUDAISM IN ISLAM: Biblical and Talmudic Backgrounds of the Koran and its Commentaries* (New York, 1980).

[3] Sura al-Ma'idah [5]:73.

would discover one day that time does indeed work wonders, and that was exactly what happened.

In time I came to know the real basis for this accusation. I discovered that it is not based on any New Testament passage whatsoever. It is rather based on a wrong perspective of trinity in one Qur'anic passage, which reads

> *And when God said, 'O Jesus son of Mary, didst thou say unto men, 'Take me and my mother as gods apart from God?' He said, 'To thee be glory! It is not mine to say what I have no right to. If I indeed say it, thou knowest it; thou knowest what is in my (inner) self'.*[4]

Obviously, in this Qur'anic text Jesus is cleared of having said that He and His mother, Mary, are two gods *"apart from God"*. Of course, there is nothing in the Gospel to indicate that Jesus said this or even hinted at it. A careful reading of the above-mentioned verse may suggest a Qur'anic misunderstanding, if not a misinterpretation, of the Trinity. First of all, it is possible that because the Syriac word *'ruh'* (Spirit) is used in the feminine, there was a misidentification of the Holy Spirit with the Virgin Mary. Attention can also be drawn to the fact that the association of Mary with the Holy Spirit may well have been taken from the lost *Gospel according to the Hebrews*, parts of which is preserved in Origen's commentary on Matthew. Here, Jesus is made to speak of "<u>my mother, the Holy Spirit</u>".

Some refer to Aphraates's interesting statement in his *Treatise of Virginity against the Jews*. Here Aphraates writes: "When a man hath not yet taken a wife, he loveth and honoureth God his father and the <u>Holy Spirit his mother</u> and he hath no other love". Others have detected in this Qur'anic verse the Nestorian voice of protest against the title '*theotokos*' (Mother of God) for the Virgin Mary. Interestingly, the worship of Mary became much more emphasised after the Nestorian controversy.

However, it is not hard to conclude from the above that the Qur'an has apparently misconceived the Trinity (Father, Son & Holy Spirit) as Father, Mother and Son, and felt obliged, in this text, to deny the divinity of the Virgin Mary.[5] Incidentally, although the Holy Spirit (*ruh al-qudus*) is mentioned in the Qur'an, He is not clearly identified.

---

[4] Sura al-Ma'idah [5]:119.

[5] See J.W. Sweetman, *Islam and Christian Theology* (London, 1945), Vol. 1, p. 32.

In fact, as in the Talmud, the Holy Spirit often seems to be identified in the Qur'an with the angel Gabriel.[6] Here the Talmudic influence in the Qur'an can hardly be dismissed.

Before I discovered the above answer, my study of the Bible was making a remarkable impact upon me. But was it an impact or something else? Looking back, I can confidently say the Holy Spirit was operating with His divine power and wisdom through the Bible as I studied it. But something unique and unprecedented began to happen when I came to the New Testament. As I read it, regardless of the few things I could not grasp, two things seemed to stand out to me so clearly: the glorious personality of Jesus and the unfathomable love of God revealed in Him.

The Uniqueness of Jesus

Of all the prophetic personalities that earned my great admiration, the personality of Jesus Christ was certainly the topmost. He is mentioned in ninety-three verses of fourteen Qur'anic Suras, a total of ninety seven times. Although, twenty-eight prophets are named in the Qur'an the uniqueness of Christ seems to dwarf them all. There were two principle reasons for my profoundest admiration for Jesus: First, my early childhood acquaintance with the Mission House and the pleasant stories that I used to hear about Jesus and His incomparable gentleness and compassion for the sick and the needy, and also His extraordinary attitude of forgiveness towards His bitterest enemies. True, as previously mentioned, at that time Jesus was the light that passed unnoticed by me. But, it seems that the personality of Jesus and His unparalleled manner of life and work were somehow unconsciously stamped on my childhood mind.

Second, my childhood admiration for Jesus and His work, strangely enough, seemed to have been enhanced by none other than the Qur'an itself. Here Jesus is mentioned in fourteen suras (chapters). But, what is uniquely interesting is that Jesus in the Qur'an rates higher than all the prophets including Muhammad. It was most probably for this reason that the great Sufi martyr, al-Hallaj, looked to Jesus rather than Muhammad as the supreme example of glorified humanity. It

---

[6] Talmud Sanhedrin 44, compare with Sura al-Baqara[2]:87; Sura al-Nahl[16]:102; Sura al-Shu'ra'[26:192-194]; see also 'Umar W. al-Da'uq, *al-Ruh al-Qudus,Jibril, fi al-Yahudiyah wa al-Nasraniyah* (Beirut, 1996) pp.61ff.

was also for the same reason that Ibn al-Arabi, another famous Sufi, called Jesus *"the seal of the saints"* or *"the seal who seals the absolute saintship".*[7] And this was one of the few things that irresistibly and finally helped to drive me to the arms of Jesus.

The Qur'an, for example, gives Jesus a number of titles, each one of which throbs with significance:

1 He is called a **'Sign'** (*ayah*) i.e. a miracle. He is made *"a Sign to the people"* (Sura Maryam [19]:21). He was such a *'Sign'* not only to the people of Israel, but also *"a Sign to all beings"* (Sura al-'Anbya' [21]:91).[8] In this context, He is identified in the New Testament as *'a Sign'* (see Lk. 2:34).

2 He is called a **'Witness'** (*Shahid*) in this world *"over them* (i.e. the disciples) *as long as I* (Jesus) *remained among them"* (Sura al-Ma'idah [5]:120); and *"on the day of resurrection, he* (Jesus) *will be a witness against them* (unbelievers)*"* (Sura al-Nisa'[4]:159). He is also described as *'witness'* in the New Testament (see Rev. 3:14). Interestingly, the term **'Witness'** is one of 'the ninety nine Beautiful Names of God' (*Asma' Allah al-Husna*), which occurs quite frequently in the Qur'an (e.g. Sura al-Nisa'[4]:33).[9]

3 He is an **'Example'** (*mathal*) in the sense of a parable or an analogy. It is stated in the Qur'an that *"the Son of Mary is used as a parable"* or *"cited as an example"* (Sura al-Zukhruf [43]:57). It is also stated, *"And we made him an example to the children of Israel"* (v.59). The New Testament also refers to Him as being an example (see 1 Pet. 2:21f).

4 He is portrayed as a **'Mercy'** (*rahmah*). God is said to have appointed Jesus *"as a sign to the people and a mercy from Us"* (Sura Maryam [19]:21). This attribute of mercy is also said to be the hallmark of His followers, *". . . and we ordained in the hearts of those who followed him compassion and mercy"* (Sura al Hadid [57]:27). The merciful attribute of Jesus is evident throughout the New Testament.

---

[7] Alfred Guillaume, *Islam* (Penguin Books, 1973), p. 145; see Muhi al-Din Ibn al-Arabi, *Fusus al-Hikam* (Beirut 1946), pp. 138-150; also his *al-Futuhat al-Makkyyah*, Vol. 2, p. 64.

[8] See Sura al-Mu'minun [23]:50; also Sura Al-'Imran [3]:50.

[9] See also Sura al-Ma'idah [5]:117; Sura al-An 'am [6]:19; Sura Yunus [10]:46; Sura al-Hajj [22]:17 etc.

5   He is portrayed as **'One brought near'** (*Min al-muqarrabin*). In the Qur'an He is *"One of those brought nearest"* or *"near stationed to God"*, according to Arberry's translation (Sura Al-Imran [3]:40). This may refer to the place that Jesus is to have in paradise, or his being raised to heaven into the society of angels. The phrase *"those brought nearest"*, in one place at least, applies to those who go before, in gardens of delight. They are said to be *"those who are brought nearest"* the divine throne (see Sura al-Waqi'a [56]:11). Could this be an allusion to Christ being *"at the right hand of God"* as mentioned in the New Testament? (see Acts 2:33-35; Eph. 1:20; Col. 3:1; Heb. 1:3-4). Interestingly, in his story of Muhammad's vision of heaven, Ibn Ishaq tells how the prophet saw Jesus in the second heaven,[10] perhaps awaiting His second coming to the world.

6   **'One of the upright'** (*min al-salihin*). The Qur'an describes Gabriel as announcing, *"He* (Jesus) *shall be* (of the company) *of the righteous"* (Sura Al-Imran [3]:46). Oddly enough, Sufi Muslims go so far as to term him as 'the seal of all pure saintly leaders' (*khatamu asfiya' al-a'imah*).

7   He is known as **'the Spirit of God'** (*ruh Allah*). More than once the Qur'an mentions that God *"strengthened* (or *confirmed*) *Him with the Holy Spirit"* (Sura al-Baqara [2]:87,253; Sura al-Ma'idah [5]:113). It also affirms three times that He was born of the Holy Spirit (Sura al-Nisa'[4]:171; Sura al-Anbya' [21]:91; Sura al-Tahrim [66]:12). These verses indicate that the Spirit was active in the birth of Jesus, and recalls the words of Gabriel to Mary in Luke's Gospel, *"The Holy Spirit shall come upon you"* (Lk. 1:35). The great Muslim mystic, Ibn al-Arabi, said that God had revealed Jesus as being Spirit, and gave him this extra gift of life-giving breath.[11] And according to the scholarly jurist, Muhammad al-Bayyumi, "The Holy Spirit is the Spirit of God".[12]

8   He is also called **'the Word of God'** (*kalimatu Allah*). It is clearly stated, *"Jesus, son of Mary is . . . His Word which He cast to Mary . . ."* (Sura al-Nisa'[4]:171; cf. Sura Al-'Imran [3]:39,45). Strangely enough,

---

[10] See Ibn Hisham, *Sirat al-Nabi, May God bless him & give him peace* (Cairo, n.d.) Vol. 2, p.13.

[11] Hayek, *Le Christ de l'Islam*   (Paris, 1959), p. 1.

[12] Muhammad al-Hariri al-Bayyumi, *al-Ruh wa Muhimmatuha* (Cairo n.d.), p. 53, also G. Parrrinder, *Jesus in the Qur'an* (Oxford, 1992), p. 50.

according to Tafsir Fath al-Qadir and Tafsir al-Baghawi, Jesus is said to be "a spirit like all other spirits except that God added him to Himself". Ibn Khaldun and Ibn Kathir, the Muslim historians, quote a letter sent from Muhammad to the Negus, king of Abyssinia, in which he declared, "I bear witness that Jesus son of Mary is the Spirit of God and <u>His Word</u> which He cast to Mary the virgin".[13]

9 Another title is **'Blessed'** (*mubarak*). He is said to have proclaimed from His cradle, *"And He (God) had made me blessed wherever I am"* (Sura Maryam [19]: 31).

10 There is the title **'Eminent'** (*Wajih*). He is expressly described as *"Eminent in this world and the next"* (Sura Al-Imran [3]:45). It is worth noting that most Muslim commentators understand Christ's *'Eminence'* in this text as a reference to his high prophetic office in this world, and his position as a mediator in the world to come.[14]

As I reflected on all these sublime titles of Christ, I found two of them extremely fascinating, and indeed most challenging – Jesus being the Spirit of God and the Word of God. These are also the titles by which Jesus is frequently known in the New Testament. Whereas in the New Testament these are titles of His divinity, in Islam they are not adequately explained.

(a) Jesus the Spirit of God

True, the Qur'an says about Adam that God *"fashioned him in due proportion, and breathed into him of His spirit"* or *"something of His spirit"*, according to A.Yusuf Ali's translation (Sura al-Sajdah [32]:9). In his commentary, the same translator says bluntly that Jesus was different. He was, as he put it, "a Spirit proceeding from God".[15] Muslim commentators fail to make a difference between Jesus who was conceived of the Spirit and Adam into whom God's Spirit was

---

[13] Ibn Khaldun, *Kitab al-'Ibar wa Diwan al-Mubtada' wa al-Khabar* (Beirut, 1992), Vol. 2, pp. 435-6; Ibn Kathir, *al- Bidayatu wa al-Nihayah* (Cairo, 1991), Vol. 2, p. 100.

[14] See al-Zamakhshari, *al-Khashshaf*, Vol. 1, p. 357; Al- Baidawi, *Tafsir al-Baidawi*, p. 99; *Tafsir al-Jalalayn* , p. 70; Ibn Kathir, *Tafsir al-Qur'an al-'Adhim*, Vol. 1, 356.

[15] A.Yusuf Ali, *THE HOLY QUR'AN: Text, Translation and Commentary*, p. 234.

breathed. They usually appeal to the Qur'anic text which reads, *"The similitude of Jesus before God is as that of Adam; He created him from dust, then said to him: 'Be', and he was"* (Sura Al-'Imran [3]:59). But I was able to note carefully the great difference between Adam and Jesus. In Adam's case, as quoted above, it is plainly stated that God *"fashioned him in due proportion, and breathed into him of His spirit"*. In the case of Jesus it is written, *"And Mary the daughter of 'Imran, who guarded her chastity; and We breathed into (her body) of Our Spirit . . ."* (Sura al-Tahrim [66]:12; also Sura al-Anbiya' [21]:91).

Now, it is worth noting that Adam was already *"fashioned in due proportion"* when the spirit was breathed into him. The spirit here, as in Gen. 2:7, means no more than *"the breath of life"*. Conversely, Jesus was not fashioned in any way when God breathed His Spirit into Mary. Therefore, unlike Adam, Jesus Christ was in His entirety the very Spirit of God that was breathed into Mary's womb. If this is not the miracle of the incarnation, then what is it?

(b) Jesus the Word of God

As previously pointed out, 'the Word' as a title of Jesus is mentioned in the Qur'an at least three times. It is clear that the term 'the Word' (Greek *Logos*) is one of the most significant titles of Jesus in the New Testament, particularly in John's Gospel: *"In the beginning was the Word, and the Word was with God and the Word was God . . ."* (Jn. 1:1f). 'The Word' i.e. *Logos* here is more than speech: it is God in action – creating (vv.3, 10), revealing (v.2, 18), and redeeming (vv.4,12). Jesus is this 'Word' (v.14). In Christian theology the title of Jesus as 'the Word of God' clearly relates to His divine character. But to Muslims that title lacks entirely the content of deity.

In spite of that, Muslim commentators are not apparently of one accord as to its real significance. Razi, for example, said that Jesus was called a 'Word' because he was the fulfilment of the word spoken by the prophets. Elsewhere, he points out, "What is in fact intended by 'a Word from Him', is Jesus". For Tabari, it points to the message, which God ordered the angels to deliver to Mary.[16] But, according to al-Zamakhshari, the title meant no more than he (Jesus) came into being by God's expressed word and command.[17] This is also the view of Ibn

---

[16] Tabari, *Tafsir*, Vol. 4, p. 47.

[17] Zamakhshari, *al-Kashshaf*, Vol. 1, p. 580.

Kathir. Quoting Shadhan Ibn Yahya, Ibn Kathir writes, " 'a word from Him (God)' does not mean that the word became Jesus, but [that] by God's word Jesus came into being, which makes it agreeable with the text wherein God said to Adam as to Jesus 'Be', and he was" (Sura Al-'Imran [3]:59).[18]

At this point, an interesting thought occurred to me. If indeed Jesus was called 'the Word of God' simply because He was created by the word of God like Adam and his descendants, then are we to designate every created human being (including every animal) by the title 'Word of God'? It is unlikely that the Qur'an – or its commentators – would agree. The title 'Word of God' is undeniably the specific, and indeed the exclusive designation of Jesus both in the New Testament and the Qur'an. The Qur'an clearly states that it is His own special name: *"Behold the angels said, 'Mary, God gives thee good tidings of a Word from Him whose name is the Messiah, Jesus . . .'"* (Sura Al-'Imran [3]:45).[19]

There is little doubt that the Qur'anic title of Jesus as the *'Word of God'* is directly borrowed from the New Testament. Muhammad must have known from contemporary Christians that this and other titles of Jesus did in fact have the content of deity.[20] Yet, his struggle to divest the title of Jesus as 'the Word' of divinity cannot be overlooked. The first reason for stripping this title of its divine significance was apparently due to the uncompromising monotheistic character of Islam and its hostile opposition to polytheism from its inception: *"God forgiveth not that partners should be set up with Him; but forgiveth anything else, to whom He pleaseth. To set up partners with God is to devise a sin most heinous indeed"* (Sura al-Nisa' [4]:48,116). The other reason probably was to bring this title (Word of God) into harmony with its brand of strict monotheism. In one verse, for example, the title *'Word of God'*, as a title for Jesus, is preceded by *"Messiah Jesus the son of Mary was*

---

[18] Ibn Kathir, *Tafsir al-Qur'an al-'Adhim*, Vol. 1, p. 579.

[19] See the translation of A.J. Arberry, *The Koran*, p. 51.

[20] There is one Qur'anic reference to a dispute between Muhammad and the polytheists of Quraysh over the deity of Christ (Sura al-Zukhruf [43]:57-61). Apparently, the knowledge of the deity of Christ was not confined only to the Christians of Arabia. The Polytheists may well have acknowledged him as one of many deities. Historically, among the pictures of the pagan deities that were drawn on the walls of al-Ka'bah there was the icon of Mary and Jesus sitting on her lap. See al-Azraqi, *Tarikh Maccah* (Beirut, 1995), Vol. 2, pp. 186f.

only a Messenger of God" (Sura al-Nisa'[4]:171). The verse that follows immediately reads, *"The Messiah will never scorn to be a slave to God . . ."* (v.172). Thus, within these two verses, five human characteristics of Jesus are used in order to dismiss any divine significance which the title *'Word of God'* might convey. With this in mind I found myself wondering if there was another possible reason why this particular title of Christ had been stripped of its divine significance. Could it be, for example, because the *'Word of God'* was simply conceived to be a written or a spoken revelation rather than something personified in an individual?

(c) The 'Word of God' in Later Islamic Theology

For a Muslim the Qur'an is neither a human nor an angelic product. It is entirely from God who revealed it to Muhammad, and there is no shortage of Qur'anic passages in which this point is made perfectly clear.[21] Moreover, it is stated that the Qur'an is a book that has its origin in a heavenly **'Mother of the Book'** (Um al-kitab): *"We have made it a Qur'an in Arabic, that ye may be able to understand (and learn wisdom). And verily, it is in the Mother of the Book, in our presence, high (in dignity), full of wisdom"* (Sura al-Zukhruf [43]:3-4; cf. Sura al-Ra'd [13]:39). This original copy is also known as **'a Tablet Preserved'** (lawh mahfuz): *"Nay, this is a Glorious Qur'an,(inscribed) in a Tablet Preserved"* (Sura al-Buruj [85]:21-22). Thus, since the beginning of Islam, the Qur'an was regarded by Muslims as the word of God par excellence.

During the hundred years after the death of Muhammad, this reverence for the Qur'an among Muslims had grown to a remarkable level. Then a fierce controversy broke out among Muslim scholars on the question as to whether the Qur'an was created or is co-eternal with God (or like God Himself, uncreated). It has been suggested that this controversy was a direct influence of the Christian doctrine of the *'Logos'*.[22] The clash was between the Mu'tazilites, a group of Muslim theologians that were greatly influenced by Greek philosophy, and the

---

[21] Sura al-Baqara [2]:2-4; Sura Al-'Imran [3]:7; Sura Yusuf [12]:1-2; Sura al-Kahf [18]: 1; Sura Taha [20]:113; Sura al-Furqan [25]:6; Sura al-Zumur [39]:1-2; Sura Fussilat [41]:2-3; Sura al-Zukhruf [43];43-44; Sura [al-Rahman [55]:1-2.

[22] See A. Abdul-Haqq, *Sharing Your Faith with a Muslim* (Minneapolis: Bethany Fellowship, Inc. 1980) pp. 62f.

Sunni Muslim scholars. The Sunni scholars believed that the 'Word of God' as contained in the Qur'an, is co-eternal with God, for there was never a time when God was without speech. The 'Word of God' (i.e. His speech) is His divine quality (*sefah*), and therefore co-existent with Him.

Abu Hanifah seemed aware of the problem involved here. In his attempt to clarify this orthodox view, he wrote: "The Qur'an is the word of God, and His inspired word and revelation. It is a necessary attribute of God. It is not God, but still inseparable from God".[23] But this would cut no ice with the Mu'tazilites, the weighty opponents of the Sunnis. The Mu'tazilites, who usually sought to combine Greek rationalism with Islamic thought, denied the eternity of the 'Word of God' as contained in the Qur'an, and argued that it is created. To suggest that the 'Word of God' is co-existent with God is tantamount to believing in two gods. Indeed, for them, it would hardly be different from the Christian belief that Jesus being the 'Word of God' is equal in eternity with God.[24] Consequently, during the prisoners' exchange with the Byzantines, Ibn Abi Du'ad, a Mu'tazilite scholar and chief minister of the Abbasid Caliph, refused the exchange of a Christian for a Muslim who believed in the eternity of the Qur'an. For him, such a Muslim was theologically no different from a Byzantine Christian.

The reign of the Caliph al-Mutawakil in the ninth century witnessed the beginning of the end of the Mu'tazilites and the ascendancy of the Sunni orthodoxy. Unlike his predecessors, the Caliph al-Mutawakil adopted the orthodox doctrine of the uncreated Qur'an. He even decreed the capital punishment for anyone who taught that the 'Word of God' was created.[25] The Mu'tazilites eventually disappeared from the stage of history and Sunni orthodoxy finally triumphed. The overwhelming majority of Muslims in the world today are Sunni orthodox, and with them the theological concept of the majestic and incomparable place of the Qur'an continued.

---

[23] Ibid. p. 62; N.L. Geisler & Abdul Saleeb, *Answering Islam* (Books, Grand Rapids, Michigan, 1993), p. 100.

[24] Interestingly, under John of Damascus, the Christians during the Ummayyad period followed precisely this line of argument with orthodox Muslims who unlike the Mu'tazilites believed in the co-eternity of the Word with God.

[25] Ibn Kathir, *al-Bidayah wa al-Nihayah*, Vol. 5, p. 866.

(d) Jesus and the Qur'an

It should come as no surprise that most people in the West do not understand what the Qur'an is apart from assuming that it is Islam's holy book. The fact of the matter is that for Muslims, the Qur'an is much more than that. It is the expression of God's will and wisdom. Ever since the ascendancy of Orthodox Islam, which began under the Caliph al-Mutawakil, the belief in the eternity of the Qur'an has been more pronounced, and it is today an axiomatic article of faith. For orthodox Islam, the Qur'an, which is God's speech, is an eternal attribute of God. It is without beginning or intermission, precisely like His knowledge, might, wisdom, and other attributes of His infinite being. Thus, the Qur'an which is God's acknowledged manifestation of speaking, did not originate in time by His special act of creative will, but has existed from all eternity.[26]

Among the points that I had found rather uncomfortable was the question of the eternity of the Qur'an. I had wondered at the time if this was an attempt to make the Qur'an as divine in relation to the Muslims as Christ is divine in relation to the Christians. It seems that I was not far off the mark. According to some modern Muslim scholars, if one wants to compare the Qur'an with anything in Christianity, one must compare it with Christ Himself. "Christ was the expression of the divine among men, the revelation of the divine will." That is what the Qur'an is in orthodox Islam.[27] Some have rightly observed that "Whereas in Christianity 'in the beginning was the Word and the Word became flesh', in Orthodox Islam in the beginning was the Word and the Word became a Book!"[28]

With all these different theological intricacies in Islam, I came to realise that after all there was something unique about Jesus Christ. His primary purpose apparently was neither to write a book nor to establish a religion. The New Testament was the product of His followers who wrote under the inspiration of the Holy Spirit, and the community in which He operated was already saturated by religion. The New Testament is a revelation about the supreme revelation of

---

[26] N.L. Geisler & Abdul Saleeb, *Answering Islam*, p. 100; also Ignaz Goldziher, *Introduction to Islamic Theology* (Princeton University Press, 1981), p. 97.

[27] See Charis Waddy, *The Muslim Mind* (New York: Longman, 1976), p. 14; also Seyyed Hossein Nasr, *Ideals and Realities in Islam* (London, 1975), pp. 43-44.

[28] N.L. Geisler & Abdul Saleeb, *Answering Islam*, p. 98.

God in Jesus Christ. St Paul reminds his readers that *"God was in Christ Jesus reconciling the world to Himself"* (2 Cor. 5:19). To young Timothy he declares, *"And without controversy, great is the mystery of godliness: God was manifest in the flesh . . ."* (1 Tim. 3:16). Jesus personally told the truth about Himself, *"I and the Father are one"* (Jn. 10:30). He left Philip in no doubt, *"He who has seen me has seen the Father"* (14:9).

These self-declared statements of Jesus could not but inspire me with a sense of awe and wonder. For me to feel this way at this stage could only indicate that I had another spirit within me. It seemed that unconsciously I was on tiptoe with expectation. In any case, the idea of a great moral or spiritual teacher saying what Christ said is out of the question. Indeed, for many the only person who can say that sort of thing is either God or a complete lunatic suffering from that form of delusion, which undermines the whole mind of man. In fact, some of Jesus' contemporaries did suggest he was a complete lunatic for the same reason (Mt. 12:22-32).

(e) The Final Verdict

For the first time, God began to reveal Himself to me in a special way. Although my faith in God was profound, in reality He was unreachable, untouchable and unknowable to me. The link between God and me was simply non-existent, and therefore there was no dialogue. I realised that in Jesus Christ alone the link is initiated and the dialogue established. For me, the message of the New Testament was crystal clear: if one wants to know what God is like he must simply look at Jesus. *"He is,"* as St Paul puts it, *"the image of the invisible God"* (Col. 1:15). I had thought that I knew God, at least through the Islamic 'ninety-nine beautiful names of God' (*Asma' Allah al-Husna*), which I knew by heart. Yet, among those ninety-nine beautiful names of God (some of which are disturbingly negative), one thing remains absent: it is God as '*love*'. In point of fact, the Qur'an plainly states that God does not love sinners of any sort.[29] His love is reserved only

---

[29] They are *"the transgressors"* (Sura al-Baqara [2]:190, those that are *"ungrateful and wicked"* (v.276), *"the faithless"* (Sura al-'Imran [3]:32), *"the wrong-doers"* (v.57). *"the arrogant and vainglorious"* (Sura al-Nisa, [4]:36), *"those given to perfidy and crime"* (v.107), *" the mischief-makers"* (Sura al-Ma'idah [5]:67), *"those given to excess"* (v.87), *"the wasters"* (Sura al-An 'am [6]:141), *"the treacherous"* (Sura al-Anfal [8]:58), *"those who exult in riches"* (Sura al-Qasas [28]:76).

for the good, and those who are good are specifically defined in the Qur'an.[30] By contrast, in the New Testament *"God is love"*, and that is undeniably its watchword and theme (Jn. 3:16; Eph. 3:14-19; 1 Jn. 4:8,16). In Jesus Christ, God has revealed His amazing and matchless love, the love that is so measureless and free. It is the love that loves the whole wide world. It is the love that loves the vilest sinners into His goodness and grace.

Of course, I was aware of the Qur'anic reminder that God is *"strict in punishment"*, and that He is also *"oft-forgiving, most merciful"* (al-Ma'idah [5]:101). God is undoubtedly *"most gracious, most merciful"*, as the words of *'al-basmalah'* (the Qur'anic invocation) puts it. These words are simply descriptive of God's attributes of benevolence and kindness. But the message of the Gospel, as I clearly discovered, is the declaration that *"God is love"*. It is not merely the declaration of God's benevolent gifts for the improvement of man's daily welfare, but of the infinite gift of Himself for his eternal well-being. So then, if *"God is love"* He is, by definition, something more than being merely the God of kindness. Indeed, "it appears from all the records," as C.S. Lewis put it, "that though He has often rebuked us and condemned us, He has never regarded us with contempt. He has paid us the intolerable complement of loving us, in the deepest, most tragic, most inexorable sense."[31] In fact, when Jesus said: *"Greater love has no man than this, that a man lay down his life for his friends"* (Jn. 15:13), He was laying bare the very heart and character of God. Here Jesus is showing in the clearest and simplest possible terms that *"God is love"* and that man is the object of that infinite and redeeming love.

With these discoveries, I finally decided that the truth undoubtedly lay with the message of the Gospel. In one sense a great burden had been taken off me, but in another, I became, as in St Augustine's experience, 'a burden to myself'. The truth can be a double-edged sword, most calming and most disturbing. I was now like a bank employee who moved in a huge store of money, but not a penny of it

---

[30] God loves those *"who keep themselves pure and clean"* (Sura al-Baqara [2]:222), *"those who are upright"* (Sura Al-'Imran [3]:76), *"those who do good"* (v.134), *"those who are patient"* (v.146), *"those who trust"* (v.159), *"those who are just"* (Sura al-Mumtahinah [60]:8), *"those who fight . . . in battle array"* (Sura al-Saf[61]:4) and *"those who follow the prophet Muhammad himself"* (Sura Al-'Imran [3]:31).

[31] C.S. Lewis, *The Business of Heaven* (London, 1984).

belonged to him. I was now in a position where I had encountered the truth, but the truth had not yet set me free.

(f) The Great Decision

The beginning of October 1959 witnessed my return to the Seminary and the start of another year of earnest study. Meanwhile, my contact with Dr Rigby and his colleagues and my frequent visits to the Mission House continued as usual. So far, I had been attending the services without fail. But with my new discovery, the enjoyment seemed to have doubled. Shortly after this change of attitude, which Dr Rigby may well have noticed, I was invited for a cup of tea with him after an evening service.

In the course of our conversation around the table, I remember cutting across country to the subject of my recent findings. I told Dr Rigby with enthusiasm the amazing truth I discovered about the scriptures generally and of Jesus Christ in particular. I pointed out that the most remarkable thing about Jesus was that He did not come only to lead man up to some religious and moral high ground. But rather it seems that He came mainly to put man right with God through His sacrificial death on the cross and justify him through His glorious resurrection (Rom. 4:25). In brief, the entire difference between religion like Islam and Jesus Christ was now abundantly clear. Simply put, religion (any religion) commends itself to man as the truth, which leads to God by way of 'thou shalt', and 'thou shalt not'. But Jesus Christ commends Himself to man as *"the way the truth and the life"* (Jn. 14:6). The path to God leads only through Him, and through what He (and no one else) has done.

Apart from his occasional quiet expressions of 'Praise the Lord' and 'Hallelujah', Dr Rigby listened attentively and enthusiastically to me as I spoke. During the brief discussion that followed, I asked, after some hesitation: "How can one become a fully-fledged Christian?" If I remember rightly, Dr Rigby's answer was something like this: "For one to become a Christian, he must simply repent and accept Jesus Christ as his personal Lord and Saviour. In doing so, the Lord Jesus Christ immediately comes and makes his heart His dwelling place and becomes his daily friend." For a moment, I thought that if this is all that it takes to become a Christian, then Christianity sounds far too simplistic, and perhaps even a cheap religion! But on reflection I was quick to recognise that that was precisely the stuff that religion is made of. Its membership always requires a price. By contrast, in Christianity Jesus has already paid the price – indeed an infinite price. Most of all, I was aware that my entire life was suffering from an aching void, which only Christ could fill. It was obvious to me that in this situation Jesus was available not to provide a solution to my deep-seated dilemma, but to be the solution to that dilemma. It was therefore high time that I should take this decisive step and cast myself wholly and unreservedly upon the loving and welcoming heart of Jesus. And so, Dr Rigby, the man who from that moment onward I designated as my spiritual father, led me prayerfully to commit my life to the Lord Jesus Christ, and to promise to serve Him to the end.

The tremendous sense of that divine transformation which I subsequently experienced is beyond human description. What happened to me at that moment was so awesome, so divine and so infinite that silence might be a more eloquent description of it than words. The Mount of Transfiguration experience was so infinitely awesome for Peter, James and John. Yet, John never mentioned it in his gospel. For him, the experience was simply beyond words. A blind man had a miraculously wholesome encounter with Jesus. Yet, his description of that encounter could not go beyond, *"I know this, I was blind, and now I can see"* (Jn. 9:1-25 NLT).

It took me a long journey to come to Jesus. But my arrival at this soul-refreshing experience of Jesus and His love did not mark the end. Indeed, another journey was about to begin, and this time not on my own, but hand in hand with Jesus Himself.

Chapter 6

BETWEEN CAUTION AND HONESTY

"Look carefully then how you walk, not as unwise men but as
wise, making the most of the time, because the days are evil."
(Paul's Letter to the Ephesians 5:15-16)

During the days and the weeks that followed, I was basking in the glorious experience of the living Christ in my life. My fellowship with the Lord was being strengthened day by day through my private devotion, which usually consisted of the study of the scriptures and prayers. In addition to this, I continued to attend the Sunday and midweek services at the Mission House steadfastly. Those services were attended by a small number of people. But I was conscious of what Jesus once said: *"For where two or three are gathered together in my name, there am I in the midst of them"* (Mt. 18:20).

There is a cultural and religious background to these words of Jesus. To this day, no Jewish synagogue can constitute worship on the Sabbath day without a *'minyan'* i.e. a quorum of at least ten adult males. The idea is apparently based on the Biblical incident of Abraham's intercession for Sodom and Gomorrah. His plea for righteous people who might be in Sodom and Gomorrah evoked the promise of God that if just ten righteous people were found there He would spare those two cities from destruction (Gen. 18:32). According to Jewish Midrash, God was ready to do this "so that there might be sufficient for an assembly of [righteous men to pray] on behalf of them all".[1] But our Lord leaves us in no doubt that God's presence in any place of worship does not depend on numbers. His presence can be real and vital among His people regardless of how many of them gather in His name.

I found the simplicity and the informality of those services at the Mission House a source of great strength and blessing. On occasions I was encouraged to participate in the worship in one way or another,

---

[1] *Midrash Rabbah: Genesis* (The Soncino Press, New York 1983), Vol. 1, p. 432.

and I did so with a real sense of joy and enthusiasm. But that sense of joy and enthusiasm was confined only to the small assembly of kindred spirits in the Mission House. Outside it the world was entirely different. I was fully aware of the risk I could face if my conversion became known. Therefore, I prayed that I might be careful and wise as I daily rubbed shoulders with all sorts and conditions of people in my hometown. In particular, I prayed in the words of the Psalmist that the Lord would set "*a watch before my mouth and keep the door of my lips*" (Ps. 141:3). In this situation a careful tongue makes a wise head, and in the words of St Francis de Sales, "There is nothing so like a wise man as a fool who holds his tongue!"

It is true that silence is the most satisfactory substitute for wisdom. But it is equally true that if silence becomes a permanent feature in a person, then wisdom may be reduced to a strange oddity. In the words of Ecclesiastes, "*There is a time for everything, and a season for every activity under heaven*", and that included "*a time to be silent and a time to speak*" (3:1,7). However, there are times also when it is unwise to be silent about the truth, and to do so is an unmitigated folly. But, in the final analysis, as Jesus put it, "*wisdom is justified of her children*" (Mt. 11:19). In other words, wisdom is shown to be right by what results from it.

The Gathering Storm

It is nigh impossible for a convert from Islam to remain incognito for long in his Islamic environment. Sooner or later he will be known. At first, things seem quite normal and people have no cause for suspicion. Yet, deep in his own heart he knows that a radical change has occurred in his life, and even the world around him has changed. Everything is calm so far; but it is an uneasy calm, it is like that sort of calm that comes before the storm. In his situation no caution or care for safety can guarantee a permanent cover against exposure.

Now, in any educational institution the spirit of competition and rivalry among students is a common feature. Such competition is often conducted in an attitude of friendship and good humour. But there are instances in which it can turn into an atmosphere of hard feelings and vindictiveness. Some students are simply incapable of taking it on the chin when they fail to meet a challenge, or when silenced in a battle of intellectual argument. For them, the idea of living to fight another day goes by the board, and the stage is set for a vindictive reaction.

It was the end of a study day, and I was walking home in the company of some of my fellow students. Such walks were often dominated by a post-mortem of what had happened that day in the classroom, or by some other subject. On this particular occasion the conversation revolved around a remark made by the History lecturer that morning in answer to a student's question. The question was whether or not primitive narratives given by famous medieval Muslim historians like Tabari, Ibn Kathir and others were reliable. The lecturer's answer came as a big surprise to some students. He told the class that a careful student should not take everything written by those eminent scholars at face value. Their writings (whether histories or commentaries), were laced with a good deal of 'Israeliyat' (i.e. Jewish legends).

The feeling among those companions was mixed. One of them who may be designated as M.S. could not hide his contempt for the lecturer's answer. He went so far as to call it 'blasphemous'. He did not explain why he found that answer blasphemous. He was noted for his long silences, which earned him the nickname of 'a smouldering fire beneath the hay', the English equivalent of 'still waters run deep'. His long silences appeared to betray a good deal of his arrogance and ignorance. But when he spoke one could not fail to discern a touch of rigidity and fanaticism about him. Above all, it was not safe to cross him. He would nurse the grudge and wait patiently for the right opportunity to strike back. I recall how on two previous occasions I happened to cross swords with him, and from what happened later on, he apparently did not forget it. Throwing caution to the wind, I decided to take issue with him for what he had just said:

"What was so blasphemous in saying that some of those distinguished scholars' writings were laced with an element of Israeliyat?" I asked with a smile. "Do we not acknowledge openly that even some Hadiths (reported sayings of the prophet Muhammad) are laced with some *Israeliyat*? Is it blasphemy to say so? Why don't you take a look at this particular subject in Shaykh Mahmud Abu Rayya's recent book on the Hadith?"[2]

"Do you also suppose" he retorted angrily, "that the Qur'an also contains some elements of *Israeliyat*?"

---

[2] Mahmud Abu Rayya, *Adwa' 'ala al-Sunna al-Muhammadiya* (Cairo, n.d. Fifth edition), pp. 117ff; see also Ibn Khaldun, *al-Muqaddimah*, p. 9.

"Never mind what I suppose," I said calmly, "my question is clear and simple, what was so blasphemous about what the teacher had said?"

At this point the guy seemed rattled as all the other students' eyes were upon him. Realising that his position was untenable, he proceeded to tone down his position, which probably surprised that company of students.

"What I said," he bounced back, "was purely my opinion and I had every right to say it. The claim that some Hadiths are riddled with *Israeliyat* might lead the enemies of Islam to say the same thing about the Qur'an itself."

"Indeed," I responded, "you are free to think what you like, but you are not free to say what you like. If everyone were to say what they think, mental asylums and jails would be full!"

On hearing this, the students burst into laughter, which did not go down well with him. Perhaps he thought that he was being made a fool of. At this point he felt that it was time for him to strike back:

"I know you agree with our teacher's statement that the Hadiths are laced with *Israeliyat*," he shouted.

"I certainly do," I said, "and I am not afraid to say so."

"Do you think then that the Qur'an might also contain some elements of *Israeliyat*?" he asked with a sharp voice?

At this point I became aware that I was being pushed a bit too far. For a Muslim to admit that the Qur'an is in any way influenced by the *Israeliyat* would be blasphemy and apostasy of the first order. I went silent for a few seconds, which looked like hours. I had to think hard for an answer to this highly charged and dangerous question. Suddenly, I thought I had an answer, which might get me off the hook.

"Orientalists and scholars of Islamic studies," I quietly pointed, "have no qualms that the Qur'an has not escaped the *Israeliyat* influence. For them, the Qur'anic stories like those of Solomon who had control over demons, spirits and winds and understood the language of birds and ants are derived from *Israeliyat*.[3] The same could be said of the story of God's threat to let Mount Sinai fall on the rebellious Israelites if they refused to accept His law."[4]

"Never mind what the Orientalists say," he interrupted, "I want to know your own opinion on this matter."

---

[3] Sura Sad [38]:36-38; Sura al-Naml [27]:17ff; compare with the *Second Targum of the Book of Esther*.

[4] Sura al-A'raf [7]:171; compare with Aboda Zarah 2.2.

"Excuse me! You sound as if you are ordering me," I answered evasively. "If this is your attitude, then I'm not going to answer."

I had just finished this sentence when I heard my grandfather calling me to come with him to the grocer's shop. That call was God sent. It rescued me from falling into a dangerous trap. I certainly had a very close shave. But that company of students had their own thoughts and the guy called M.S. was ready to exploit them, and exploit them he did. Within a few days the gossip spread in the Seminary suggesting that I had some grave doubts about the Qur'an. Their suspicion was also re-enforced by the fact that I had not been seen at the Friday prayers for a long time. It was now obvious that a gathering storm was looming on the horizon.

A Brief Pause

During the few weeks that followed, I was becoming an object of suspicion. A group of students led by M.S. were relentless in their whispering campaign that I had a dim view of the Qur'an. They also blamed me for allowing myself to be influenced by my missionary friends. Others did not believe that those British missionaries could easily influence me in this or in any other respect. In their opinion, the whole thing is a misunderstanding. In my absence, my closest friends did not hesitate to defend me as vigorously as they possibly could. But bad news has no shortage of adherents, listeners or even promoters, and behind the scene M.S. was obviously active.

A couple of weeks later people were saying that only a person who courted atheism or embraced another faith would have negative views of the Qur'an. At home the atmosphere was quite uneasy on one occasion. Grandfather and the rest of the family wanted to know what was going on, for there was no smoke without fire. In my response I tried to say as little as possible. I told them that there were some wicked students who were trying to smear me as a result of an argument I had with some of them. Grandfather sat in a pensive mood listening as I told them what happened. Until now, the old man did not know his grandson had been a frequent visitor to the Mission House, but a number of my fellow students knew. When I finished speaking, grandfather left the house muttering some words I could not make out.

Later that day, I visited the Mission House and briefed Dr Rigby and his colleagues of what was happening. I strongly urged them to uphold me in their prayers, for Satan seemed to be spoiling for an attack. Happily, their prayers were answered. The rumour began to die down, and for a few weeks everything was quiet. But this did not mean that the issue had been forgotten. The reason for this probably was that attention was diverted to a schoolteacher who had converted to Bahaism and recently recanted under pressure. As a result the whole town was in a state of excitement about that incident. People's curiosity and suspicion about me seemed to have been put on the back burner. All I could do in that situation was to exercise careful discretion and keep a very low profile.

Spring had arrived and the students were ready for their spring vacation, which that year happened to coincide with a Muslim festival. A group of about fifteen students decided to organize a day's picnic during that vacation. A couple of my closest friends urged me to join them, which I gladly accepted. I even suggested that the picnic place should be my family's huge orchard with its fascinating citrus groves, which was roughly three kilometres east of the town. The orchard was situated on a hill overlooking the Locus valley with its long serpentine river, and a short distance beyond it stood the ruins of Lixus, the ancient Roman city.

Permission was granted by grandfather, and early on Friday morning we made our way to the picnic place. On arrival we had breakfast and afterwards we went to explore the orchard with its many fruit trees and several running streams. By mid-day we gathered for a lavish lunch of couscous, which the orchard caretaker's family had prepared. The students rewarded them generously for it afterwards. The time spent together so far was full of jokes and laughter as they teased one another and played friendly tricks on each other. In all this, I seemed to be in my element. I was sure that the rest of the other students who were absent would be sorry when they realise what they had missed. It was indeed an enjoyable time. But little did I know that it was only a brief pause.

The Gathering Pace

After lunch we retired to enjoy some aromatic glasses of Moroccan mint-tea. At this stage the conversation seemed to be relaxed as we talked about various subjects. Then unexpectedly, the case of the schoolteacher who had recently recanted from Bahaism cropped up. I was not happy that this subject had come up. Inwardly I felt agitated, and wondered if that enjoyable day was about to be spoiled. There was only one option of safety open to me. I must keep completely silent. It was not in my best interests to get involved in that dangerous conversation. The schoolteacher about whom the conversation revolved was well known to me. In the early years he and I were both in same the Qur'anic school. He belonged to a very prestigious family. His father was a scholarly imam at the main mosque of the city. In their conversation, he was both the object of condemnation for his apostasy and commendation for having recanted afterwards. And it was obvious that their condemnation outweighed their commendation.

However, the conversation quickly moved to the question of Bahai scripture, which no one knew, and concluded that Bahaism had none. Then the focus turned on the uniqueness of the Qur'an, its purity and authenticity compared to other scriptures. That was exactly the subject I did not expect to be raised on that pleasant day. I felt that if this subject did not stop at this early stage, the day would inevitably be entirely ruined. And that precisely what happened. In comparing the Qur'an with Jewish and Christian scriptures in particular (which none of them had ever read), the derisory remarks they made about them were so shocking that I had a battle keeping my mouth shut. Two of the students who were mostly vociferous in vilifying the Old and New Testaments went a step further. They claimed that these so-called scriptures were man-made. The original Jewish and Christian scriptures were lost. They no longer existed. At this point, my longsuffering reached its limit. Silence may be wise, but too much silence is tantamount to courting cowardice. Caution may be safe, but honesty is far safer. I felt that I must speak out.

"What real evidence do we have that those books were lost?" I quietly asked. "And if so, when were they lost, before or after the Qur'an? If before the Qur'an, then we have a serious problem. In the Qur'an the prophet was ordered to seek help from those who have the scriptures so as to eliminate any existing doubt. He was told: *And if you* (Muhammad) *are in any doubt concerning that which we reveal unto you, then ask those who read the scripture* (that was) *before you'.*[5]

---

[5] Sura Yunus [10]:94.

"We don't know," came their reply. "But there are those who believe that they were lost."

"There isn't the slightest historical hint that they were lost," I argued. "On the contrary, recent Qumran discoveries refute this allegation. The Qumran community belonged to the first Century BC. Among the treasures found in the Qumran caves in Palestine, in 1947, was a list of the books of the Jewish scriptures (Ar. *Taurat*), containing all the books that are used today in Jewish synagogues. The manuscripts discovered there are no different from what is in the hands of the Jews and the Christians today."

"Do you mean that those ancient scriptures still exist?" they asked.

"Yes, they do," I responded. "As a matter of fact, when a Muslim denies the existence of those divine scriptures, he perhaps inadvertently undermines his own faith."

"What do you mean?" asked one of them.

I looked at him and said, "The Qur'an clearly states, '*The Apostle* (Muhammad*) believeth in what hath been revealed to him from his Lord (as do) the believers. Each one believeth in God, His angels, His books and His Apostles.*'[6] The Qur'an also states elsewhere, '*O ye who believe! Believe in God and His Apostle, and the scripture, which He hath sent to His Apostle, and the scripture which He sent to those before (him). Any who denieth God, His angels, His books, His Apostles, and the Day of Judgment, hath gone far, far astray.*'[7]

Now, if one believes in the existing reality of God, His angels, the historic prophets, and in the Last day that awaits all humanity, how can one deny the existence of His holy books that are in circulation today? It is ludicrous to believe in the unseen things and dismiss as non-existent the things that are evidently seen today. The Muslim who does this undermines his own faith. It is extremely paradoxical for a Muslim to believe in the former revelations, as an article of faith, and at the same time deny their existence. Can anyone believe in something that does not exist?"

There was a sign of anxiety on the faces of the two students who denied the existence of Jewish and Christian scriptures. Surprisingly, there was a relaxed smile on the faces of two other students. It appeared to be a smile of approval. After a mild dispute between them, which involved a lot of cross-talking, one of those

---

[6] Sura al-Baqara [2]:285.

[7] Sura al-Nisa'[4]:136.

who smiled approvingly spoke up. He may be designated as A.Q. in this particular account.

"It is probably wrong to say that the scriptures of the People of the Book no longer exist. But do you agree that those scriptures have been in some way falsified according to Islamic consensus?" he asked.

"With all respect," I answered, "this assertion has never been substantiated. In fact, there have been dissenting voices among some highly distinguished Muslim scholars regarding this claim."

"Like who, for example?" he asked.

"For example," I pointed out, "this claim, according to the famous Shaykh Muhammad Abduh, makes no sense at all. He writes, 'It would not have been possible for Jews and Christians everywhere to agree on changing the text. Even if those in Arabia had done it, the difference between their book and those of their brothers, let us say, in Syria or Europe, would have been obvious.'"

"It is interesting that such a statement should come from a highly distinguished Islamic scholar like Muhammad Abduh. In any case, he must be a one off," he said with a smile.

"By no means," I replied. "As a matter of fact, Muslim scholars in India examined this matter in detail in the light of the contents of the Qur'an, and were convinced of the authenticity of the scriptures of the Old and the New Testaments. They had no doubt that these books have not been changed or corrupted as is generally alleged.

"According to them, there are indications that some of the Jewish scholars have acted wrongly in their interpretations. Therefore, the falsification lies not in the sacred text, but in the Jewish interpretation of the sacred text."

"How did they come to know that?" he asked.

"Those eminent scholars," I replied, "based their conclusion on the writings of Muslim scholars like al-Razi, al-Jalalain, al-Tabari, al-Baidawi and others. Their interpretations of Sura al-Baqara [2]:75; Sura al-'An'am[6]:61; Sura al-Nisa'[4]:46; Sura al-Ma'idah [5]:44; not to mention others, are well known. It might be a good idea to take a look again at these invaluable commentaries on this particular point."

There was a period of utter silence. Apart from looking at each other, some with a faint smile and others with a straight face, no one said a word. I wondered if I had said more than enough and therefore given them a cause for suspicion. I wished I could know what was going through their minds. Then some of them suddenly broke the silence.

"Do you personally and honestly believe that those Jewish and Christian scriptures are authentic today?" he asked.

"I certainly do," I replied.

"Have you read them?" one of them asked.

"Indeed," I said "I've read them and found them fascinating."

"Do they sound like the Holy Qur'an?" He asked.

"In some ways they do," I answered, "but in many ways they don't."

"So then," asked a student sitting beside me, "do you suppose that they really contain the pure word of God"?

"I don't suppose it," I calmly said, "I sincerely believe that they are the word of God."

"Do they sound better than the Holy Qur'an?" asked another student.

"Now, just a minute," I promptly replied. "Is this an inquisition or what? We'd better change this subject once and for all. Let us talk about something else."

The atmosphere was now electric. And amidst what could only be described as a sombre mood, the students started getting ready to leave as the sun was beginning to set. Whatever doubts those students had had about me in the past, this last dialogue did much to clear most of it. They were now certain that a change had occurred in me. They could hardly disguise their indignation. Walking back home that day, I overheard one of the students a few yards behind me hurling one of the vilest insults on the missionaries. I knew that they were angry both with me and with the missionaries whom they believed had damaged me beyond repair. However, as I looked at the sun setting over the horizon, I was certain of one thing. Most of those students were not going to let the sun go down on their anger. A few weeks earlier, I had felt that a gathering storm was looming on the horizon. But now that storm appeared to be gathering pace. Yet, far from throwing prudence to the wind, I was determined to remain calm, cautious, and above all honest in the face of the storm, which was about to break.

Chapter 7

THE STORM OF ADVERSITIES

"Prosperity is the blessing of the Old Testament; adversity is the blessing of the New."

(Francis Bacon)

Ever since I embraced the offer of the grace of God, I was never unmindful of the fact that faith in Jesus Christ has its own price. The relatively quiet period in which I was enjoying my faith was not to last forever. Trials and adversities were inevitable. Jesus did not hesitate to tell His own followers what to expect. *"In the world you shall have tribulation,"* He told them. Then He added, *"But be of good cheer, I have overcome the world."*[1] Interestingly, God does not take away trials or carry us over them, but strengthens us through them. In time of adversity, the certainty that Jesus has overcome this world of trials and strife is in itself a source of tremendous strength. As a child I had been quite nervous by nature, but in my youth I learned to hide it and keep it under control. During my open stand for Jesus and the hardship that followed, my nervousness suddenly disappeared completely.

I still look upon that recovery as a divine touch, which prepared me to face the inevitable adversities with amazing fortitude and strength. There is a sense in which my adversities were the means by which I was being identified with Jesus. He once said, *"A disciple is not above his teacher, nor a servant above his master; it is enough for the disciple to be like his teacher, and the servant like his master. If they have called the master of the house Beelzebul, how much more will they malign those of his household?"*[2] The New Testament teaches that nothing will show more accurately what a Christian is than the way he meets trials and tribulations.[3]

---

[1] Jn. 16:33.

[2] Mt. 10:24-25; 1 Pet. 4:12-19.

[3] 1 Pet. 1:7.

An Insult as Compliment

"What's In A Name?" wrote Shakespeare.[4] There may or may not be much in a name for Westerners. The sound of a name seems to matter more than its meaning. But for the Arabs as for their ancient Semitic relatives in Biblical times, names are more like what we would call today nicknames. A name is given to one as a description of his present or future character. In Biblical times, for example, one of Isaac's sons was called Esau because he was hairy.[5] His brother was called Jacob because he was a supplanter.[6] There are also cases in which the name given to a person is intended to signify his destiny. God, for example, changed the name Abram to Abraham, for he was to be the father of a multitude of nations.[7] Likewise Sarai's name was changed to Sarah, Jacob's to Israel, and Simon's to Peter.[8]

A name could often be given at first as a term of contempt. In time, however, that name may be adopted as a title of honour. For example, among themselves, the Christians of the first century used the term 'belonging to the Way', 'disciples' and most of all 'believers'.[9] The name 'Christian' is found only three times in the New Testament, and was used as a term of reproach for the early followers of Jesus by their opponents.[10] Apparently when the nickname 'Christian' as a derogatory term was first given to the early believers, they must have felt deeply insulted. Peter then was able to tell his readers that in such a situation they should do what he and his friends did – "glorify God in this name" (1 Pet. 4:16).

The week of that spring vacation was over, and the students were returning to the Seminary on a bright and beautiful Saturday morning. They were walking in groups. I was walking alone after I had tried to join one of those groups and felt a peculiar chill from them. I knew that something was afoot. As I walked alone I could feel that all eyes were upon me. I was just a few yards from the Seminary gates when

---

[4] Romeo & Juliet, II, 2.

[5] Gen. 25:25.

[6] Gen. 27:36.

[7] Gen. 17:5.

[8] Gen. 17:15; 35:9-10; Mt. 16:18.

[9] See Acts 9:2,26; cf. 5:14.

[10] For them, 'Christian' was a Latin word meaning 'partisans of Christ'. See Acts 11:26; 26:28; 1 Pet. 4:16.

a voice rang out *"Masihi!"* (i.e. Christian). At this point I felt as if my heart sank into my boots. I refused to look around to see where that voice came from or who was responsible. With my heart pounding, I simply kept my head down as I walked into the Seminary.

In the classroom I could hardly concentrate. I realised that my position was fast becoming untenable. What if I were challenged directly as to whether I really was a Christian? For a moment I toyed with the idea that if that happened I could reply with a flat denial as long as my heart remained firm in my newfound faith. But I quickly realised that this would be more agreeable with the Qur'anic concept of *'taqiya'* than with the New Testament teaching.[11] In Islam *'taqiya'* is an act whereby a Muslim, out of fear, conceals his real faith or opinion by resorting if necessary to a flat denial or a lie.

In my dilemma, I was reminded of the words of Jesus in the New Testament: *"For whoever is ashamed of me and of my words, of him will the Son of man be ashamed when he comes in his glory and the glory of the Father and of the holy angels."*[12] The words of St Paul to the Philippians also were not far from my mind, *"For it has been granted to you that for the sake of Christ you should not only believe in Him but also suffer for His sake."*[13]

As I pondered these words, a tremendous sense of serenity and courage came upon me. In the silence of my own heart I decided that if I were ever challenged about my newfound faith, I must be honest and truthful. I must not be afraid of people or ashamed of Jesus whatever the cost might be. I felt calm and confident that He who brought me out of darkness into His marvellous light was also able to protect me from all harm. No doubt, at first I felt like those early believers, who probably felt insulted when their opponents gave them the nickname 'Christian'. But like them also I came to consider it a real compliment.

Confrontation and Victory

At the recreation ground afterwards, a number of students seemed to eye me as though I was a totally new student. I tried to engage some of them in conversation, but their frosty attitude towards me was too

---

[11] The Qur'anic verses relating to the concept of *'taqiya'* are: Sura Al-'Imran [3]:28; Sura al-Nahl [16]:106.

[12] Lk. 9:26.

[13] Phil. 1:29.

obvious. Others simply distanced themselves from me. Suddenly, that voice again rang out, "*Masihi!*", which apparently drew the attention of a good number of students. At first, I did not know where that voice came from. But the cast of one student's eyes towards a group of four or five students some distance away was enough to pinpoint the source of that voice. In that group of students I saw M.S. my bitter opponent, who was obviously their instigator and ringleader.

At first I strongly felt that I should go immediately and tackle them. But on reflection, I thought that to do that at this particular time and place might be extremely precarious. I decided instead to wait for the right opportunity, which as a matter of fact, was not far off. On the way home that very day, I spotted that notorious group of students walking together and joined them. And without a moment's hesitation I tackled them head on.

"Hey! Lads," I said, "one of you today has shouted '*Masihi*' twice, presumably referring to me."

"Presumably?" they asked with a laugh. "If it is a presumption, here is your chance to clear yourself, for the feelings against you are running very high, as you probably know."

"There is one thing that bothers me about you, guys," I said somehow angrily. "What concern is it of yours if I decide to become a Christian, a Jew or even an atheist? The matter is entirely between God and me. And if you believe that by so doing I'm going to hell, that's my business. I'm taking none of you with me!"

At this stage a number of other students overheard the conversation and joined them. Some of them were my closest friends. But, with the exception of two who remained steadfast, the rest had distanced themselves from me since the last talk at the picnic. The battle of words continued.

"Don't be so evasive," they argued, "we know that you are smart and have a way with words. Give us a straight answer. Have you become a Christian? There are indications to suggest that you may well have. If you haven't, then tell us."

"I'm not evasive or afraid of anyone". I replied. "If you really want to know, then here is my answer without hooves or horns: 'Yes, I've become a Christian', and if anyone at any time wants to persuade me otherwise, he (or they) would be more than welcome. I'll not run away."

My unambiguous announcement of my newfound faith came as a bombshell to that group of students whose reactions varied. Some were simply stunned into silence, others worked themselves into a fury of indignation; but as for M.S., their ringleader, he was wearing a smirk. For that fellow, the scene seemed to be quite enjoyable. Looking at him, I felt sad that here was a guy whose quiet nature spoke peace, but war was in his heart. His smirk signalled that he was pleased with his victory. But in this confrontation the one who became the object of anger and vilification was the real victor. I was fully aware that in Christ there are no victories without conflicts, no rainbows without clouds and storms.

A Help in Time of Trouble

As one of my two steadfast friends who happened to be there whisked me away, I realised that what had happened was just a foretaste of things to come. We walked briskly but silently until we reached the quiet town promenade that overlooked the Atlantic. Here I broke the silence by asking my faithful companion if he was hurt or offended by what had happened a little while ago. He looked as though he was close to tears. He was certainly distressed. His reply was that regardless of his personal feelings, what mattered was that he was both astonished and worried. He was astonished by the honest conviction and courage I had shown in that highly dangerous situation. And he was also seriously worried by the grave consequences that would inevitably follow. Apart from this, he offered no advice and hardly said anything more. However, he remained with me until dusk and then took his leave of me with words something like, "When you get home, go straight into your bedroom, close the door and go to sleep. Forget what happened today, and if possible forget what might happen tomorrow. I remain your friend. Don't forget that." These last words did much to boost my spirit. Here indeed was a friend, who unlike the rest, instead of pointing a finger he held out a hand.

After my friend had left, I stayed a little while praying as I gazed upon the ocean's angry waves. As I looked on, the Lord seemed to remind me that He was the Master of the sea. He both rebuked its angry waves into silence and walked triumphantly over them.[14] If I ever felt like the disciples sailing a tempestuous sea, Jesus would

---

[14] Mt. 8:23-27; 14:22-27; Mk. 6:45-52; Jn. 6:16-21.

always come to me across the storms of life with hands outstretched, and with His calm clear voice He would bid me take heart and have no fear. I must only be careful not to be like Peter who took his eyes off the Master and set them upon the waves, and was immediately overwhelmed by them.

These two uplifting experiences followed almost immediately after my first confrontation. As a result, I felt calm and my courage renewed, and that was a refreshing moment. C.S. Lewis once wrote, "Our Father refreshes us on the journey with some pleasant inns, but will not encourage us to mistake them for home."[15] Indeed, "In this world you will have trouble," Jesus said. Then He added, "But take heart! I have overcome the world."[16] I was aware that the journey, which I had begun recently, would not be easy, but I was confident that the presence of Christ with me would be my unremitting source of help and support.

I made my way home. When I arrived I was asked if I needed something to eat. I quietly replied that I was not hungry. I thought perhaps the atmosphere at home was slightly sombre. Had the family heard anything? If they had, then nobody let on. The person more likely to do so in this situation would have been grandfather and he was fortunately out of town. I then went straight into my bedroom, closed the door and went to bed. As I lay down, I recalled how in the events of that day, the Lord was indeed "a very present help in trouble".[17] And with these words of the Psalmist echoing in my mind, I was fast asleep.

Paying the Price

Next day, I woke up early in the morning after a good night's sleep. In the privacy of my bedroom I was able to spend a quiet time of devotion. I was aware that it was going to be a unique and extraordinary day and I must expect the unexpected. I prayed that the Lord might keep His protective hand upon me and bless me with His wisdom and peace. I then made myself a quick breakfast and left for the Seminary. I had not gone ten yards from home when I saw my loyal friend together with the second friend (who was absent at the

[15] C.S. Lewis, *The Business of Heaven* (Collins 1984), p. 18.

[16] Jn. 16:33 NIV.

[17] Ps. 46:1.

confrontation the day before), waiting for me. I was deeply touched to realise that in that difficult situation, they were caring and thoughtful enough to make sure I did not walk to the Seminary on my own. Throughout that day, students often eyed me whispering to each other and keeping their distance from me. But my two friends hardly left my side. Strangely enough, in view of what had happened the day before, nobody yelled *"Masihi"* at me. It transpired that the night before, my two friends had caught up with the real culprit and strongly warned him not to do it again.

Just before the start of the final class that day, the lecturer took me aside and told me that the Principal wanted to see me in his office after the class. I knew then that things were out in the open, and that the signs were not good, but I kept calm and ready for any eventuality. At the same time, I was uniquely conscious of the God's presence. I was fully confident that come what may, the Lord would not let me down. And those who put their trust in Him would not be disappointed. To crown it all, the reassuring words of St Paul were a source of great encouragement, *"If God is for us, who can be against us?"*[18]

When the class was over, my two friends came running, wished me well and went away looking rather pessimistic. I waited a little until all the students had left and then made my way to the Principal's office. In the office there were six members of the Faculty sitting – the Dean, the Principal and four lecturers, two of them seemed to glance at me with what could only be described as a very faint smile. The one, though a graduate of the ancient Islamic university of Qarawiyyin in Fez, was noted for his liberal socialist stance. The other was an Algerian member of the resistance movement who had recently got political asylum in Morocco. The rest of them sat stony-faced. Then the Principal came in and sat at his desk. He brought an envelope out of his pocket, placed it on the desk before him and without any preliminaries he got into the subject as he looked me straight in the face.

"I guess you must have an idea why you're summoned here today," he said in a gruff voice.

"Yes, sir," I replied.

"According to reliable witnesses, you've openly and unashamedly announced your conversion to Christianity. Is that true?" he asked.

"Yes, sir," I replied.

---

[18] Rom. 8:31.

"Has it occurred to you," he said, "that by doing this you've done irreparable damage to yourself and your future? Do you realise that what you've done has brought the good name of your family into disrepute and given a bad name to this institution? The people in this town are scandalized and furious at what you've done? I have a letter before me signed by a huge number of students expressing their anger and demanding that drastic action should be taken against you.

"Sir," I answered, "I'm fully aware of the consequences of my decision. I can imagine how angry people are at me, and had I been in their place I would've felt the same. As a matter of fact, sir, I never went out of my way to confess my newfound faith. I did so only after being pushed into a difficult and inescapable position by certain vindictive fellow students.

"And why didn't you deny it?" he angrily asked. "In that way you could've spared yourself and all of us this unprecedented tragedy."

"I could not possibly do so, sir" I responded. "The concept of 'taqiya' has no place in the Christian faith, otherwise, the blood of countless martyrs would not have been shed in the early Christian centuries. Christ has expressly said, *So everyone who acknowledges me before men, I also will acknowledge before my Father who is in heaven; but whoever denies me before men, I also will deny him before my Father who is in heaven.*[19] The denial of the truth is a serious issue; and since I hate to be deceived, I would hate to deceive others. The words of Christ are clear, *'And as you wish that men would do to you, do so to them'.*[20]

At this stage, one of those lecturers that sat stony-faced could no longer contain his fury. He asked permission to say something and was granted.

"This is outrageous," he thundered. "I simply can't believe what I'm seeing and hearing. Do you realise that your apostasy is a serious insult to Islam? It is a clear declaration that Islam is a false religion and that is why you've turned your back on it. Isn't that so? Come on admit it."

With this question, I felt somehow cornered. I also felt this lecturer was trying to put words into my mouth, which might lead to a greater indictment. And what could be a greater and more serious indictment than a verbal admission that Islam is a false religion? In

---

[19] Mt. 10:32-33.

[20] Lk. 6:31.

the silence of my own heart I prayed for help in this difficult situation. In seconds I was ready with the answer, which neither that lecturer nor the faculty expected.

"With all due respect, sir," I replied, "I've never insulted Islam in my entire life. But in the market place of this city men can trade daily insults and invoke curses on each other's religion, which is Islam. But no protest has ever been heard. In this city also there are certain self-confessed atheists, who are pretty vocal in treating Islam with nothing less than disdain, as you know. Yet, such people pass with total impunity. But when one changes from Islam to another faith, then all are out to get him as though he had committed something worse than murder."

"Apostasy is indeed worse than murder," he shouted back. "What you've done is most outrageous both to your family and your Muslim community in this city. I therefore understand why apostates must suffer capital punishment according to Shari'a law unless they recant. It is regrettable that this law is not implemented today."

"Of course, as we all know," I replied with a slight sense of indignation, "this particular law is not cancelled, but only postponed. Islam is the only religion in the world that has capital punishment for apostasy. At present this is not implemented, and that's probably to Islam's own advantage. In fact, the execution of apostates does Islam no good, because in the final analysis, this law produces either martyrs or hypocrites."

At this stage, the Principal intervened to stop the exchange. By this time that lecturer's temperature seemed a bit too high. As a last attempt, the Principal decided to resort to a more tactful and ego-massaging method to soften me and finally reclaim me to my ancestral faith.

"Everybody in this Faculty," he said in a soft voice, "can testify that you are a highly diligent and brilliant student. You, among a few others, have been the pride and joy of this Institution. As a Faculty, we value you so much and want you to reconsider your present position. We implore you not to eclipse your bright future. We also implore you to give some thought to your honourable family. Do not inflict so great a shame upon them. Come back to your ancestral faith, and may God curse those evil missionaries that have poisoned your mind with their 'shirk'".[21]

---

[21] 'Shirk' means polytheism – the belief in many gods. In this context, the Principal was referring to the Christian Trinitarian belief.

"I beg to differ, sir," I responded. "Those missionaries did nothing of the sort. My conversion is the outcome of my own research study, in which they had no hand whatsoever."

"And what was your discovery?" he asked.

"I discovered that the popular Islamic concept which views the Bible as a corrupted text is utterly unfounded," I politely said. "There is no hint of this allegation even in the Qur'an. That was the starting point of my journey to Christianity. Once I became absolutely sure of the authenticity of the Bible, I started reading it, which consequently led to my conversion. I am fully convinced that Jesus Christ is, as He Himself has said in the Holy *'Injil'* (Gospel), *'the Way, the Truth and the Life. No one comes to the Father but by me'*."

After these last words, there followed a brief hush. Then the Principal, looking quite angry, asked me to wait outside until I was recalled. Outside the office there was nobody around except the janitor standing at the gate a few yards away. As I sat down my eyes looked with intense curiosity at the walls and marble pillars as though I was a new student on my first day at the Seminary. I possibly did that on the first day I entered that institution as a new student. I was now instinctively doing the same thing, but for the last time.

As I sat there waiting to be recalled, I was suddenly seized with a combined sense of agitation, anxiety and self-doubt. For the first time I realised the harsh reality of the position I was in. Did I really count the cost when I first embraced Christianity? Was I so reckless as to ignore the social rejection, ostracism and God knows what else that would follow? Could it be that I was like one who was sleep walking my way into an abyss? With such thoughts things looked as dark as midnight, and I began to feel extremely vulnerable. But surprisingly the thought of looking for a way out of this acute dilemma never occurred to me. Instead, the very thought of Jesus and His never failing love and power began to flood my heart in a unique manner. Why should I yield to such devilish thoughts? Of course, I must have counted the cost when I received Christ into my life; and far be it from Him to let His own people down or forsake them in any way. With these thoughts I felt the reality of Christ with me, even sitting next to me in that darkest moment. Indeed, I was now confident that the Lord never fails to follow close upon the heels of those who might either be unconsciously drifting, or fearfully running away.

The door of the office opened and I was called in. I glanced at the Faculty members as if trying to read the verdict on their faces. I noticed that the two lecturers, who had earlier glanced at me with a faint smile, had their arms folded and their heads bowed. Their posture signalled either sympathy or embarrassment or both. The others seemed anything but unhappy or indifferent to the decision that had just been made.

The Principal took one look at me and in two brief and curt statements he spelt out the decision of the Faculty. "As an apostate from Islam," he said in a rather sharp tone, "the Faculty has hereby decided that you be dismissed from this Seminary. A letter confirming this decision will be sent to you soon. We hope you realise the enormity of your action for which you're paying a heavy price. You may be excused." I left the office with those last few words still ringing in my ears ". . . you're paying a heavy price". The price was indeed high, I thought, but the price Jesus paid was infinitely higher.

Chapter 8

WITH THE GOD OF TOMORROW

*"I have learned to live each day as it comes, and not
to borrow trouble by dreading tomorrow. It is the
dark menace of the future that makes cowards of us."*

(Dorothy Dix)

As I left the Seminary for the last time, I felt that the blow I had just suffered was indeed hard to bear. I was also aware that many would be gloating when they hear the news of my expulsion. But my greatest worry was the reaction of the family when this shocking piece of news reaches them. As the saying goes, 'It's much easier to borrow trouble than it is to give it away'. In the back of my mind, grandfather was still out of town, and that in some way provided me with a breathing space, but little did I know that he would return home that evening.

For the time being, I made my way to the Mission House. I felt in need of some spiritual encouragement and comfort after going through the wringer a little while ago. Dr Rigby and his colleagues met me with a warm welcome as usual. They were quite aware of my situation, and who was not? Indeed, the whole town was abuzz with the news of the recent young apostate. I informed them of my dismissal from the Seminary a few hours earlier, which came to them as no surprise.

In the peaceful and hallowed atmosphere of that place, Dr Rigby spared no effort in assuring me of his love, prayer and support in the situation. He reminded me of the fact that he considered me his son in the Lord and that I was welcome at his home anytime. He also urged that I should never have any reason to feel alone or isolated in any way. The Lord was with me and I had nothing to fear. Indeed, in that meeting I felt renewed and refreshed by the ministry of help and encouragement I received. As I left the Mission House afterwards I was more certain than ever that I was in the firm grip of Divine Providence and that my steps into the future would be *"ordered by the Lord"*.[1]

---

[1] Ps. 37:23.

God's Safety Net

On my way home under the cover of a dark evening, I was under no illusion that the stakes were high. But on the whole I was not worried by what the future might hold. I knew that things in my life were on the verge of an unprecedented change. But my faith was deeply rooted in the Lord, because in Him there is no variation or shadow of change.[2]

I was half way home when I decided to pay a visit to my maternal grandmother. I had not seen her for nearly three weeks. Before then I used to stay with her a few days at a time. I thought that it would be interesting to know her feelings about the latest event. I was certain that she would be quite upset by the news of my conversion to Christianity and my expulsion from the Seminary. But I was equally certain that the upset would be nothing compared to that of my paternal grandfather and his household. My grandmother loved me so dearly and had a deep affection for me. This was so because on one the hand I was the son of her only daughter, and on the other I bore a striking resemblance to her, as many knew. She often told people that as long as I lived, her dear daughter was not dead.

As I entered the house, though I was welcomed, the element of fuss which usually crowned my visits was missing. During supper, she told me with tears in her eyes how deeply distressed and angry she was at what I had done. My action, she said, had brought shame and social disgrace upon both families. True, she added, the feuding of the two families since my mother's death had left a scar on both of them. But, the wound that my action (my conversion) had inflicted was incurable. It would remain for both families a painful and festering sore for life.

"Did you consider the consequences of your foolish and disastrous deed? What would become of you now?" she asked. My response was one of utter silence, partly out of respect for her, and partly because any honest reply from me might exacerbate the situation. I could not possibly say anything that might upset her more. Instead I put my head on her shoulder and sobbed my heart out, and so did she. Probably the unbearable ordeal of the last few days was now giving vent to this flood of emotional grief. In the midst of that tearful situation, I realised how true the words of Jesus were, *"I have not come to bring peace, but*

---

[2] Jas. 1:17.

a sword. For I have come to set a man against his father, and a daughter against her mother, and a daughter-in-law against her mother-in-law; and a man's foes will be his own household . . ."[3] Meanwhile, in my heart of hearts I always knew that of all my relatives, grandmother had been the most loving and affectionate for reasons already mentioned. But now that I was a convert to Christianity, I would no longer hold the same place in her heart. However, what followed next showed that I was totally wrong.

The few minutes' silence which followed that emotional moment was broken by grandmother's unexpected statement. She told me that after what I did the prospect of my continued stay in my grandfather's house was extremely slim. My expulsion was inevitable. She was not sure that my grandfather would be satisfied with that alone. In her opinion he was so vindictive and unscrupulous as to stop at nothing. Therefore, in view of such a gloomy prospect, she suggested that I would be more than welcome to live with her. But first of all, I must wait and see what grandfather would do. If he expelled me, she said, I should collect my belongings and come home. Under no circumstances would she want to see me, the son of her only daughter, out in the street hungry and homeless.

As she said that, I was deeply moved and could not but give expression to my heart-felt gratitude to her, and that was the first time I had spoken since I came in. Then before I left, I kissed her good night promising to keep her informed of whatever happened. As I walked out, I asked the Lord in the silence of my own heart, to let His blessing abound towards grandmother. I also thanked Him for His instant provision of a safety net that would protect me from falling upon a hard time of homelessness.

The Edge of Rejection

It was near mid-night when I arrived home, having walked slowly in order to play for time. In that way I hoped everybody would be asleep and that might save a lot of hustle. To my surprise, the lights were on and there were signs of activity within the house. I put my ear to the door to find out what was going on side, when suddenly I heard my grandfather's voice. I simply could not believe my ears. I had been under the impression that he was still out of town for at least

---

[3] Mt. 10:34-39.

another day or two. What had made him return so quickly? Could he have got wind of what had happened that day in my home-town? This was possible because the distance between Alcasar and Larache was only 25 km, and bad news travels fast. However, one thing was certain. On his arrival from Alcasar early that evening, the letter from the Seminary confirming my dismissal had already been delivered by hand. One could only guess how he felt when he knew its contents.

Meanwhile, I was in a great dilemma. Should I return to my grandmother rather than face the inevitable wrath of the old man? Or should I take the bull by the horns and face the music in all its jarring discord? But returning to grandmother at almost mid-night would be inappropriate. It would be utterly unfair to disturb her peaceful sleep after an upsetting day. After much prayer and consideration, I decided to go in, being mindful of the New Testament words, *"Cast all your anxieties on Him, for he cares about you."*[4]

Words would be inadequate to describe the atmosphere inside the house. I recall that as I entered an extraordinary silence suddenly descended upon the house. Everybody (paternal grandmother, paternal aunt, her husband and family) had all disappeared into the safety of their own bedrooms. As I walked towards my bedroom, the angry voice of grandfather resounded through the house as he stormed out of his own bedroom and walked towards me.

"Where do you think you are going?" he asked angrily. "Do you realise what time this is?" I tried in a quiet voice to apologise for coming home so late. The old man immediately seized on the term 'home', and with his trembling finger pointed close to my face, he launched his bitter diatribe against me. In the course of his long and bitter denunciation, he declared, "As an apostate you no longer belong in this family. As far as we are concerned, you are dead and buried. In this way," he added, "the family honour will be restored and its shame wiped clean from your unforgivable act of apostasy. Now," he concluded, "you have a few minutes in which you can collect all your belongings and leave the house for good." As he turned to walk away, he bitterly grumbled, "Alas, would to God I had never taken you to that infidel English doctor. Your death would've kept our honour unblemished for posterity."

As I hurriedly collected as many of my belongings as I could find, it was apparent that I had no hard feelings toward grandfather.

---

[4] 1 Pet. 5:7.

Instead, I had so much love and sympathy for him that I was moved to tears. In the first place, I felt deeply sorry for a man who had no higher goal than to love his family, to ensure their well-being and to safeguard them against any sort of harm or disrepute. In his fury he must have been thinking that all his efforts had been like ploughing the sand or sowing the ocean – a meaningless vanity and vexation of spirit. It was simply unbearable to see a man in the twilight of his life being crushed beyond measure.

In the second place, the pleasure and the delight of being at home was now at an end. Would memory be kind to me from that day onward? It is certain that memory is not always kind. True, it can take one by the hand and walk him through the glorious avenues of a lost paradise. But it can also put him on the rack of a bad conscience. Yet, I did not feel myself on the rack of a bad conscience; I was rather fortified by the fact that my conscience was clear before God. I was sure that there is always a smile of God's approval on one, who *"for conscience toward God endures grief . . ."*[5]

As a matter of fact, what I had lost was something that can simply be described as a happy and secure home wherein the warmth of love and contentment surrounded me. The sun looks down on nothing half so good as a household laughing together over a meal, planning for a holiday somewhere, and sharing in all that concerns them whether it be bitter or sweet. There is a sense in which the happy home of my childhood was a paradise gift of God to me, and I was now about to leave it. In my situation, I was not aware of St Francis de Sales' beautiful dictum, "She is an all-pure soul who cannot love the paradise of God, but only the God of paradise."

It was in the early hours of the morning that I left home never to see it again. With a bundle of my belongings under my arm I had nowhere to go except to the small and very quiet port of the town. I was very tired by that time. I lay on one of the benches and tried to close my eyes for a little sleep. But the cold air of the sea at that early time of the morning, plus the rough wood of the bench made it impossible for me to dose off. Instead, I sat up and decided to spend time in prayer during which I felt a tremendous sense of fortitude and serenity. Time also seemed to pass very quickly. At the break of dawn, I made my way to my grandmother, who welcomed me home. She made me some breakfast during which I informed her of what had

---

[5] 1 Pet. 2:19.

happened. Then, feeling quite exhausted I went to bed. It was time to close the door on the trials of the last couple of days, including my first-hand experience of the rough edge of rejection.

Some More Losses

I woke up about sunset, and for the first time I realised that there was nothing for me to do. The Seminary's door was closed to me, and in the current atmosphere of hostility the chance of getting a job in town was virtually zero. The thought that another phase of trouble might be ahead was not far from my mind. But, I decided to brush it aside and "*not worry about tomorrow, for tomorrow will worry about itself*".[6]

After dinner in the evening, I walked under the cover of darkness to the Mission House. The fellowship there was cheerful and most uplifting, and the stress and strain of the last few days seemed to pale into insignificance. I mentioned to Dr Rigby the hardships that might yet be in store for me in town, and that a trip to another town or city for a time might not be a bad idea. After all, Jesus Himself told His followers, "*When they persecute you in one town, flee to the next.*"[7] In any case, I would return home once the popular indignation had subsided. After praying with me about this and other matters, I left.

Arriving home late that evening, I found grandmother terribly worried about me. In the current situation, she told me, it was dangerously unwise for me to be out in the street so late at night. I agreed and apologised for causing her undue anxiety. Then I shared with her the possibility of me leaving town for a while until things had calmed down. She was unhappy with the idea, and wondered which town or city I had in mind, and how I would manage to live there. I replied that the city of Tetuan might be a good choice.[8] On my arrival there I would try my best to find some work. Until then I would manage on the little money I had in my savings. Grandmother said no more, but looked at me silently. Her silence suggested that she was reluctantly in favour of the idea. She could probably see that my temporary absence from town might very well keep me out of harm's way. This became clear when she broke her silence and pointed out

---

[6] Mt. 6:34.

[7] Mt. 10:23.

[8] Tetuan lies north-east of Larache and is approximately 115 km from it.

that she would agree on one condition. I had to give her my solemn promise that in the event of finding myself in some grave difficulty, I would return home at once. And I did promise her that without reservation.

Two days later some of grandmother's friends reported that I had been officially disinherited, which came as no surprise. According to Shari'a law an apostate does not inherit his Muslim family or relatives. This law is based on the Prophet Mohammad's instruction, "The Muslim will not inherit the infidel or the infidel the Muslim."[9] The loss was noted but did not seem to affect me. Deep in my own heart I believed that in spite of this additional loss, my gain was infinitely greater. In the words of Samuel Rutherford, "They lose nothing who gain Christ."

In spite of everything my faith remained unshaken. It was neither a blind faith, nor a faith that induced me to play ostrich. On the contrary, I was fully aware that because of my faith in Jesus Christ I was being gradually stripped of all the things I enjoyed and cherished so much. But the loss of these things did not impoverish me. As a matter of fact it was by no means a loss to give all that up for Him who gave up heaven itself for people like me. But there was one thing I prayerfully tried to come to terms with. It was the aching void of loneliness created by the loss of my many friends and companions. Mother Teresa once wrote, "Loneliness and the feeling of being unwanted is the most terrible poverty."[10] But even in such a situation, the Lord does not forget to intervene in some way or another.

The following day, there was a knock at the door. I could hardly believe my eyes when I opened the door and saw my two faithful friends. I had last seen them just shortly before going to the Principal's office. I remembered how they had come running, wished me well and left looking quite pessimistic. It was a real joy to see them again. They hugged me, kissed grandmother's hand and sat down. Grandmother then made us some Moroccan tea and left us together. They handed me a small envelope from the Algerian lecturer who had been present at the Principal's office and who seemed to be sympathetic and sorry for me. When I opened it, I found a small piece of paper containing the Arabic translation of article 18 and clause 1 of the Universal

---

[9] *Zad al-Muslim fima itafaqa 'alayhi al-Bukhari wa Muslim* (Cairo n.d.), Vol. 5. p. 371.

[10] See *Time Magazine*, 'Saints Among Us', 29 Dec. 1975.

Declaration of Human Rights. It was a statement pertaining to religious freedom, which was adopted and proclaimed by General Assembly resolution 217 on the 10th Dec. 1948. I thought it was extremely kind of that lecturer to send me such an important item. I slipped it into my pocket without telling my friends what was in it. I did not know how useful the content of that paper would soon be.

During our conversation, I was curious and even eager to know the level of people's reaction towards me. They were tactfully selective in their report, but nevertheless quite truthful. Whilst admitting that feelings among the people were running high, the diplomatic tone of their report tended to play down the high level of that reaction. They were also quick to add that there were a few who were privately expressing their admiration for the courage of my conviction and for my intellectual prowess in the debate. In this way they were trying to give me some sense of uplift and gratification.

In my reply, I thanked them for their sincere friendship and steadfast loyalty. I mentioned with deep regret how that, apart from them, many other so-called friends had parted company with me. But their genuine friendship reminded me of the Biblical text, which says, *"There are friends who pretend to be friends, but there is a friend who sticks closer than a brother."*[11] When I said that, a smile was drawn upon their faces, but made no comment on that scriptural quotation. The conversation soon shifted to other subjects, and those that were humorous were the most preferable. Obviously, they were keen to cheer me up, and to that end there was no shortage of recalling some hilarious Seminary incidents. Their visit was undoubtedly quite therapeutic, and indeed God-sent.

As they were preparing to leave, I noticed that, for some reason or another, my friends seemed to be feeling slightly awkward. They looked as though they were trying to say something, but did not know how to put it. Finally, they managed to speak. They wanted me to know that I was the best friend they had ever had. In terms of sincerity, loyalty and trust I was incomparable. They told me that it was noticeable to them that since I had embraced Christianity the quality of my friendship seemed to have gone from better to best. Therefore, they were determined to remain my friends, and that hopefully their friendship would match mine. They drew my attention to the fact that although the atmosphere in town was quite charged, their visit

---

[11] Prov. 18:24 (RSV).

that evening just to see me was a risk worth taking. Some people in town, they said, were already blaming them for continuing as friends to me. Indeed, their families had warned them not to have anything to do with me. They continued, albeit emotionally, that owing to the circumstances they had decided to pay me this last visit, which I must not take as marking the end of their friendship. With these last words, they hugged me goodbye and left feeling very upset and near to tears. As for me, I greatly appreciated my friends' kindness and honesty. I was only sorry that my ordeal had not left them unaffected psychologically and socially. I appreciated the fact that it was in their best interests to keep their distance from me. They deserved it.

With this last incident, it occurred to me that although God's providence is merciful and gracious, it could also be hard to cope with. It was a troubling thought. Yet, at the time I did not know that if God is love, then by definition, His love must be something more than mere kindness. It took me a long time to learn that troubles are often God's tools by which He fashions His own people for better things. But what I learned then, in the face of one loss after another, was enough to keep me safe under that very hand of Providence. I learned to *count everything as loss because of the surpassing worth of knowing Christ Jesus . . ."*[12]

Before the Governor

It was a rainy cold mid-January morning 1960. After a small breakfast, I retired to finish reading the Arabic translation of the book *The Pilgrim's Progress*, by John Bunyan. In my current situation, the book was a source of great spiritual strength and encouragement, next only to the Bible. In the intervals, I was thinking over my possible trip to the city of Tetuan. For me, life in my hometown would certainly be difficult and probably insecure. As things stood, apart from my visits to the Mission House under the cover of darkness, I was staying permanently at home. It was like being under house arrest. Nevertheless, the possibility of something new happening unexpectedly was always in the back of my mind. And I was not far wrong.

Grandmother had just finished talking to a neighbour at the door when a gentleman appeared asking to see me. I rushed to see who that

---

[12] Phil. 3:8.

person was. At first sight I gathered that the gentleman might have been an official of some sort. It soon transpired that he was a civil servant from the Mayor, who was the governor of my hometown and its adjacent districts. He told me that the Mayor wanted to see me that day in his office at 3 p.m. My poor grandmother was in a terrible state. Although she did not show it, the colour of her face and her stony silence spoke volumes. The summons was something completely new, although in the back of my mind, the possibility of the civil authorities getting involved one day had not been far from my mind.

Looking at the clock, I noticed I had only a couple of hours before seeing the Mayor. My level of tension and anxiety was beyond endurance. My mind was in turmoil. And there were reasons for me to feel that way. Morocco became a fully-fledged independent state after the withdrawal of the French and Spanish colonial powers in 1956. Since then everything about that country was becoming different. However, in the midst of my mental ordeal, the Lord seemed to inspire me with a thought, which did much to lower my level of tension and anxiety. If the Mayor had intended to take drastic measures against me, would he not have sent me a policeman instead of a civil servant? The more I thought about this point the calmer and more confident I became. By now, the time for the appointment was drawing near, and I made my way to the Mayor's administrative building that was roughly about 400 metres away. As I walked, I could feel most people's eyes were on me, and I determined to look neither to the right nor to the left, but just keep walking with my head down.

I arrived at the Mayor's place a few minutes early and was told to sit and wait until I was called. It was a God-given time for me to renew my courage in a quiet word of prayer. I asked the Lord to give me strength and wisdom, and most of all, to enable me to speak the truth in love when I meet the governor. During that prayer the bell rang and my name was called. Incidentally, the Mayor was surprisingly a native of the city of Tetuan and quite unpopular among the people of Larache for his hard line methods. His attitude of bullying and scare tactics was such that people had often written to the Ministry of Interior in Rabat requesting his removal from office. I was about to have a taste of his brusque and tactless attitude.

As I stepped into the office, I saw the Mayor sitting behind his desk browsing over some papers or documents in front of him. I greeted him politely with the phrase, "Good afternoon, sir." In reply, I was curtly told, "Sit down." As a matter of fact, what followed amounted to a disconcerting session of rancour and veiled threats from this high ranking official. It seemed also that he was probably of the opinion that he who shouts the loudest wins the argument! The following was roughly how that meeting began and ended:

"I've never met or seen an apostate in my entire life," he said with a straight face. "Unfortunately, now I have one in front of me."

"I understand that, sir," I replied in a low voice.

"I don't think you do," he said in a sharp tone of voice. "For me as for many in this town, coming across someone who has openly renounced Islam and embraced Christianity is an insult to everything that we hold dear in this country. No, indeed, you don't understand how deeply offended I am by you. What in the world has induced you to abandon Islam, the religion of your forebears, for an entirely foreign one?"

"Sir," I answered, "it's the dictate of conscience that has induced me to do so."

"Are you trying to insult my intelligence or what?" he sarcastically asked. "I'm speaking about the faith of your birth and you're telling me about 'the dictate of conscience'. What conscience? Are you trying to be smart with me?"

"Sir," I responded, "Islam is indeed the religion of my birth and upbringing. But it's not the religion I chose. Christianity is the faith I've now chosen to embrace, and I've done so only after a thorough comparative study of the two faiths. It is never a crime for one to obey his conscience when the truth becomes crystal clear. Indeed, sir, in such a situation one should have absolute freedom to do so."

"What freedom are you talking about?" he angrily asked. "And who's given you this freedom to leave the faith of your birth for another? Who do you think you're talking to? You're indeed the most insolent individual I've ever met."

"Sir," I respectfully said, "you've asked me what freedom I'm talking about. With your kind permission, I can answer that question."

"Go ahead", he shouted. "Give me more of your philosophical nonsense, veneered over with your soft Christian missionary-like talk. Go ahead, I'm listening."

"With all due respect, sir," I carefully explained, "the freedom I'm talking about is the one enshrined in the Universal Declaration of Human Rights, which was adopted and proclaimed by the General

Assembly resolution 217 A (III) on the 10th December 1948. And as you know, sir, our country, Morocco, is a signatory to this Declaration. Article 18 and clause 1 clearly states: *'Everyone has the right to freedom of thought, conscience and religion; this right includes freedom to change his religion or belief, and freedom either alone or in community with others and in public or private, to manifest his religion or belief in teaching, practice, worship and observance . . .'"*

I had barely finished the last sentence when the Mayor exploded in anger pouring out a torrent of insults upon me, and pointing out that I was there to answer for my evil apostasy and not to act like a self-styled lawyer. He went on to say, albeit indignantly, that my understanding of article 18 and clause 1 of the Declaration was totally wrong, and that Morocco had its own interpretation of that statement. But he never told me what that interpretation was, and I never asked. In fact, in that outburst I was too stunned for words. Finally after a shouting monologue, the Mayor ordered me out of his sight, muttering what sounded like, "Something has to be done . . . !"

I left the Mayor's office with a strange combination of distress and relief. On my way home, I was mindful once again that although following Jesus was by no means an easy pursuit, nevertheless it was the noblest of all pursuits. In the world, I would perhaps have some more tribulation; but I was of good cheer that Jesus Christ has overcome the world.[13] Meanwhile, the Lord was with me and the plans for my future were in His hands. By way of divine consolation, it occurred to me that what had just happened should be taken as a real privilege. It might even, in a small measure, put me amongst those to whom Jesus foretold, *". . . you will stand before governors and kings for my sake to bear witness before them."*[14] And whatever else should happen in the future, I had no fear for the Lord was with me. He is the God of yesterday, today and tomorrow.

---

[13] Jn. 16:33.

[14] Mk. 13:9; cf. Mt. 10:18.

Chapter 9

WHEN NEW DIFFICUTIES BECAME NEW OPPORTUNITIES

"God comforts us, not by changing the circumstances,
but by changing our attitude towards them."
(S.C.B. Masterman)

A couple of days later I visited the Mission House to bid Dr Rigby Godspeed on his imminent journey to Britain for a brief visit. The one to take over from him was Mr John Hutchinson, from Northern Ireland. He was a pleasant man and had a remarkable singing-voice. The fellowship in the Mission House that evening was spiritually most edifying. At the end of the meeting a special prayer was offered for my forthcoming trip to Tetuan. By that time I was certain that it was God's will that I should take that trip soon, probably about the weekend. Life in my hometown was becoming very difficult, and for me a change would be as good as a rest. In any case, I was given the address of certain missionaries in Tetuan, and was advised to visit them. Just as I was leaving, Miss Monde, one of Dr Rigby's colleagues, thrust a small envelop into my pocket. Inside it was a small amount of money together with a note to say that the enclosed was from the Lord and that it might be of some help to me on my journey. I was deeply moved by that kind gift, which to this day I still remember with much appreciation.

I returned home not as late as before. I was careful this time not to cause grandmother any anxiety. During supper, I told her of my intention to leave for Tetuan on Friday night that week. She reminded me again of my solemn promise that in the event of finding myself in a grave difficulty I should return home immediately. She was very worried about me. However, all that I wanted at that moment in time was to get away. My hometown had turned its back on me, and there was nothing left in it for me. Yet, a question crossed my mind: could I be jumping from the frying pan into the fire?

Before I could address myself to that question, my brother who had just become a professional printer after a few years as an apprentice, came to visit me. It was a real joy to see him. Throughout the recent ordeal, his entire reaction had been one of complete silence. My brother was cast in a different mould. Opting out of school at an early age, he preferred the company of some Spanish youth with whom he played football, and eventually became a semi-professional footballer for a time. With such company, his religious stance differed from the rest of the family. As a matter of fact, it was most gratifying to learn how greatly he disapproved of the way in which his elder brother had been treated. It just happened that due to the bitter reaction of grandfather and the rest of the family, he found himself in an awkward position. In that intricate situation, he obviously thought that it was safer to remain silent. But deep down he was profoundly sorry for what his brother was going through. All this became clear from his conversation with me during that visit. Among the things he shared with me that evening was the news that the Mayor was to be transferred somewhere else. In the silence of my own heart, I thought that God's ways are beyond our comprehension.

However, after informing him confidentially of my imminent trip to Tetuan, I wondered if I could correspond with grandmother through him. The old lady could neither read nor write, and telephones in those days were a rare commodity. He gladly agreed and gave me the address of his work place. After a while he left wishing me all the best on my journey.

Arriving at Nowhere

On that cold Friday evening, I walked to the bus station with no luggage except a small Bible, an Arabic copy of D'Aubigné's "*History of the Reformation*" and the clothes I was wearing. I had hoped that with the little amount of money in my pocket I would be able to buy some clothes later. I had arrived at the station just a few minutes before the 10.30 p.m. bus left for Tetuan, and in no time was on the way to its destination. As the traces of my city receded, a tremendous sense of relaxation filled my heart. The bus was not full and the mood of the travellers seemed to vary. Some were engaged in conversation, some were in fits of laughter whilst others were sitting back with their eyes closed. It was not hard to feel that most of them were in high spirits.

Some perhaps were returning home, others visiting their friends and relations, or attending to some business. It struck me also that those people were in fact going 'somewhere'. But where was I going? The answer, which I struggled hard to avoid, was 'nowhere'. Then, I realised that whereas in fact I was 'going nowhere', I certainly was 'going with someone'. I smiled as I visualised myself like one of those men who were travelling to Emmaus. As they walked and talked anxiously with each other, *"Jesus Himself drew near and went with them."*[1]

At 2.00 a.m. the bus arrived at Tetuan bus station, which was almost empty. The climate in that northernmost Moroccan city felt naturally colder than in my hometown, and I was pleased I had brought my winter coat with me. At that early hour of the morning, I decided to sit on one of the benches and have a snooze until daybreak. It was no use walking before daylight in a city I had never seen except through the pages of history books. The Phoenicians founded the city in the 3rd century B.C.; and around 1305 it was built by the Moorish king, Abu Tahbit, of the Mirinid Dynasty. By the end of the 15th century, it was rebuilt and settled by Arab refugees from Andalucia. Many houses there belonged to the aristocratic Arabs, descendants of those expelled from Andalucia some centuries before. In any case, I looked forward to seeing the city for what it was. Although anxious at what the future might hold, I was nevertheless confident that God was in control of all events.

As daylight broke that Saturday morning, I left the station for an exploratory walk in the city. I walked for hours until I arrived about noon at a very small Moroccan café facing a small mosque in a cobbled street. I went in and ordered a pot of Moroccan tea. The café was empty, but the owner, who also acted as waiter, did not seem to be unduly concerned. Indeed, he looked cheerful and relaxed. The reason, as it transpired later, was that the business usually flourished in the evenings.

The name of the owner was Ridwan. Being the only customer around, the cheerful owner, with his southern accent, asked me who I was and where I came from. The conversation that followed was long and covered a number of subjects. From time to time he would go to serve one or two new customers who had just arrived and then return for what he described as 'a gripping discussion'. In the end, Ridwan

---

[1] Lk. 24:13-14.

was clearly impressed by me as a visiting stranger and seemed to take kindly to me. Finally, he could not restrain himself from asking what was such a well-bred, proper-spoken and educated young man like me doing in a strange city alone, and what brought me there. In reply, I acknowledged that there was a long story behind it – a story albeit free from any element of crime or misdemeanour. In any case, I suggested that I would prefer not to go into it. I was, after all, very tired and must go and look for a cheap place where I could sleep at night.

Ridwan was deeply touched by what he heard, and as it transpired later, my dilemma was a vivid reminder of his own dilemma not too long ago. About ten years earlier, he had arrived alone in Tetuan from Safi in the south to escape the war of independence against the French. He had a long story to tell about the hardships he endured as a stranger in Tetuan. His situation also was not helped by the fact that he was a southerner. In those days, there was widespread prejudice by the northerners against their compatriots in the south. However, after a long and hard struggle, Ridwan finally made it. He was now happily married with two little girls, and his house was just around the corner. Owing to his experience, he had vowed never to be unkind to strangers, and he seemed to have been true to his word.

As I was preparing to leave, Ridwan insisted that I should stay and share with him some sandwiches that his wife was bringing shortly. Then, he suggested that, if he did not mind, his wife would be pleased to bring me a couple of blankets, and I could use one of the sofas in the café as a bed for the night. In his opinion, that would save me whatever money I had for sustenance. He went on to assure me that being an educated person, my circumstances might change for the better in the near future, God willing. After all, he added, in this world nothing remains the same. I was deeply touched by Ridwan's kindness and benevolence. To this day, I still remember that gentleman with the profoundest possible respect and affection.

On that day, I became acutely conscious of the fact that the hand of the Lord had been active behind all that Ridwan had done for me. I recalled the words of Proverbs, *"A man's mind plans his way, but the Lord directs his steps."*[2] I had thought that on reaching my destination, I would have 'nowhere to go', but the Lord had already found me 'somewhere to stay!'

---

[2] Prov. 16:9.

The Unfailing Christ

I woke up next day (Sunday) at 8 a.m. just as Ridwan was opening the café door. After a little breakfast, I dropped a line to my brother and let him know where I was. Afterwards I told Ridwan that I would be going out and hoped to return that evening before closing time. Ridwan apparently thought that I was going to look for work, and wished me well.

As I left the café, my first task was to look for the Mission House. Surprisingly, according to the address that was with me, it was roughly about one kilometre from the café. I knocked at the door and an English Missionary lady opened. I introduced myself and was immediately recognised. The lady then informed me that the Sunday service would begin shortly, and led me to a room where the service was usually held. There I sat waiting until a few Moroccans, mostly women, together with the Missionary staff came in, and then the service began.

It was a time of spiritual uplift and encouragement for me as I listened to the speaker expounding the words of St Paul, which began, *"who shall separate us from the love of Christ?"*[3] For me, the entire passage was a gentle challenge to realise again the sublime value of the unfailing love of Christ. The passage was also a reminder that there was a guaranteed safety in that love. To be a Christian in the first century was both difficult and dangerous. In that precarious situation, only the sovereign power of God's love could protect and preserve the believer to the uttermost. Meanwhile, I was unaware that with these thoughts the Lord was preparing me for a severe time of testing. After the service, the missionaries, who had a prior knowledge of me, greeted me warmly. And after a brief chat they gave me a list of their weekly services and hoped to see me again. Curiously, I noticed that none of them asked what I was doing or where I was staying. But at the time I attached little or no importance to that observation.

It was my tenth day in Tetuan when I received a parcel by post from my grandmother. It contained some clothes together with a brief letter from my brother, which made a distressing reading. I learnt that the day after I left, my frail octogenarian grandmother walked for a mile to the Mission House carrying that parcel. She had hoped that the missionaries would perhaps know where I was staying and deliver

---

[3] Rom. 8:35f.

it to me. Sadly, the man who had taken over from Dr Rigby left her sitting at his doorstep only to appear almost two hours later with a negative response. One could only imagine how the old lady had felt then. In fact, had it not been for my brother, who received my address three days later, the clothes I so desperately needed would never have arrived. Surely, with Mr Hutchinson's own means of communication and transport, which were rare commodities among the natives, he could have easily helped a brother in adversity.

I found that incident hard to swallow, and some questions did arise: what about the Christian's obligation to go the *"extra mile?"*[4] Are not Christians supposed to be helpful and good to all people, *"especially to those of the household of faith?"*[5] However, owing to Christian love, which *"thinks no evil"*, I decided to waive the issue on the basis that there might have been a harmless motive behind it. In this way I allowed *"no root of resentment (rancour, bitterness, or hatred) to shoot forth and cause trouble and bitter torment . . ."*[6]

It was now my third week in the city, and all attempts to find work seemed to have failed. But thanks to Ridwan's encouragement my hope did not collapse. More importantly, I prayed daily and fervently that the Lord might open doors, but although every door remained firmly closed, my faith did not waiver and my hope remained alive. Meanwhile, my attendance on the worship of God at the Mission House on Sundays and Wednesdays continued faithfully. I was always on good and brotherly Christian terms with the missionaries. Nevertheless, it was extraordinary that all that time the question of where I was staying or how I was living never once crossed their lips. They were certainly aware of the causes that had brought me to Tetuan. Was their silence deliberate, or perhaps the opportunity did not arise?

These were the questions that were bombarding my mind at times, and to which I could find no answer. In any case, I thought it wise that I should drop this matter at once. My duty was to learn to overlook others' shortcomings and failings from which I myself was not totally free. Indeed, failure is the only thing that can be achieved without much effort. It was safer for me to keep my eyes on the unfailing Christ.

---

[4] Mt. 5:41.

[5] Gal. 6:10; 1 Thess. 2:11-13; 5:15.

[6] Heb. 12:15 Amplified Version.

Almost Over the Edge

The first part of February had signalled the start of my fourth week in the city, and so far there was no sign of a job. In addition to this, the little amount of money I had kept for sustenance was about to run out. Ridwan, who had often been kind enough to ask if I was all right for food, was leaving soon forSafi with his family for two weeks' vacation. Meanwhile, he instructed the man who was to stand in for him to make sure that I was in before closing the café at night. Also the day he was leaving together with his family (and unaware of my financial position), he offered to lend me some money if I needed it before setting off. But I politely declined on the basis that, as the saying goes, "a person who accepts favours or loans from others is placing a mortgage on his peace of mind." I was confident that in some way or other the Lord would take care of me.

Two days later, the money ran out completely, and hunger consequently stared me in the face. I shall never forget the first night going to bed on an empty stomach, and the next day trying to kill hunger with too many glasses of tap water. Yet, water can never be a substitute for food. I shall never forget that day when I was so hungry that I could hardly stand on my feet too long, which recalls the words of Cervantes: "It is not the legs that carry the stomach, but the stomach the legs!"

However, after nearly two days of hunger I was beginning to feel slightly disorientated. In such a situation, even the spiritual side of my life was at very low ebb. "In the Lord's prayer," wrote T. Woodrow Wilson, "the first petition is for daily bread. No one can worship God or love his neighbour on an empty stomach." Of course, it did occur to me that the Lord might just be testing me. In any case, that test was simply beyond endurance and no divine intervention seemed to be in sight. After all, is it not written that in such a situation God would be faithful to *provide the way of escape*?[7] Or could it be that God might just be trying to push me over the edge?

Back from the Brink

It was Friday afternoon. The sun was shining that February day, so I decided to pull up a chair and sit outside the café. I was feeling

---

[7] 1 Cor. 10:13.

very tired, my mind in turmoil and hunger gnawing at me all the time. I seemed to have finally come to a dead end. I regretted not having accepted Ridwan's help when he had offered to lend me some money before leaving. But why cry over spilt milk when it is already four-fifth water?! My situation had not been good since my first week in Tetuan, and I should have known that something like this predicament would be inevitable. However, now that I was in it, should I not fulfil my promise to grandmother and return home at once? But how could I do that since there was not a penny in my pocket for the bus? In any case, all these thoughts were of no relevance whatsoever. What mattered now was that I must find something to eat – something that would appease my raging pain of starvation.

As I sat in that almost empty street nursing my stomach pain, I noticed a wave of worshippers pouring out of the small mosque facing the café. In my desperate state, a thought crossed my mind: why should I not approach one of those worshippers for help? As a total stranger I would have no reason to be ashamed. If I were rebuffed, then nobody would know who I was or where I came from. I realised that my situation was so dire that unless I threw my pride to the wind and stepped forward and asked one of those people for help, the consequences would be much worse.

By this time all the worshippers had gone except one. He was sitting at the doorstep of the mosque tying his shoes. I arose from my seat and with much trepidation walked right up to him; and with my head bowed out of embarrassment and hardly able to articulate my words, I said something like this: "Sir, I'm a complete stranger in this city. I've been here for some weeks during which I've been unsuccessful in finding work. All my money has now run out, and I'm suffering the ravages of hunger. I ask you for no money. I only beg of you to take me to the nearest shop and buy me some food. And may God never let you and your posterity suffer hunger or beg for bread."

For a few seconds the man was speechless and seemed close to tears. "I'm sorry to hear that, son," he whispered. "But forgive me if I'm unable to take you somewhere and buy you something to eat," he added as he dipped his hand into his pocket and came up with a sum of money. "I hope this little amount will be helpful, my son," he said as he slipped what felt like a piece of paper money into my hand. "If I had more I would've given it to you," he assured me. And as he turned to walk away, he repeated the Qur'anic verse, "*wa man qudera 'alayhi rizquhu falyunfiq mimma atahu Allah, la yukallifu allahu nafsan illa ma ataha*" (and the man whose resources are restricted, let him spend according to what God has given him. God puts no burden on any person beyond what He has given him).[8] Then that gentleman, who was presumably local, simply disappeared into the crowd. I had never seen him before and was never to see him again. When I turned to look at the piece of paper that he had slipped into my hand, I could not believe my eyes. It was a note of something equivalent to twenty pounds sterling (a little over $35) in today's currency. I was over the moon with joy. It was obvious that at last the hand of God had reached out and pulled me back from the brink.

The Incomparable Christ

Holding tightly to my money, I rushed to the nearest grocery shop, purchased some food and brought it to the café where I ate it as quickly and greedily as if I had never seen food! Having washed it all down with a glass of Moroccan mint tea, I felt relaxed and able to think straight. I could not get that good man who helped me out of my mind. He had probably rescued me from what could have been a damaging impact on my health because of my excruciating hunger.

But gradually, my thoughts shifted from that man's noble deed to what felt like a self-administered lecture. It seemed almost like a voice saying, "What a ridiculous end! How could you allow yourself to go so far? Do you really think that your newfound faith has done you any good? I'm afraid the answer is 'No'. From the day you embraced it you've been at the receiving end of one painful calamity after another. Certainly, religion, any religion, consists of more than devotional exercises. Good works such as caring for the needy and helping those who have fallen on hard times, are binding obligations on the adherents of most religions. Now, oddly enough, all the help that you've so far received has come almost entirely from those whose faith you've already renounced. Yet, those whose faith you've embraced, albeit at a great cost, don't seem to care. I agree that this attitude is inconsistent with the Christian message of brotherly love, which should not be '*in word or speech but in deed and in truth.*'[9] The idea that Christianity with its high moral and ethical demands

---

[8] Sura at-Talaq [65]:7.

[9] 1 Jn. 3:17-18.

outshines the rest of world's religions seems fictitious. For example, the theme of sacrificial love or sacrificial help for one's fellow man is quite often conveyed in hyperbolic terms in the New Testament. But in practice it is quite unworkable. In fact, one can help his fellow man only if he is truly able. You can't help someone else uphill without getting closer to the top yourself. And that is precisely the position where that gentleman was in when he helped you. By contrast, your Christian friends who live comfortably seem utterly indifferent. I hope that your present experience has shown you that Christianity with all its splendid set of ethics is no more than a gigantic humbug? The best thing you could do now is to pick yourself up and return to your home and family. Your security and future well-being lie only with them. Tell them that you've made a disastrous mistake, and that you bitterly regret the hurt and the shame you've inflicted on them. Now, don't think for a moment that this would backfire on you. You know how warmly welcomed the renegades and apostates are when they return to the Islamic fold. And don't be surprised if they welcome you with feasting and jollification!"

Suddenly, I came back to myself as though I had been in a trance. But whatever it was, the thoughts sounded very reasonable and I wondered why they had not crossed my mind before. I had no doubt that such thoughts made sense and I must act upon them at once. But little did I know at the time that the enemy was up to his old tricks again.[10] In any case, time was of the essence. It was about 4.00 p.m. and I must catch the bus for Larache. I reckoned that if the bus left the station an hour from then I could be in my hometown three hours later, and under the cover of darkness I ought to head directly for grandmother's house. The next day I should make my way to grandfather's house to declare my recantation, beg for the family's pardon and be reconciled to them. I had it all worked out. And without any further delay I got up to leave for the bus station. "See you later this evening," shouted the man in charge of the café. I pretended I did not hear him.

On my way to the bus station, I was suddenly in a flood of tears. Were they tears of joy for the approaching re-union with the people who hated me for what I had done, or tears of grief for the Christ I was now turning my back on? Facing this question was simply too much for me. Then I slowed down until I came to a bench by the way

---

[10] Gen. 3:1ff.

side and sat down wiping my tears. It was as though a hand had gently stopped me from going any further.

"What are those tears for?" was the question that seemed like a silent echo in my mind.

"I don't know," I answered moving my lips but making no sound.

"Do you mean you don't know, or you prefer not to know? Obviously, there is a conflict inside you, and you can't handle it. You see, when you first embraced Christianity, you did so not because you found it primarily helpful, but because you found it true. Weren't you essentially searching for the truth? Indeed you were. And you finally found the truth, and the truth has set you free.[11] So then, the Christian faith is about the truth, even if it gives you no material help. Apparently, in your ordeal, you seem to have allowed your desperate need to undermine your firm hold on the truth. I know your fellow Christians have hurt you. They've hurt me too.[12] Now, be fair. If you've become a Christian because of Christians, then you have the right to go back; but if you're a Christian because of Me, you really have no right to do so. What harm have I done to you? Can't you give Me some credit for the fact that I was behind all those who came to your help?"

Suddenly, I realised that something extraordinary had happened. The silent echo in my mind was as real as if it was coming from a person sitting next to me. That made me quite agitated. After a few minutes of calm reflection, I realised that I had just had what could only be described as an awesome encounter with the living Christ. Then without hesitation, I stood up, took a deep breath and returned to the café. On my way, I recalled the words of Jesus, *"No one who puts his hand to the plough and looks back is fit for the kingdom of God."*[13] These words had a unique significance for me that day. My eyes should never be fixed on mortals that are prone to failure but on Christ who never fails. With Him every difficulty is an opportunity for success and victory. Christ is and will always remain wholly incomparable.

---

[11] Jn. 8:32.

[12] Mt. 25:31-46.

[13] Lk. 9:62.

Chapter 10

WINNING THROUGH WEAKNESS

*"The acknowledgement of our weakness is
the first step toward repairing our loss."*

(Thomas à Kempis)

I returned to the café, and as it was beginning to rain, I went inside and sat down. I was entirely resigned to the fact that I had now truly burned all my bridges behind me, and I had no regret or doubt about it. Indeed, after that unique encounter with the living Christ, I could not do otherwise. The sense of confidence, joy and serenity that came upon me as I sat there was beyond description. I was also filled with optimism that something very good was in the pipeline. There is a sense in which optimism is one of the chief members of the faith family.

The next day after breakfast, I decided to go for a walk. I had not gone twenty yards from the café when I heard someone calling me by name. As I turned to look, I noticed a Caucasian looking gentleman on a bicycle coming towards me with a broad smile. As he got closer, I realised that the gentleman was none other than Joseph Trindle, an American missionary in Tetuan. I had met him a few times before.

"Where are you?" he asked, "I've been looking for you these last couple of days almost everywhere." After a brief conversation, he seemed eager to know where I was living. When I had told him, he looked so sad and indeed so upset that he could hardly speak. He put his hand on my shoulder and said, "That's not where you belong. I want you to go, fetch your belongings from that café and come back immediately. You're coming home to stay with us. That's where you belong."

I could hardly believe what I was hearing. It was not difficult to recognise the Lord's hand in what was happening. Meanwhile, it became immediately clear to me that, whereas before the Lord had been behind those non-Christians who came to my help, this time

He was behind this fine Christian gentleman. In my crisis, I had been in my spiritual infancy, and when one is at this stage, the limitation of one's strength and the poverty of one's vision are enormous. "It is natural for a baby," wrote C.S. Lewis, "to take its mother's milk without knowing its mother. It is equally natural for us to see the man who helps us without seeing Christ behind him."[1] However, my recent crisis and the events that subsequently followed were a stepping-stone towards my spiritual growth and towards what God had in store for me.

A Blessed Atmosphere

While Joseph Trindle waited, I rushed to the café, collected my belongings and told the attendant that I was simply going away. Then I sat down and scribbled a note, put it in an envelope and asked the attendant to deliver it to Ridwan when he returned from his journey. In that note I briefly thanked him immensely for all that he had done for me. I pointed out that a new door had been opened for me elsewhere. I assured him that I was indebted to him and his family for the kindness they had shown me since my arrival in Tetuan. I also wished that the good Lord might richly reward them for their noble deeds. Finally, I hoped to see them again one day.

On the way home, and in the course of our conversation, I was itching to know what made Joe Trindle get on his bike and go looking for me in the city. After all, I had not seen him in any of the services I had been attending since my arrival in Tetuan. When I eventually asked him, his answer revealed the extent to which the hand of Providence had been at work. It also revealed something of Joe Trindle's character and the stuff he was made of. He was, as I discovered later, quite an outspoken and even blunt man at times, yet without malice. But underneath, he was kind-hearted, humble and quick to apologize when at fault. In any case, it transpired from his answer that he had returned just the week previously from a couple of months furlough in the USA.

On hearing of me having been in Tetuan for some weeks already, and the circumstances under which I had left my hometown, he asked where I was staying. When told by his colleagues that nobody knew, the conversation between them became somewhat heated. After that,

---

[1] C S. Lewis, *The Business of Heaven*, p. 307.

he determined to do all that he could to find me. With this brief answer he switched to another subject. He must have bluntly expressed his deep disapproval at his colleagues' lack of interest in the predicament of a fugitive young convert in a totally unfamiliar city. What he had said further might not have gone down well with his colleagues, and a heated conversation developed between them.

On our arrival home, his wife Naomi, a medical doctor, warmly welcomed me. Then after a brief conversation I was shown my bedroom, which was immaculately clean and comfortable. At dinnertime, I sat down to enjoy my first decent meal in weeks, during which we talked and laughed together. When bedtime came, I entered my room and knelt in prayer before going to sleep, but words failed me. Instead, I seemed to forget myself in an ecstasy of sheer joy that the wonder working power of Christ was as real that day as it had been in ancient times. My overwhelming joy made all my words suddenly vanish, and that was a soul refreshing way of praising Him. Words are indeed useful, but on that occasion, I was sure the Lord understood the language of my heart and soul.[2] Soon afterwards I tucked myself into my comfortable bed and fell fast asleep. For me, the entire atmosphere of the house that evening seemed to be saturated with a remarkable sense of God's love.

Unity in Christ

In the weeks that followed, the Trindles regarded me as a member of their family, and included me in almost all of their home activities, which began daily with the family devotions. Then I either worked in the garden, or looked after John, their baby boy, or did whatever else I was asked to do. At least twice a week I gave them lessons in ways of improving their Arabic.

On Sunday mornings we attended the worship meetings without fail. And I still recall the first Sunday I went to the worship meeting with the Trindles. There were smiles all round. Interestingly, those who had once shown no interest in asking where I was staying were now all over me. Of course, there were no verbal apologies. But there were many ways of saying sorry, and their extraordinarily sweet courtesy to me that day was obviously one of them. On my part what had happened must be put behind me. They were part of my family

---

[2] Rom. 8:26-27.

in Christ. From now on I must allow nothing to erode the love of Christ that binds all believers together. The unity of the people of God is absolutely essential if the cause of Christ is to triumph in the world. Such unity is so important that our Lord included it in His high priestly prayer.[3]

During one of my discussions with Joe Trindle I learnt something that surprised me. I learnt that the missionaries in Morocco did not all belong to one particular church. Until then I had been under the impression that Christianity was divided only into the Catholic Church and the Protestant Church. I had thought that just as Catholicism was a uniformed ecclesiastical body so was Protestantism. But that was not the case. With rapt attention, I had learnt from Joe Trindle that several churches were represented in the Moroccan mission field. He pointed out that, with the exception of Dr Rigby and his colleagues, the bulk of the missionaries operating under the umbrella of North Africa Mission in Morocco, Algiers and Tunisia, belonged to different denominations. There were Episcopalians and Presbyterians (among them Joe & Naomi Trindle). There were Mennonites, Plymouth Brethren and Baptists. Dr Rigby and his colleagues, who covered the northern towns of Larache, Asila and al-Hoceima, belonged to Emmanuel Holiness Church and operated under its support and supervision.

When I asked whether such denominational differences meant also that there were differences among them regarding the proclamation of the gospel, his answer was clear. He told me that these denominational differences had to do only with some theological issues, which did not affect the substance of the Christian faith. For example, all of them believed the Old and New Testaments to be the Word of God and the supreme rule of faith and conduct. They all believed in the incarnation, the virgin birth, the deity of Christ, His death for our sins, His resurrection, His ascension and His return. They all believed that salvation comes only through repentance and faith in Jesus Christ. As to the issues in which these denominations differed, they had never been a problem. Their unity in the cause of Christ had always been kept intact.

What I had just heard was a valuable piece of information, which I greatly cherished. I could indeed see that all those missionaries in Morocco worked as one organisation. They had one conference, one

---

[3] Jn. 17:1ff; Eph. 4:1-3.

Christian camp to which missionaries brought their converts and one Christian rally in which their converts received baptism by emersion. They were so noted for their oneness and togetherness in the witness of Christ that an outsider would think they all belonged to one uniformed ecclesiastical body. This was precisely what Jesus prayed for, *". . . that they may all be one: even as thou, Father, art in me and I in thee, that the world might believe that thou hast sent me."*[4] The work of God's kingdom will go with leaps and bounds when the people of God are united together in the cause of Christ.

Tragedy and God's Love

On February 29 that year (1960), a huge earthquake measuring 6.7 on the Richter scale, hit the southern Moroccan city of Agadir at 11.39 pm. Most of the 'new town' area of the city was completely destroyed, and the heavily populated Talborit quarter was believed to have been the hardest hit. The earthquake lasted for more than ten seconds and was accompanied by a massive tidal wave, which added to the devastation. Eye-witnesses reported hearing screams and cries for help from those trapped. Thousands of people perished. The entire nation was rocked by that tragedy. I recall how the then reigning king, Muhammad V, wept on camera as he witnessed the devastation. Two days after the earthquake, the Moroccan authorities ordered the total evacuation of Agadir in a bid to avoid the spread of disease. The final death toll was 12,000, not to mention the wounded that probably exceeded that number. The earthquake was the worst ever to hit Morocco.

Like all my fellow-countrymen, I was shocked and deeply saddened by that unprecedented tragedy. For the first time I was faced with serious questions: Was God responsible for that catastrophe, or was He simply a spectator who did nothing to stop it happening beforehand? And if either were the case, then what had become of His attributes of compassion and love? These questions could not possibly have crossed my mind prior to my conversion. As a human being, my reaction to that calamity would certainly have been one of shock and dismay. In the past as a Muslim, the question as to whether God's hand had been responsible would never have arisen. And to delve into it might be regarded as calling the absolute divine sovereignty

---

[4] Jn. 17:21.

into question, and that would be blasphemy. All I could have done was to attribute this painful tragedy to '*al-Qada*' and '*al-Qadar*' i.e. God's eternal preordination and decree.[5] This means that everything, be it fortune or misfortune, which occurs in the inner or outer world is the immediate and isolated act of God.[6] A careful examination of this Islamic doctrine would show that it is tantamount to a rigid determinism, or an uncompromising fatalism, as some would call it.[7] Here a Muslim must live up to his name, for '*Islam*' means submission, and a '*Muslim*' is one who unreservedly submits, among other things, to the irrevocable decree and eternal will of Allah.

But I was now a Christian, and if Christianity stands for anything it most certainly stands for the unfathomable love of God for the whole world. How could I then reconcile this shattering disaster with God's love? I simply could not, and an inner struggle with this question ensued. True, I was still new in the faith and not acquainted with Christian theological studies then. Yet, as I now know, even if I were a seasoned theologian, a true answer to this question would have been impossible. The saying is probably true that, "theology is an attempt to explain a subject by men who do not understand it. The intent is not to tell the truth but to satisfy the questioner."[8]

I did not share this inner struggle with anybody but tried to negotiate my way through it in the silence of my own heart. In a simple way, I realised that there are things that are beyond all human comprehension, and this was one of them. Certainly knowledge can be a wonderful thing, but there is a sense in which knowledge is a power only if a man knows what facts not to bother about! After all, St Paul was right, "*For now we see in a mirror dimly, but then face to face. Now I know in part; then I shall understand fully, even as I have been understood.*"[9] With this simple discovery I was able to rest my case. Most of all, I resolved from then on to keep myself in the love of God – the love which transcends all that is beyond the range of my

---

[5] See Sura Al-'Imran [3]:145; Sura al-Anfal [8]:17; Sura al-Tawba [9]:51; Sura al-Ra'd [13]:31; Sura Ibrahim [14]:4 .

[6] See *Mukhtasar Sahih Muslim* (Beirut 2000), p. 20.

[7] For a comprehensive discussion on this point see G. F. Moore, *History of Religions* (T & T Clark, Edinburgh 1965), pp. 425ff; also Ibn Warraq, *Why I am not a Muslim* (New York 1995), p. 245.

[8] Elbert Hubbard, *The Philistines*, XX.

[9] I Cor. 13:12.

human mind. Indeed, God is love, and by definition "He is something more than mere kindness."[10]

A Curious Turn of Events

As a result of that tragic earthquake in Agadir, military and civilian assistance flooded in from around the world in the weeks and the months that followed. During May, a British Aid Organization approached Dr Naomi Trindle and asked her if she could be of some medical assistance to the victims of the earthquake in Agadir. Both she and Joe at once felt that the approach was from the Lord, and they prepared to leave within two days. They told me that I was coming with them to Agadir, because the Lord might have some work for me to do there. Now, in the days when highways hardly existed in Morocco, the route from Tetuan to southern Moroccan cities normally led through my hometown. And I was pleased when I took a glimpse of it on the journey. On our arrival in Agadir we were shocked by the devastation we saw.

Dr Naomi's voluntary assignment in some of the hospitals round Agadir had taken three months. Joe had also been involved during that period in various other works, with me helping when needed. At the end of that period, which was the beginning of September, their assignment ended and they decided to return home. As an ex-officer in the US Air-Force, Joe decided that we stop for lunch at the Bengrir American military base near Marrakech. Here I was astonished to see black American soldiers everywhere. Until then I had thought that all Americans were white. Slightly amused, the Trindles told me that the USA was a multi-racial country, and for me, that was a valuable piece of information. In fact, my stay with them had been as much a source of information as it was of spiritual blessing, but all that was about to end.

The hope of returning to my hometown one day when the furore had cooled down had never left me. The news from my brother had recently indicated that the popular reaction to my conversion was now one of indifference rather than hostility. Some were even asking kindly about me. Combined with this was my deep longing to see my grandmother again and also to renew my fellowship with my spiritual father, Dr Rigby, and his colleagues. Having thought prayerfully about

---

[10] C.S. Lewis, *The Business of Heaven*, p. 24.

this matter, I concluded that the time was now ripe for me to return. The Lord also seemed to approve by giving me peace and resignation about it. During lunch I shared this matter with the Trindles, adding that the Lord might well have a purpose in my return to my hometown. Reluctantly, they agreed to stop there and drop me at the Mission House. Moreover, I was profoundly moved when they told me that if hostilities were renewed against me, I should return to them at once.

Although I was sad to say goodbye to the Trindles, I was nevertheless comforted to see Dr Rigby and soon afterwards my dear grandmother. However, now that I was back in my hometown, how was I to spend my days? I thought of my favourite pine forest outside the town where I could spend every day with my books. In this way I could avoid meeting people, who might cause me problems. And that is precisely what I did. But about a week later, I began to realise that this abnormal kind of life would consequently lead me nowhere. I should therefore take the bull by the horns and walk into the city centre with my head held high. I should never doubt God's protective care. The courage and serenity with which I did that the following day could only have come from above. I was aware that all eyes were on me as I walked into an open-air café, sat down and ordered some tea.

To my great surprise, I had not been sitting long when four of my former fellow-students pulled up their chairs and joined me. The warmth of their friendship and their excitement at seeing me after a long time seemed utterly unbelievable. Some former acquaintances smiled and nodded their heads to me as they passed by. For me, such a turn of events was beyond all my expectation. Remarkably, neither those who joined me in the café nor those who stopped to greet me as they walked in the plaza raised the issue of my conversion. Indeed, in the days that followed, apart from a few who ignored me, the rest were kind and civil to me.

I was puzzled at this turn of events. Some of my friends, particularly those who had visited me at home before leaving for Tetuan, could only guess. They reckoned that some might simply have been tolerant, others trying to show the best side of Islam, and yet others seeing me as an eccentric young student whose brilliant knowledge had made me an oddball. This last remark made me chuckle with laughter. It reminded me of Festus who described Paul as being out of his mind for his great learning![11] However, what my friends had said left a

---

[11] Acts. 26:24.

lingering doubt in my mind. This change of popular attitude towards me was indeed extraordinary, and only time would reveal what lay behind this curious turn of events.

Unconscious Drift

It was the start of the year 1961. As far as my faith was concerned I was as steadfast as before. I never stayed away from the worship meetings at the Mission House, and my fellowship with Dr Rigby and his colleagues remained as strong as ever. But as far as my renewed acquaintance with my former friends was concerned, I was once again one of the boys. I joined them in almost everything including the drama club where I became a sort of celebrity in comedy plays in the town's theatre. Incidentally, to this day I am not sure if the missionaries had been aware of this particular development. On my part, I never told them anything about it.

Surprisingly, however, my former Seminary Principal, who often watched me on the stage, met me once and congratulated me "on the artistic parts" I played, as he put it. Oddly enough, he even expressed his wish to see me back in the Seminary one day. And from what he said afterwards, he seemed to imply that before this happened "some groundwork had to be done". That made me feel uneasy, and I wondered what exactly he had in mind. When I asked my friends' opinion about it, they shrugged it off. They seemed either not to have a clue, or if they had, they would not say it. Could it be that something was either afoot now, or would be in the not too distant future? Time would show that my suspicion was not unfounded after all.

On a drizzly November day that year, a fellow-student told me that the Algerian lecturer had heard that I returned home and was looking forward to seeing me. I took that as an opportunity to visit him at home, and enquire after his wife who was recovering from illness. During my visit they were hugely appreciative of Dr Rigby's medical care of her. They were equally appreciative of the fact that it was I who had been instrumental in bringing Dr Rigby to visit her in the first place. After a while, I leaned forward slightly and told my former lecturer, in a rather low voice, that I had something to ask his opinion about. He then signalled to his wife and daughter to leave us alone, which they did. The amiable lecturer listened carefully as I told him of the puzzling reaction of the public since my re-appearance in town after a long absence. People had been kind, civil and quite helpful to me. I had been taking part in several social activities including acting on the stage in the local theatre, which earned me some acclaim. But I was now seriously wrestling with a burning question: why during all this period, the subject of my conversion had never been raised, or even hinted at? I then went on to mention my recent encounter with the Principal, who had expressed his wish to see me back in the Seminary, but not before 'some groundwork' was done.

After a brief pause, the liberally minded lecturer spoke. He stated that from what he could gather, my sudden re-appearance in town and what followed thereafter, had led most of the public to conclude that I must obviously have abandoned Christianity, otherwise I would have stayed away. In reaching this conclusion, people might have considered it superfluous to raise the question of my conversion. As to his opinion about what the Principal had said, he confessed that the wish of the Principal and the entire Seminary faculty to have me back was quite genuine. But as to what he meant by 'the groundwork' that must first be done, it was beyond him. In any case, he promised to find out what the Principal really meant by that intriguing sentence.

On that note, I left my former lecturer, wishing his good wife a swift recovery. I was worried and troubled by what I had just heard. I could not help thinking that with my re-appearance in town I might well have inadvertently compromised my new faith. It seemed to me that I might now be more vulnerable than before. I also could not help feeling that some things unknown to me might be at work behind the scene. In this situation, I could only ask God to keep His protective hand on me.

Next day, I met a group of Spanish youths who introduced themselves to me as members of the Catholic Guild. I happened to have heard of them. As trained theological debaters, their task was to win back former Spanish Catholics from Evangelical Churches. After independence, these Churches in Morocco were left undisturbed, whilst in Spain under Franco they were constantly harassed. They told me that they had heard of me and wished to meet me one day. Then, rather than standing talking in the street, they invited me to a nearby canteen for some refreshment. They were so friendly to me that for a moment I hoped that they were not seeing me as a future catch for Catholicism! However, during the conversation they asked me to tell them the story of my conversion, which I did. To my great surprise, they were deeply touched by what they heard. I was even more surprised when they informed me that they had in fact been following the news about me from the outset and had been praying for me! At the end they invited me to visit their Youth Fellowship and join them in their games and sport at the Maristas.

The Maristas, which was near the Mission House, was partly a college for the training of priests and partly an educational institution for Spanish youths. In reality, the affinity between them and me seemed to transcend all Catholic/Protestant theological disagreements. After all, we both belonged to the same household of faith. In addition to that, their positive response to my testimony gave me a measure of encouragement and renewal. The recent events had left me with some sense of spiritual weakness, as a result of what I believed was an unconscious drift on my part. A tiny spark from the light of Christ, might have at least accompanied my re-appearance among my former friends in the city. Instead, that entire light was unconsciously placed under the bushel.[12] Consequently, in the darkness I was no longer recognised for what I really was at heart. Acknowledging my weakness was the first step toward restoration. It is an extraordinary experience to win the victory through weakness.[13]

---

[12] Mt. 5:14-16.

[13] 2 Cor. 12:10.

Chapter 11

BEYOND HOME AND COUNTRY

"Weep not for him who is dead, nor bemoan him;
but weep bitterly for him who goes away, for he
shall return no more to see his native land."

(Jeremiah 22:10)

In Christianity, winning a spiritual victory does not mean reaching a state of perfect invulnerability. If so, a Christian's continued dependence upon God would be utterly superfluous. It was a remarkable experience for me to gain a vital spiritual victory. But in spite of that I still had a lingering worry. It is said that worry is like a rocking chair; it keeps you busy, but gets you nowhere. So then, it is not true to assume that those who are in Christ are free from worry. In my case, I could not help worrying about what the Principal had meant by suggesting that "some groundwork had to be done" before I could be back in the Seminary. What could be the nature of that 'groundwork'? The phrase was dangerously loaded, and I could not wait to find out from that eminent Algerian lecturer. In any case, in spite of my worry I was confident that the Lord was in full control of the situation.

Meanwhile, I decided to curtail my visits to the town centre. In this way I would begin the process of a gradual break with the people, many of them were good friends and companions. Yet, subconsciously I was resentful of their conclusion that I had abandoned Christianity. But on reflection, I had only myself to blame. True, I had said nothing wrong to create that impression. But, as Marcus Aurelius once said, "A wrong-doer is often a man that has left something undone, not always he that has done something."[1] However, that was the past. After all, he who has never made a mistake has never made anything. My task now

---

[1] Marcus Aurelius, *Meditations*, VIII.

was to adopt St Paul's own programme: *"Forgetting what lies behind and reaching forward to what lies ahead."[2]*

A Period of God's Choice

The breaking of relationship with my friends and companions was inevitable. If my voluntary and innocent re-appearance had led my town-folk to conclude that I must have abandoned Christianity, what would be the outcome if they discovered one day that I was still a Christian? Indeed, as long as I remained a Christian that day was bound to come. Fortunately, my renewed relationship with my town-folk had no immediate impact on my own spiritual life. But, far from being like a bucket from which the bottom had dropped out, it had rather been like a bucket with a hole in it. My spiritual life-blood had slowly been draining away until the Lord made me aware of it. At present however my frequent absence from the circle of my friends did not pass unnoticed, and some of them were even perturbed about it. But as far as I was concerned there was no turning back. All I had to do now was to keep a low profile and proceed with my plan accordingly. Then something happened which promptly brought about the final break.

On a cold mid-January day 1962, I accidentally met the Algerian lecturer. He had been looking for me in the last few days. He indicated that he had something important to tell me, and I had better come and see him at home that very evening, which I did. After a brief exchange of greetings, the lecturer told me that what he was about to say must be kept strictly confidential, otherwise his credibility among his colleagues at the Seminary would be irreparably damaged. I promised that what he was about to tell me would never cross my lips.

After his brief pause, his statement as I quite remember was as follows: "The Principal and the faculty are very keen to see you back in the Seminary. And to that end they've started doing some 'groundwork,'" he said with a sarcastic smile. "And I now have a clear idea what that 'groundwork' is," he continued. "They've already planned to hold a meeting at the Mayor's office next Wednesday at which the newly installed Mayor himself, including a few distinguished men, will be present. Incidentally, Mr Allal al-Fasi, the minister of state for Islamic affairs and founder of the Istiqlal party, would be arriving in the city

---

[2] Phil. 3:13.

that same day to address his party members. He'd already been asked to honour that meeting with his presence, and he had agreed. Last but not least, you will be invited to that meeting. Now, the original plan was to invite you and your grandfather for the purpose of effecting a reconciliation between you both. But your grandfather had declined stating that nothing you do can ever make good the damage you have done to the family's good name. He also dismissed the rumour that you've abandoned Christianity describing it as a wishful thinking."

As the amiable lecturer stopped to sip his Moroccan mint tea, I asked him if any of those involved believed his statement. "Oddly enough," he responded, "some members of the faculty seemed to believe it. Nevertheless, they're optimistic that when the honourable Allal al-Fasi and the distinguished guests in that meeting present you with the radiant face of Islam things will change."

I smiled thinking how over-optimistic those gentlemen must be. Either that or they must be determined to get me by hook or by crook! "But there is something else," the lecturer said. "It is agreed that the invitation will be issued to you on the very day the meeting is scheduled to be held. An emissary will convey it to you first thing in the morning from the Mayor's office. They apparently suspect that if they were to invite you a few days earlier, you might have ample time to reflect on it and decide not to attend. In other words, they're determined to strike while the iron is hot".

The gentle lecturer sat back, took a deep breath and said, "I've told you all this in deep gratitude for what you've done for my wife. She is today a recovered woman because of you and because of what Dr Rigby has done for her. Now, what you plan to do is entirely your own business. But whatever you decide, you will always be our friend." I responded by expressing to him and his family my deepest gratitude for their kindness. I assured them that I was and would always be fortified by their unwavering friendship.

On my way home that evening, I decided that I should now terminate my association with my town-folk and withdraw myself from them completely. My days would be better spent in reading and prayer at my favourite pine forest outside the town. For me, it was the spot where the consciousness of God's presence could not be more real. And what could be better than making a start next day in the morning? I did that for the next two days during which I felt spiritually refreshed and renewed. On the third day, which was Sunday, I went to the Mission House for worship as usual. Afterwards I briefed Dr Rigby and his colleagues of the latest developments and urged them to pray that I might be guided wisely in the next few days. That guidance was not long in coming. As I lay in bed that evening I felt strongly that come what may I would not attend that meeting. Then, I committed myself to God in prayer and was fast asleep.

Early on Wednesday morning, the day the meeting was to be held, I took my Bible and a couple of other books and left for the pine forest. The morning was cold and drizzly, and I hoped the canteen at the forest gate would be open where I could have some breakfast and wait for the weather to improve. On my arrival the canteen was open and I was the first client that morning. Shortly afterwards the weather improved and I was able to spend a peaceful day in the forest which was virtually empty.

Here I decided to close the door of my mind on any speculation about what might or might not be happening at the Mayor's office that day. With God's help, I was able to focus my mind on reading, meditation and prayer. At sunset I made my way to the Mission House for the midweek service. Of course, in the back of my mind concern and even fear of what measures the authorities might take against me could not be easily dismissed. But, I was greatly heartened and encouraged by the love and prayerful support shown to me in that meeting. Here the one vital lesson I learned was that though there is much in the world to make us afraid, there is much more in our faith to make us unafraid.

Returning home at night, my grandmother told me that someone had called twice in the morning looking for me. I knew immediately that he could have been none other than the emissary from the Mayor's office. Surprisingly, he had given her no reason for his calls nor left any message for me. For the next couple of weeks I heard nothing, neither from the Mayor's office nor from anywhere else. By the middle of March and the beginning of spring, I was certain that the whole issue had died a death. The Algerian lecturer confirmed this to me. One day he told me laughingly that he had heard it said, "The Mayor, the Principal, the Faculty and many town-folk are now agreed that you no longer have a place with them. Like all apostates, your real place is in hell! But, there is a small element of liberal intellectuals and Arab nationalists who are vocal in defending your right to believe what you like, and I'm one of them. They never fail to stress your intellectual aptitude and your ardent Arab nationalism."

The most remarkable thing was that as a convert to Christianity, the only hardship I endured came from all but the government. The reason for this is not hard to find. Morocco is one of the signatories to the United Nations Declaration of Human Rights (1948). Its geographical closeness to Europe and centuries of its long historic interaction with Europeans might have done much to make it averse to any form of Islamic extremism. Instead Moroccans by their spiritual nature and disposition are more inclined to Sufism. But there was another factor. Pan-Arabism was the ideology of the Arab world in the 1950s and 1960s. Secular Arab nationalism was in its heyday. Prominent among its champions in those days were Arab rulers like President Nasser of Egypt. Interestingly, Arab nationalism was also strongly promoted among those Middle Eastern Arab countries with large Christian Arab minorities. In those days what mattered most was the individual's Arab identity. Indeed, there was the phrase of the time, "Religion belongs to God, but the motherland belongs to all." That was the period in which the idea of a resurgent Islamic fundamentalism was unheard of. Secular Arab Nationalism was at its zenith. My conversion to Christianity coincided with that period. It was a period of God's perfect choice.

The First Love

My exclusion became a bittersweet experience. On the one hand, it brought me tranquillity, which would not have been possible had I remained among the crowd. On the other hand, a life of loneliness was giving me a painful sense of social emptiness. As I quoted earlier, "Loneliness and the feeling of being unwanted is the most terrible poverty." This was a heavy cross for me to bear.

One afternoon, whilst walking in my beloved pine forest I suddenly remembered something. The Spanish Catholic youths had recently asked me to visit their Youth Fellowship. In my current situation, I was more than happy to go. But little did I know that there were some unexpected surprises awaiting me. The first was the warm welcome accorded to me by the sizable Catholic Youth Fellowship consisting of male and female, and particularly by the two Dominican priests who were in charge. Now, with the exception of attending Mass, the

Fellowship gladly involved me in all their games and sport activities. I was never once excluded from any discussion organised by the priests. This was so even when the subject of discussion happened to be doctrinal or theological.

At times when discussions involved doctrinal issues unique to Roman Catholicism, I was tactful enough to say precious little or keep completely quiet. Surprisingly, the Fellowship seemed to appreciate my discretion. Then one day they asked me to tell them how I became a Christian, which I gladly did. As a result, a number of them were greatly impressed, among them Beatrice, a fine young lady whose radiant face and graceful demeanour made an enormous impact upon me. As she stood talking to me once, I could hardly hear what she was saying because I was entranced by the loveliness of her personality. My heart was instantly captivated. The whole encounter was like being hit by a mighty whirlwind. Of course, this is not an uncommon experience to those who find themselves for the first time thrust into the strange world of romance. I was astonished to learn later that the admiration had been mutual. Indeed, love is like chickenpox, we all have to go through it!

During the few weeks before the Fellowship closed for the summer break, our friendship was becoming stronger. And by summertime we were in love with each other. For me, the sun simply arose and set over Beatrice. It was a glorious thing to feel that the entire meaning of the universe was summed up in her. They say that love is blind, but to be in love for the first time in one's life is to be blind, deaf and stupefied! Prudence simply disappears. It was Disraeli who once said, "The magic of first love is our ignorance that it can ever end." However, all that mattered to me at that time was that I now had someone who could fill the aching void that loneliness had created as a result of my conversion. I even comforted myself with the belief that God's hand must have been in it. Bringing God into my first love experience seemed an effective way of keeping my head firmly in the sand!

Dusk was always the time of our rendezvous, and the place was one of the town's gardens overlooking the Atlantic Ocean. This venue was suitably convenient for us. It kept us a little distant from the town-centre and out of the public eye. Our talks were always about past or present matters, but never about future things. Doubt or fear, or perhaps both, might have prevented us from peeking into the unknown. In any case, those were the sweetest and most wonderful days in my life. Words are perhaps inadequate to describe the glorious feeling of being head over heels in love for the first time. There is nothing in this world that is so utterly sublime as to love and to be loved. Indeed, if this was a dream, as I often imagined, then I preferred not to wake up. Yet, I did not know that a rude awakening was not far off.

In addition to her calm and pleasant nature, Beatrice was a resolute and reserved person. She felt deeply for me, but tried not to be emotionally demonstrative about it. Unknown to me however, a tug of war was going on between her and her family who were bitterly opposed to her current relationship with me. Indeed, they were determined to put an end to it by hook or by crook. I only knew much later that their opposition was based on, what they described as the incompatible relationship of their Catholic daughter with a Moroccan Muslim turned Protestant! And for a Spanish conservative middle class family under Franco, that was intolerable. But, Beatrice never told me a word about it. Maybe this was due to her reserved nature. Maybe she thought that I was hurting already from my social exclusion, and to tell me of what was happening might be more than I could take.

The scorching North African summer was coming to an end and autumn was announcing its approach. In autumn God paints all the leaves and the flowers, and at the end of it, He puts them all to sleep, and they are no more. There is also a proverb that says, 'The cuckoo comes in April, and stays the month of May; sings a song at midsummer, and then goes away.' It seems that in autumn a good number of lovely things come to an end. In my case, the love that had grown in spring and blossomed in summer time was about to fade and blow away in autumn.

On that Tuesday autumn evening, the rendezvous area was dark and chilly, and the breeze from the ocean was not helpful. Beatrice was sniffing occasionally, which sounded as if she had a touch of cold. Looking back, it seemed more likely that she was having a fierce battle trying to control her emotions. In the dark I could not clearly see her face. It seemed as if the darkness itself was being kind enough to shield me, at least for that moment, from the inevitable blast. Thus, I knew nothing of what was going on, and in that case ignorance was bliss. But one thing I still recall vividly. Her grip of my hands that evening was unusually tight. Was she trying to comfort me in advance of the bombshell that was soon to hit me? Or was she, at least in mind, stubbornly refusing to lose that which was already lost?

Previously, whenever the time to go home had arrived, Beatrice would cross the road, stand underneath the streetlight and wave to me briefly then go away. But this time she did something different. Having crossed the road rather briskly, she stood beneath the streetlight and waved longer than usual. In her hand there was a handkerchief with which she was wiping her nose and face, which made me think her cold was probably getting worse. In fact, as I looked on from a distance, it never occurred to me that she was crying. As she turned around and walked away, I had no idea that I was never to see her again.

For nearly two weeks I waited every evening in the usual place for the lady who never came. In my growing anxiety I began to prepare myself for the worst, which was not long coming. One of Beatrice's closest friends, called Lolita, met me one Sunday evening and dropped the bombshell. She informed me that Beatrice had recently been sent to Spain with her aunt to continue her studies there. The news was a shattering blow to me. I felt as though my world was suddenly engulfed in utter chaos and darkness. Recovery however was slow but sure. In the process of recovery I came to realise how fragile and transient human love was compared to God's strong and enduring love. Time and circumstances might eclipse one's love, but the light of God's love remains forever shining.

The Calling of God

Memory is a frightening thing. There are so many pictures that remain unobliterated in the human mind. Psychology suggests that everything one has ever seen or done is buried in one's mind. It may not be there on the conscious level, but it is buried deep down in the unconscious. And even there it has its effect upon one. Similarly, in spite of my remarkable recovery the memory of Beatrice was still fresh in my mind. It was about that time that the Lord saw fit to channel my mind and energy elsewhere.

To begin with, I was entrusted with the task of helping the missionaries improve their diction in Arabic. The atmosphere during those lessons was almost always full of joy and humour. Among those present was a missionary lady who had recently come from England. I affectionately called her 'Aunty Lily'. She was a dedicated nurse and a Christian of the finest spiritual fibre. Her love and care for me had done much to shape my future. As a matter of fact, she was a lady whose faith and love were no abstract issues, but practical realities. In the words of Martin Luther, "Faith like light, should always be simple and unbending; while love, like warmth, should beam forth on every side and bend to every necessity of our brethren." Her kind and steadfast support for me continued far beyond her short period in Morocco. Indeed, it continued until the closing days of her life. I was profoundly grieved when she passed away on the 24th January 2009 at the age of 94. On my part, I shall remain eternally indebted to her for the significant part she played in my life.

However, in those days a couple of missionaries from North Africa Mission asked me to record some gospel messages to be broadcast from Radio Monrovia, Liberia. Although I gladly agreed to do so, I was unaware that this was the first and new signal that God might have been calling me to some kind of service. But the Lord had another way of making this abundantly clear to me. As my recorded gospel messages were being broadcast from Liberia, word reached me that some in my hometown thought they had heard what sounded like my voice on Radio Monrovia. But they were not sure due to the poor quality of the sound waves. My reaction was one of concern. I was aware that whilst Morocco might turn a blind eye to one who changed his faith to another, it could not tolerate his attempt to convert others to his own new faith.

Having shared this matter with Dr Rigby and some of his colleagues, I was wisely advised to keep a low profile. Meanwhile, Dr Rigby had for a while been quietly and prayerfully busy inquiring about a suitable Bible school for me in Beirut, Lebanon. And it was precisely about this time of great concern that he happened to have found one and was able to break the news to me. He told me that the Nazarene Bible School in Beirut had agreed to accept me freely as a resident student for a three-year course. All biblical and theological studies were taught in English. And as my knowledge of English was next to zero, the School had agreed to give me an intensive course in English before starting my theological studies.

At first, I did not know what to make of that piece of news. My initial thought was that I had never been outside my own country. How would I cope with being a total stranger in a totally foreign land? But have I not been a stranger already in my own country? Was it not therefore possible that in this way the Lord might have been preparing me for this very thing? After all, it might not have been a co-incidence that this door opened at the very time I was involved in recording those gospel messages for Radio Liberia. If so, could it be that God might have been sending me a signal calling me to prepare for service? But service to do what and where exactly?

The more I became certain of God's calling the more I became reluctant and quite uneasy about it. At least on one occasion I even thought of brushing aside this divine overture all together. As I look back now I realise that such a reaction is quite natural when God truly puts His finger on an individual. It is hard to find a Biblical prophet who did not want to run for miles when God called him. However, slowly but surely I came to realise that there was no other way to be happy in Jesus but to trust and respond obediently to His summon. That was precisely what Abraham did, and that was precisely how he became a blessing to many.[3] This was a memorable experience for me. It taught me for the first time the spiritual value of being sensitive and responsive to God when He beckons or calls.

Preparing to Leave

A few years earlier, Morocco had gained its independence from France and Spain (1956). With the gradual departure of the French and Spanish population during this period, Moroccans began to feel the pinch of unemployment. Many were leaving for European countries, particularly Germany, in search of work. The government was apparently unhappy with that slow exodus so soon after independence and decided to place some tough restrictions on applications for passports. How could I now get over this hurdle?

It was now 1963. After much prayer and consideration, I decided that I should in any case send my application together with other required documents and hope for the best. A few days later I was summoned to the Passport Office in Tangiers to explain my purpose for wanting a passport. The interviewer, apparently a high government official, looked at me with a half smile and asked for a good reason why I wanted to have a passport. Tense but fully in control of myself, I answered calmly and succinctly: "An American college in Beirut, Lebanon, has accepted me as a student for a three-year study course,

---

[3] Gen. 12:1-3.

beginning in September. I should therefore be grateful if my passport could be issued soon so that I can be there in two months time." I was careful not to use the term 'Bible' in connection with the college.

The official looked at me with a broad smile and said, "Congratulations on your admission into that famous and highly renowned academic American Institution in Beirut. I have two Syrian friends who are graduates from there". I was baffled and did not know what he was talking about. In fact, I thought he had either misunderstood me or that he was being sarcastic. He then leaned slightly forward and told me that I would get my passport next week, and with that he rang the bell for the next interviewee.

I left feeling confused and utterly pessimistic about the outcome. To begin with I knew of no successful applicant who had ever received his passport after a month let alone a week. Moreover, I could make no head or tail of what that official had said. What famous and highly renowned academic American Institution was he talking about? That was certainly not the description of the college I was going to. Obviously, there was nothing to suggest that the official was serious in what he said, and so the chance of getting my passport seemed highly remote. In this situation it was purely human to feel despondent.

Four days later, the postman arrived at my door and asked me to sign for a recorded envelope, which contained my passport. The floods of joy that overwhelmed me at that moment in time are beyond description. I could not but realise that the good Lord was most decidedly in charge of this whole case. Later, I was fascinated by the way the good Lord seemed to have gone about it. Because I was careful not to use the word 'Bible' in connection with the 'American college', the government official immediately thought that the 'American college' was none other than the prestigious American University of Beirut!

At the time, I was at a loss trying to figure out what the official was getting at during the interview. As a matter of fact, I had never so much as heard of what he called this "highly renowned academic American Institution in Beirut". With this mind-boggling statement, the promise to send me my passport next week had sounded quite hollow. But the man was as good as his word. The Lord was obviously behind that official's action. Sometimes it is natural for us to see the person who helps us without seeing the Lord behind him or her. The passport for me was the key to freedom and the key to what God had in store for me. From the outset, I was aware that my application for a passport was not going to be easy. But God in His wisdom and power was able to override all obstacles in the most unimaginable way. His thoughts are not our thoughts neither are our ways His ways (Isa. 55:8).

Time For Departure

I had never been out of my country, and the prospect of doing so soon brought me a great sense of joy and excitement. But this feeling was soon followed by some sober and constructive thoughts. I realised that rejoicing in what God had just done for me must not be taken as an end in itself. There are times when our Heavenly Father refreshes us on the journey with some pleasant inns, but will never encourage us to take any of them as our permanent abode. God saves us not to sit but to serve. It is dangerous to take God's gift of grace lightly. Much is expected from those to whom much is given.[4] The period of my hardship in Morocco was now almost at an end, but hardship as such might not be over. The road before me might be hard. And God's servant must be ready to *"endure hardship as a good soldier of Jesus Christ"*.[5] That was a brief but unforgettable moment of sobering thoughts.

My flight from Tangiers to Beirut via Madrid and Rome was scheduled, if my memory serves me well, for the 15th of August 1963. To this day I do not know who paid for the ticket. But whoever that person might have been, the Lord was firmly behind his or her noble action. In the final analysis I could rest assured that the Lord was the real source of that provision. By this time, Dr Rigby had left the mission field for a new post in the UK, but his keen and prayerful interest in me remained unchangeable. He was kept fully informed of my progress by his successor Mr Reg Davies, a man of unique spiritual calibre. His wisdom, gentleness and pastoral care did much to prepare me for what lay ahead. A few days before my scheduled flight, both he and his wife suggested that I should spend the eve of my departure at the Mission House. In that way Mr Davies would drive me early next morning to Tangiers's airport. I would get there in good time for my afternoon flight. It was a good idea, and I agreed to it. As a matter of fact, spending that evening in the Mission House proved most comforting after a very sad experience that very day.

---

[4] Lk. 12:48.

[5] 2 Tim. 2:3-7.

I had already informed my grandmother of my forthcoming departure for Lebanon. Her reaction at the time was one of silence and tears. But next day she had a hearty talk with me, which I still remember. "Although it is the hardest things for me to see you go," she told me, "it is in your best interest that you go. There is nothing left for you in this town. And if you continue the way you are, your future in this country as a whole would be bleak." She went on, "You've suffered long enough, and we have suffered along with you."

When I asked her what she meant by this last sentence, she replied, "What you did, my son, has been like a massive flood. It has swept us all along with you. A good number of my friends and relations have cut all contact with me. They are angry that I allowed you to stay with me." That was news to me, and I was sad to hear it. However, the saddest and most painful moment in my living memory was that evening when I bid her my final goodbye. Having packed my suitcase, I sat down for my last meal with us. Being of delicate sensibilities I decided that the best way to avoid breaking down was to keep talking about anything except my approaching departure.

It was an impossible task. She listened to me in utter silence. Perhaps the weight of her grief was beyond words. Moreover, from the way she looked at me, I suspected that because I bore the likeness of my mother, she might have been taking a good look at her daughter's image for the last time.

Shortly thereafter my suspicion was confirmed. As I leaned forward to kiss her goodbye I heard her say in a voice choking with tearful emotions, "Today I feel as though I'm burying my daughter all over again. Never mind, son, hurry up and go. Your English friends must be waiting for you. Take care of yourself, son. May Allah be with you." As I walked out of the house, I could hear her sobbing. It was difficult for me to negotiate my way down the narrow cobbled street that evening, for tears were blinding me. That incident was simply too much for me, and I consider it so even today when I remember it.

Arriving at the Mission House that night, Mr Davies and his wife could discern that I was heavy-hearted. They may well have understood why, but asked no question. Instead, they surrounded me with the warmth of their love and laughter until I regained my composure and was greatly uplifted. After a time of prayer together, I went to bed and was fast asleep.

Early next morning Mr Davies drove me to Tangier. After a brief stop off at the Missionary Hospital in the district of Marshan for something to eat, he ran me to the airport. A few hours later I was on the plane to Madrid. The tense feeling of being on a flight for the first time was soon overcome by the joyful awareness that such a flight was a flight into freedom and liberty. I wondered for a moment how ancient Israel felt when God reminded them, *"You know how I brought you to myself and carried you on eagle's wings."*[6]

As I watched the shores of Morocco recede until they disappeared from view, the memory of my sad farewell visit to grandmother the night before did not disappear from my mind. On that sad evening, the words "Keep in touch" or "Don't forget to write" never crossed her lips. Could it be that she wept partly because in her heart of hearts she knew that I would never be back? If so, then one can understand how Jeremiah felt about King Jehoahaz's exile to Egypt when he said, *"Weep not for him who is dead, nor bemoan him; but weep bitterly for him who goes away, for he shall return no more to see his native land."*[7]

---

[6] Ex.19:4 (NLT).

[7] Jer. 22:10, see also 2 Kg. 23:33; 2 Chr. 36:1-4.

Chapter 12

THE SPLENDOUR OF LEBANON

"The righteous shall flourish like the palm tree;
he shall grow like a cedar in Lebanon."

(Psalm 92:12)

After spending a night in Madrid, next day in the morning I flew to Rome, and from there I flew to Lebanon in the afternoon of the same day. On my arrival in Beirut airport, Revd Donald Reed, the principal of the theological school, was waiting for me accompanied by a Jordanian Christian as an interpreter. He must have been aware that my English was either very poor or that I could not speak it at all. After greeting me with a warm welcome, they drove me to the Bible school in the district of Ashafia, and on arrival I was shown my room in the students' residence.

Afterwards during the conversation over coffee and sandwiches, Mr Reed asked me about my first name, which he strangely enough knew already. When I replied that it was *'Muhammad'*, the Principal politely wondered if I would prefer to have a Biblical name. I replied that in Morocco a missionary lady named Delis Hughes had tried to have me change my name to *'Samuel'*. But as this name was popular only among Moroccan Jews, I was reluctant to accept it. I felt that with a name like that some people might conclude that I had now gone over to Judaism! After a roar of laughter, the Principal looked at me and said, "From now on your name will be *'Samuel'*". And indeed from then to this day *'Samuel'* has been my proper name.

This Biblical name has been of great spiritual significance to me. Many Christians maintain that the name *'Samuel'* means 'heard of God'. True, *Samuel* was a child of prayer, and for Hannah, his mother, his birth was a clear answer to her prayer.[1] But, when Hannah *"called his name Samuel, saying, because I have asked him of the Lord"* (v.20),

---

[1] 1 Sam. 1:1-20. Strangely enough the prophet Samuel is mentioned once in the Qur'an but not by name, see *Sura al-Baqara [2]:246.*

she was not giving the actual derivation of the name. She was simply expressing assonance, not an etymology. The name, *Samuel,* literally means *'name of God'* suggesting the boy's close affinity with God. The name therefore has proved to be of great spiritual challenge to me. There is a sense in which my conversion was indeed an answer to many a prayer. But now that I was a Christian, my solemn responsibility was that I should walk in close affinity with the Lord. And the name *'Samuel'* has kept me mindful of that solemn responsibility.

Learning English

The study course began about the middle of September. Apart from one or two theological students who were in their second or third year, the rest were new like me. All of them were Middle Eastern – Lebanese, Syrians, Jordanians and Palestinians – and all from Christian backgrounds. I was the only student of Muslim origin and from the North African country of Morocco, in the westernmost part of the Arab world. Whereas those students seemed to have had a good start in English from somewhere, I was at a disadvantage. I was starting from scratch. I certainly had a good command of Spanish, but the help I derived from it in my study of English was infinitesimal. There was however no shortage of helpers. Principal Reed, Mr Huff and other diligent teachers at that Bible school were a great help to me. Moreover, the morning worship conducted entirely in English every day of the week was another great help.

In a situation where English is used almost exclusively in the classroom or church services and Arabic for the rest of the day, the possibility of gaining a good grasp of that foreign language may be slim. That was precisely what used to go through my mind from time to time. Looking back I realise that for those whom God loves, he can at times be lovingly challenging and even provocative. Their victory or defeat may be determined by their response to the circumstances they are in. And there is a sense in which the power to victory is reached by way of weakness, which was St Paul's own experience.[2]

I was often asked to preach at the Sunday Arabic Church service. Here, my sermons were delivered spontaneously and eloquently in refined classical Arabic. As a former Muslim Seminarian steeped in the pre- and post-Islamic Arabic literature and well versed in the rules

---

[2] 2 Cor. 12:9-10.

of the Arabic grammar, preaching in this way was quite natural to me. But to the worshippers it was an object of fascination. Fellow students would privately admit that in terms of eloquence and rhetorical abilities in Arabic I was by far superior to them. Conversely, I had no qualms to admit even openly that where my English was concerned I was the least of them all. This was a point of my greatest weakness – a weakness that kept me in a state of humility and reliance on the Lord. In the words of Hannah More, "We should keep up in our hearts a constant sense of our weakness, not with a design to discourage the mind and depress the spirit, but to drive us out of ourselves in search of divine assistance." That was precisely what I did, and within a year I was able to speak, read and write in English, albeit imperfectly. In getting to this stage, I realised that by God's help I was now on course.

A Friend Indeed!

During my time in Beirut, there were a number of people whose kindness and help I still remember with much gratitude. Among them was the Revd Bishara Zabaneh, a Palestinian Anglican clergyman and a full time English teacher at the Bible school. He was a gifted preacher, an outstanding translator from English to Arabic and vice versa, and above all a dedicated gentleman. As regards his relationship to people he was sociable, kind-hearted, benevolent and extraordinarily humorous. It is very seldom that a bond of friendship between two strangers can be struck at first encounter; and that is exactly what happened when I first met this amiable gentleman. A remarkable sense of affinity developed between us in the course of our first conversation and continued far beyond my three years study in Beirut. Indeed, our bond of friendship and brotherliness continued from that time (1963) until his death with Leukaemia in February 2007 in Amman, Jordan.

His kindness and generosity could not be underestimated. Both he and Rosette, his Lebanese wife, regarded me as their adopted brother, and their home was always open to me. In this way they were careful to protect me against the ravages of loneliness in a foreign land. In doing so, Mr Zabaneh was ever so compassionate, and most likely because he knew *"the heart of a stranger"*.[3] As a refugee himself, he seemed to live with the painful memory of the Palestinian tragedy

---

[3] Ex. 22:21; 23:9; Lev. 19:34; Deut. 10:19.

of 1948. Having known him personally, it is almost certain that when he died he took that painful memory with him into his grave.

As one coming from the westernmost part of the Arab world, I had fully shared the sympathy that my native country of Morocco had felt for the Palestinian cause. But, in Lebanon, as in the neighbouring Arab states facing Israel, I found the feeling for the Palestinian cause acutely sharper. For almost all the Arabs of the region, Muslims and Christians, the 1948 Palestinian tragedy (Ar. *Nakba*) was and still is a festering wound. And Palestinian refugee camps in most Arab countries of the region were always there to keep that painful memory alive.

But, what about the painful memory of those who were directly involved? When he could be persuaded to talk, Mr Zabaneh would tell of how he was born and brought up in the city of Ramalla, Palestine, of distinguished parents. He would recall how being the son of an outstanding elder of the community he received a good education in the local Anglican school. He would go on to tell how as a teenager he was an eyewitness to the havoc that the Zionists (the Haganah & the Stern Gang) wrecked upon his city and its Arab population. Then, he would come to a part of the story when his eyes will fill with tears. It is the part when his father locked the front door of their lovely house, and together with his terrified family, they were escorted by the armed Haganah into an already packed truck and driven to the Jordanian border where they were dumped. Even there, Zionist gunmen did not hesitate to shoot overhead to make their victims move inside the Jordanian territory quicker. As for life in Jordan, he could only say that his father "died there in austere circumstances".

That seemed to speak volumes about the scar that the 1948 Palestinian tragedy had left upon his soul. The Palestinian tragedy as told partly by my friend and partly in the history books which I started reading was enormous. Yet, for Mr Zabaneh, that tragedy had a positive side. It seemed to bring out the best that was in him. It apparently made him sensitive and full of compassion for the underprivileged, the dispossessed and the alien. And in his eyes, the Moroccan student seemed to fit into all these three characteristic features. It may well be that he was seeing something of himself in me, and therefore he did not hesitate to befriend me. And the way he befriended me could only recall the Biblical phrase, "... *there is a friend who sticks closer than a brother*".[4] That friendship lasted until he left this scene of time

---

[4] Prov. 18:24.

in the winter of 2007. In the Apocrypha book of Ben Sirach we have a beautiful description of true friends, *"A faithful friend is a sturdy shelter: he that has found one has found a treasure. There is nothing so precious as a faithful friend, and no scale can measure his excellence"* (6:14-15). Revd Bishara Zabaneh was that friend indeed!

The Lebanon of the Sixties

When I first arrived in Lebanon, in the mid-summer of 1963, it was, as some called it, 'the Paris of the Orient' or 'the Switzerland of the Middle East'. It was no doubt a land of freedom and liberty. Compared to the rest of the Arab countries, which were mainly secular nationalist, Lebanon was the only Arab country where freedom really reigned. Here freedom and democracy governed almost every aspect of Lebanese life. Yet, the residue of the 1958 civil war was still discernable in the country even after President Shihab had restored its equilibrium. The one thing that seemed to colour this remarkable freedom in my eyes was the widespread amount of firearms among the Lebanese people.

In Beirut particularly, there existed what could only be described as Mafia-like chiefs, each controlling his own district. People with grievances tended to go to these district chiefs for justice rather than to the police. And strangely enough in most cases justice was not only done but also seen to be done and quickly. On one particular occasion, the Bible school had some serious problems with certain delinquent youths from the nearby Armenian district. Principal Reed tried to get the local police to do something about it, but to no avail. In the end he was advised to approach the chiefs of that Armenian district, which he did. The problem was promptly dealt with, and the delinquent youths were never seen again around the Bible school.

Freedom in Lebanon included freedom to bear arms; and as a result the country was awash with weapons, something that was undreamed of in my native country of Morocco. And in this situation, quite often intrigues and tensions between those chiefs and their gangs exploded into violence and bloodshed.

The press or television reports of such events were often most disturbing to me as a Moroccan student. In my native country a riot of any sort would be ruthlessly put down. In time, however, I observed that this factionalism existed even among politicians. Such politicians could be seen arriving at the parliament escorted by their heavily armed factional militias. It was easy to conclude that the problem of Lebanon was by no means dictatorship, but a weak state totally unable to govern itself firmly. The seeds of full-scale civil war, which broke out in the 1970s, had already been there. When that happened, state institutions swiftly crumbled, the army fell apart and militia violence ruled the roost.

Sadly, the victims of that calamity were the Lebanese population. The Lebanese people were the best that the Arab world could produce. They were, as I knew them, a people of the finest possible qualities – very tolerant, kind and hospitable to a fault. I still cherish the memory of a number of fine Christian friends among them. After many years, I still remember with much admiration the beauty and the loveliness of their spiritual life and character. In brief, there are so many things I still remember about the Lebanon of the sixties. Some are happy memories that the mind never tires of them, but others are often sad to remember. It might have been better had they never occurred or even existed.

When Attitudes Change

On vacations students went back home somewhere in Lebanon, Syria or Jordan, whilst I stayed at the Bible school. For me it was a time for work in the campus, occasional visits to the Bishara home and study in the school's library. Here I would often reflect upon the level of my work-study so far and upon my relationship with my fellow students.

This last one seemed to cause me a great deal of concern. There were two ethnic groups of students – Arabs and Armenians. The Armenians tended to keep themselves apart. Understandably, their language and their sense of ethnic identity kept them together. Apart from two or three who were rather odd, most of them were on good terms with the Arab group. The odd fellows were not keen on mixing with the Arab groups generally and the Moroccan student in particular. One Armenian student was even reproached by these odd fellows for trying to befriend me personally. In fact, the attitude of one of them towards me had been so intolerable that an unpleasant encounter between us was unavoidable. Their behaviour was most disconcerting. But I soon came to know the possible reason for this attitude.

In the early 20th century, over one million Armenians were killed in Turkey. Fleeing the mass killing, hundreds of thousands of Armenian refugees came to Lebanon, Syria and other Arab countries. The memory of that appalling massacre still burns deep in the soul of the Armenian people today. In the opinion of some Arab students, the memory of that appalling incident may well have been behind their dislike of me. But how could they dislike me when I was not even a Turk? Apparently, for those odd fellows, the presence of a Muslim, or one from a Muslim background, was enough to conjure up a Turk in their mind! According to Mr Bishara, some years earlier the Bible school had a Turkish student of Muslim origin who was treated by most Armenian students in the same way.

Now, one can understand how non-Christians feel or react towards their past or present persecutors. But it is terribly hard to envisage a professing Christian nursing old grudges. Principal Reed was very unhappy with the hard feeling that most Armenian theological students had towards the Turks. He would often point out to them openly and privately that one could not be a Christian minister of the Gospel and at the same time nurse a hatred for the Turks because of what their grandparents had done decades ago. He would often stress that the ministers of Christ must be characterised by forgiveness and love towards all people including their enemies. Sadly, some were indifferent to his words and others even resentful. This might even have played some part in the bitter hostility that was unjustly directed against me later, and might have finally led to Principal Reed's departure from the field. What happened to him was a stain upon the character of the culprits. I thought highly of Principal Reed. He was a man of the finest moral and spiritual fibre.

Until now, the people I had a great affinity with at the Institute were the Arab students, among them Waheeb Antakly, a fine Christian young man from Syria. The relationship between him and most Armenian students can best be described as normal. But then something happened that caused a dramatic change of attitude. In the summer of my second year at Bible school, I went down with yellow jaundice and had to spend a few weeks in hospital. Suddenly, those Armenian students were deeply touched by the fact that here was a fellow student who hailed from a far off country and who had no relative or next of kin to visit him in hospital. And so they decided to visit me in hospital one day. During that visit the warmth of their brotherly love touched me profoundly, and before leaving they prayed for me and assured me of their continued prayers for my recovery.

For me, that was an overwhelming and indeed an unforgettable experience. It marked a turning point in my relationship with them. Indeed, as time went on, some of them became my best and closest friends among them, including Gricor Garabedian, whose memory I still cherish today. "You are far dearer to God than all of us here, Sam", he used to tell me. "You converted to the faith of Christ from another religion at a great cost. We were born as Christians and there was no cost involved."

Well-meaning though he was, what he said seemed to create for me another spot – a proud spot – capable of inflating my ego if I stayed there long enough. To leave that proud spot I took my strength from the words of the blind man to whose Jesus had given sight. *"I was blind, but now I can see,"* he said.[5] There was no pride in what that blind man said. He was merely describing his experience.

The Value of Togetherness

Doubtless Lebanon was (and still is) the only Arab country where freedom of religion has existed. Missionary organisations of all stripes operated freely in the land. Yet, it was easy for me to notice at that time that with all that existing freedom, missionary activities (including the activities of Lebanese evangelicals), were being focussed almost exclusively on the Christian population of the country. Missionary work among the Muslims was almost non-existent. I often wondered if this was an easy way out. Evangelising Muslims would almost be like walking into a minefield.

There might have been another reason. Muslim and Christian communities had two radically opposed ideologies. The former was all for Arab nationalism and Nasserism in particular. By contrast, the Christians, and mostly the Maronites, were averse to Arab nationalism and strongly pro-West. Could that be the reason why Western missionaries felt quite at home working among the Christian population? Arab nationalism (and Nasserism) was obviously unpopular in the West at the time, and such a political perspective must have rubbed off on them. But concentrating entirely on the Christian community was neither wise nor helpful to the cause of

---

[5] Jn. 9:25.

Christ. Perhaps if the same missionary effort had been channelled into the Muslim community of Lebanon, the history of that country might have been different today.

Incidentally, it may come as a big surprise to many that the rise of Arab nationalism (in mid & late nineteenth century Middle East generally and Lebanon in particular), had to a great extent been inspired by Western missionaries. It is hard to see why the role of missionaries in the twentieth century Lebanon became different. This was another dark spot where my search for an answer was a futile attempt.

Freedom can be wonderful, but it can also be dangerous. It can either be rightly used or badly misused. Moreover, freedom is not a question of doing what one likes but doing what one ought to do for the good of all. In the glorious sphere of the religious freedom I was now enjoying, I noticed something quite disturbing, and this was not an exercise in fault-finding. In that free and democratic society there were plenty of other strange and intriguing things for me to see. Among them was something I had discovered just a few months after my arrival in the country – something from which I derived a valuable lesson.

I was very surprised to discover that Missions from different Christian denominations (mostly from the USA), were blatantly in hot competition with each other. As a result the spirit of Christian fellowship and co-operation between them was virtually absent. It was painfully clear to me that the situation in Lebanon stood in glaring contrast to that which existed among the Christian Missions I knew in Morocco. Missionaries there were able to find unity and togetherness as their source of strength in a predominantly Muslim country. Victory belongs to those who *"make every effort to keep the unity of the Spirit in the bond of peace . . ."* [6] It seems that the enemy is never as victorious as when he is fighting God's people separately. On signing the Declaration of Independence (4th July 1776), Benjamin Franklin remarked, "We must indeed all hang together, or most assuredly, we shall all hang separately!"

In the book of Ecclesiastes 4:9-12 I found a solemn yet simple lesson, which Christians cannot afford to ignore. In this passage the author points out that far better than the successful rivalry that places a man above his fellows and keeps him aloof from them are the

---

[6] Eph. 4:3-6 RSV.

advantages that come from unity and co-operation. Warmth, comfort, security and protection flow from togetherness and association with others. Unity was precisely the request that our Lord offered in His High Priestly prayer for His Universal Church (see John 17:20-26). To live otherwise would be tantamount to wishing He had never offered that prayer.

Light for the Future

Life at the Bible school, after some rough and bumpy rides at the beginning, turned out to be pleasant. The school was not exclusively a theological training institute for future pastors. Part of it was a sort of primary school for Lebanese children. And in this part some theological students were quite useful, as for example, in helping with sport, or filling in for an absent teacher or in starting a sort of Christian drama group. I still recall how on occasions I was asked to stand in for the teacher of Arabic grammar when absent. I was certainly very much at home with this subject, and indeed most gratified to earn the appreciation of both staff and students. But I would perhaps be more remembered for being put in charge of the Christian drama group, which consisted entirely of theological students – Arabs and Armenians – who performed their parts with diligence and enthusiasm. Interestingly, a number of individuals were won for Christ at the close of some of the plays. Of course almost all the plays contained a good deal of humour. After all, Christianity is the faith that brings joy and laughter simultaneously into the human life.

Life at the Bible school was in many ways wonderful, but in terms of studies it was not easy for me as all the subjects were in English. Unlike my fellow students, I had never had any crash course in English before coming to this Institute. Looking back I can unashamedly confess that with regards to English I was the weakest of all my fellow students. But in spite of the difficulties I refused to be discouraged. I passionately believed that the Good Lord did not bring me all the way to this Institute for nothing. Therefore, I resolved to do my best and leave the rest to Him.

In addition to my resolve, I received an extra boost from Principal Reed in one of my conversations with him in his office. "My English is an insurmountable problem," I told him. "Although I manage to understand the lessons, I find it is quite difficult to put down what I know in English, especially during exams." "Well, Samuel," he replied, "you just have to put down what you know in the way you know, and we'll understand what you mean!"

His advice was just what I needed. Before that it seemed as though I had begun to stare at an abyss, and as Nietzsche once said, "If you stare too long at the abyss, the abyss will stare back at you." But with God's help I was determined to press on and hope for the best.

The course at the Bible school ran for three years, and so far I had been there two years during which I had done not so badly. Until then, apart from my studies and other school activities nothing else concerned me. But at the start of my third year, I began to consider for the first time the question of what to do after I graduated in eight months' time. The question was partly evoked by some of my fellow students who spoke openly of their desire to emigrate to the USA after graduating. Others were quietly preparing to do so when the time came. For me, staying in Lebanon after graduating would be out of the question. I had no work permit, and even if I had one I certainly had no professional qualification. And supposing I found a job of some sort, housing would be a huge problem in an already small but crowded country like Lebanon. To crown it all, life in that wonderful land was quite expensive.

After much prayer and consideration, I realised that staying in Lebanon would not be a good idea. As I was still young and the road before me was still long, the best thing for me was to further my education. But to further my education where? For a short period I felt the attraction of the USA, but the pull of the United Kingdom of Great Britain was by far stronger, and not without some good reasons. I had always been in contact with some Emmanuel missionaries, chiefly among them Mr Reg Davies and Aunty Lily Randle. The photographs I had often seen of Dr Rigby and some of his peers in fine Emmanuel uniform on the college campus had left a remarkably permanent impression on me. The same could be said of all the fascinating things I had heard about Emmanuel College itself. I was confident that should I decide to go there, I would not feel like a fish out of water. In a sense it would be my spiritual home and environment. After all, I was the fruit of Emmanuel Mission, and the people there who had prayed for me all those years would love to have me there. On my part, I simply longed to see them and be among them.

When Principal Reed heard of my preference to go to Britain after graduating, he hardly stopped teasing me about it. "What in the world made you prefer Britain to the USA?" he used to ask me with a giggle, "it's a cold, sleety, snowy, damp and wet country. As for food, the Brits are the worst cooks in the world. If they get confused about anything in the kitchen, they simply boil it!" On the whole he seemed happy with my choice. But I had the feeling that perhaps he would have been happier had I chosen to further my education in the USA.

The remarkable thing was that in all the ups and downs of my theological school days in Lebanon, the Lord was my guiding light. And when the time came for me to look beyond the present, I could count on Him to give me some light for the future.

Chapter 13

LAND OF HOPE AND GLORY

"We may be a small island,
but we are not a small people."

(Sir Edward Heath)

During my three years at the Nazarene Bible School in Beirut, I had never lost touch with Emmanuel missionaries, as previously stated. Among those missionaries was Aunty Randle of blessed memory. At that time she had been a sister nurse at a Birmingham hospital. When she had learned of my keen desire to enter Emmanuel College in Birkenhead, she prayerfully decided to do something about it. Now, both she and Dr Rigby belonged to Emmanuel Church in Birmingham, whose founder and minister was the Revd Cecil Shelton, a very amiable and godly gentleman. Being a very influential member of Emmanuel Council, Aunty Randle approached him to ask the Council to accept me as a student at Emmanuel College. The Council, she suggested, might be happy to admit me as the first fruit of Emmanuel Mission into its College.

When Mr Shelton brought the matter to the Council, the first reaction was one of silence. As for those in leadership, the sign of reservation was quite obvious on their faces. However, having made a strong case in favour of admitting me into College as a student, the Council agreed to do so, albeit reluctantly. This last word, when it first came to my attention, either due to my thrill of being admitted or my ignorance of its real import, did not sink in. But a few years later, I came to know its real implication, and my reaction was one of deep sadness; but more of this shortly.

When the news that I had been accepted as a student at Emmanuel reached me, I was overjoyed. Meanwhile, I was not unaware that this would mean a new phase and a new adjustment to a completely different environment. I had a clear idea that in terms of culture and way of life, Britain stood in glaring contrast to the world I had hitherto known and cherished. But I was determined to do my very best to adapt to the new situation. Moreover, the idea of a permanent stay in Britain was out of the question. My sole ambition was to return to serve the Lord in Lebanon after finishing my education in Britain.

Graduating Under a Cloud

Sadly, this joyful prospect was marred by a very unfortunate incident that occurred at the Nazarene Bible School a few months before graduation. The atmosphere was suddenly full of rancour and agitation. Principal Reed, who was also a supervisor of the Churches of the Nazarene in Beirut, found himself in head on collision with four pastors, three Arabs and one Armenian. And it was rumoured at the time that an important person, who shall remain nameless, was behind them. At any rate, the conflict was not a mere clash of personalities as some had suggested. It was rather a clash of discipline and indiscipline, a clash of selflessness and selfishness, and a clash of truth and falsehood. As an eyewitness, I still recall the noble qualities that adorned the life and ministry of Principal Reed – the qualities of sincere spirituality and practical discipline, self-sacrifice and deep abhorrence of hypocrisy and lies. His opponents were apparently not cast in the same mould, and neither could they be squeezed into it. He was simply too much for them. And when all the invectives and character assassinations had failed, a plot was hatched to remove him from office. They accused him of being pro-Israel.

Such an allegation was not only preposterous, but also extremely dangerous to make against anyone in Lebanon at that period. His opponents were aware that for any resident alien (especially an American), in an Arab country, his days of stay would be numbered if he were daubed with a pro-Zionist smear. Consequently, Principal Reed was summoned to appear before the Evangelical Synod of Lebanon regarding this absurd allegation, but the outcome was inconclusive. Like my fellow students, I watched helplessly as Principal Reed went through the wringer. None of them ever doubted his innocence. His profound love for the Arab people and his unremitting sympathy for their cause were undeniable. Yet, oddly enough, neither the Nazarene Mission Board in the USA (which was already involved), nor the Evangelical Synod of Lebanon had ever called any of the students as a witness.

Finally, after much pressure on the Mission Board, particularly from the above-unnamed figure, who was the real instigator, Principal Reed was recalled to the USA in the summer of 1966. And with his removal, the healthy and vigorous spiritual and educational life of the Bible school started to decline. Perhaps one of the saddest incidents, which I still remember, was the day Principal Reed was leaving for the Airport to fly to the USA. I was standing at the upper gate of the School, when Principal Reed and his family appeared and were making their way to the car that was waiting to take them to the Airport. To say that they looked sad would be an understatement. It seemed that their visible sadness was but the tip of the iceberg of what lurked inside them. "Well, Samuel," said Principal Reed with a fatherly smile, as he shook hands with me, "Take care and I hope to see you soon." I felt a big lump in my throat. I knew how indebted I was to that good man. He was a father figure to me. It was hard to hold back my tears as the vehicle left and eventually disappeared into the distance.

A couple of weeks before this, a group of American tourists who happened to be in Lebanon came to visit the Bible school. With all the students left after the graduation, I was the only one remaining at school. Having welcomed the group, Principal Reed asked me to get some refreshments for the guests as he showed them around the school. As I served the guests, I noticed one elderly lady pointing towards me as she talked to Principal Reed. She was obviously asking him who I was. Shortly before they left, she called me and handed me an envelope and wished me a safe journey to Britain. When I opened it later I found a $25 cheque and a note saying, "I shall be mindful of you in my prayers. Please write and let me know how you are progressing with your studies in Great Britain."

Her name was Mary Vaughan. Principal Reed had obviously told her about my imminent trip to the UK for study. I certainly kept in touch with Mary Vaughan until she passed away in her early nineties. I shall never forget her prayerful support and kind generosity. Her kind-heartedness was such that when I married Shirley she flew all the way from Florida to be at my wedding in Skelmersdale, England. She was a good and godly lady. I still treasure her blessed memory and will continue to do so as long as I live.

There is also another thing I still remember. Before leaving Beirut, Principal Reed was determined that the task God had called to do was fully carried out before he left. Under the circumstances, he had managed to arrange the final exams and organize the graduation of his theological students, including the celebration that normally followed. He might have lost trust in people, but he never lost heart in serving them through Christ. Throughout the celebration that followed the graduation the niggling thoughts of the recent event seemed to rob a good many that day of the joy of the occasion. That was precisely my personal feeling. But what intrigued me most was the paradox of the whole thing. The graduation was a happy one, but at the same time it was a graduation under a dark cloud.

A New Destination

With Principal Reed's departure for the USA, and when all the students had left shortly after graduating, I was the only student left at the school building. I could not resist thinking how three years earlier I was the first student to arrive at that Bible School, and three years later I was the last one to leave. However, a week later I was driven to Beirut Airport accompanied by two of my closest friends, Revd Bishara Zabaneh and Krikore Garabedian. After less than an hour there, my London-bound airplane called for boarding. It was time to say goodbye in which my friends gave me their warm and tearful embrace.

It was indeed a highly emotional moment. It brought back the sad memory of three years earlier when I had bidden my final farewell to my dear grandmother. I wondered, as I walked to the aircraft, if one day I would see my two good friends again. I took my seat in the aircraft and after a little while it took off. Flying over Beirut, and watching it disappear beneath the clouds, did not help me emotionally, for I was already feeling the pain of leaving my two friends behind. It was not until the plane was over the Mediterranean a couple of hours later that my emotional grief began to subside, and I was fast asleep. When I woke up, the plane was hovering over the great city of London. As I looked down to see it, I naively assumed that most, if not all, people down there must be as good Christians as the missionaries through whom I was converted. My naivety was like a flu virus, which one discovers as soon as one begins to sneeze. It was indeed quite disappointing for me to discover a few days later that only a minority of the British people were really Christians.

At Heathrow Airport, the secretary of Emmanuel College, Mr Frank Salt, was waiting for me. I had met him a couple of times years earlier in my Moroccan hometown during his visits to the Emmanuel missionaries there. For the first time I noticed that his habitual gestures and way of speaking were rather peculiar. I certainly did not recall seeing this idiosyncrasy in him during his visits to Morocco. I either failed to notice it when I first met him in Morocco, or this was something he had developed since then. In any case, the constant contortion of his face and rapid blinking of his eyes appeared to be a ploy designed to cover up something that had to do with his hitherto unknown strange personality. A few years later he left office

However, together we took the London-Liverpool train, and some hours later we arrived at the Liverpool train station. It was early evening, but because it was mid-summer it looked as though it was still afternoon. The sun was still shining, but well on the way to sinking into the west. Coming from the scorching summer heat of the Middle East, I might have been surprised by the chill of the Liverpool air as I boarded the boat to cross the river Mersey to Birkenhead. I was now in a different world, and so far almost everything I saw was a surprise to me in some way or another. But the biggest surprise of all was awaiting me at Emmanuel Bible College.

A Strange Welcome

My arrival at Emmanuel College was during summer vacation. As in Lebanon three years before, I was the first student to arrive, and had to remain there a few weeks before the students returned. Arriving at the College gate, I looked forward excitedly to meeting and greeting the people there. Now, the familiar manner in which one greets his relations, friends or even total strangers in the Arab world is usually warm and full of courtesy. All the missionaries I knew were no different from the natives in this respect. The absence of such warmth in one's greeting could be taken as a discourtesy or even a veiled insult. Yet, that was precisely how I felt when I met the college staff. With the exception of one who shook my hand, the rest simply nodded to me with what looked like a thin smile. I was taken aback and wondered for a moment if my arrival was at all welcomed.

On reflection, what I had just seen might simply be typical of a staid British temperament. Mr Zabaneh and others in Lebanon had warned me that, unlike the Arab people, the British were quite a self-restrained and reserved people. In this way I was able to find an excuse for them. A few weeks later, the students, male and females, returned to college from their summer vacation to begin a new term. New students like me joined them. Some of them came from as far as Ghana, Barbados and India, but most of the students that particular year were from Northern Ireland.

Watching the arrival of students, I noticed with interest the remarkable warmth and joy with which the college staff met them. I could not help thinking, with some degree of astonishment, that that was not the way they had welcomed me a few weeks earlier. Refusing to make an issue of it, I assumed that they intended no harm. The fact that my command of English was quite poor could have prevented them from engaging me in a conversation which I would not have been able to maintain. Perhaps they thought that I had just arrived from a very long journey, and they would rather leave me alone to relax first. There was plenty of time in which they would get to know me. But all these and other excuses seemed to evaporate when most of the students rushed to welcome me fervently. I could not avoid noticing that the attitudes of the staff and the students towards me in this respect were clearly different. Why? Did I unintentionally do or say something that might have put them off? These and other questions kept gnawing at me until I finally decided in a self-deprecating way to close the door on this issue at once. I thought that I was just being downright childish about it.

During the months that followed, I did my very best to integrate into the life of Emmanuel College, about which more will be said later. The students, and particularly the Irish students, were simply excellent. In terms of godliness, spiritual zeal, diligence and brotherly love they were exemplary. They seemed to be quite aware of the problems that surrounded me at college, whereas I myself was not fully aware of them.

The memory of one particular occasion still lingers in my mind. I was sitting alone in the study room when Brother M.H., as he was called, came in and sat next to me. He looked slightly pensive, giving the impression that he came either with a complaint or bad news. "How are you doing, Sam?" he asked in a rather low tone of voice. "I hope you're settling in reasonably well in this new environment." I answered that I was settling in quite well. However, adjusting to a completely different culture and environment, I told him, was never easy for a foreigner like me. But, with God's help, I added, all would be well in the end. Brother M.H. nodded his head vigorously in agreement as his eyes filled with tears. He then laid his hand on my shoulder and offered a prayer. All that I recall from that prayer is the first verse of a familiar old hymn, which says:

> When upon life's billows you are tempest tossed
> When you discouraged thinking all is lost,
> Count your many blessings; name them one by one,
> And it will surprise you what the Lord hath done.

When brother M.H. had left, it became pretty clear to me that for some reason or another he seemed deeply concerned about me. Why he should feel that way at this early stage of the college term I simply had no idea.

When Ignorance is Bliss

A transition from one culture to another is not quite easy. For example, misunderstandings, mistrusts and a number of other disadvantages are expected in the life of any immigrant. But there are certain ways in which he might feel safe and reasonably sheltered from any hardship. There is of course the rule of law such as exists in western democracies, which can guarantee him his human rights. Another way might be the existence of close friends and relations in his newfound country that can protect him and act as his safety net. But there is a third way – his utter ignorance of the odds that may be against him.

The main cause of this ignorance may be his failure to learn from reliable sources something about the world he is migrating to. He is in too much of a hurry to bother with such a thing. All he wants is to get to the place where he could earn a reasonably good living, or get a good education, or simply escape political or religious persecution. His pre-conceived image of Westerners can be most re-assuring. They are, as he always viewed them, kind, polite, gentle, fair, sympathetic and honest people. They would not do anything to harm him. Finally, he arrives in the country with a language problem and with a psychologically huge load of his own culture.

These and perhaps much more can serve to cloud a lot of serious issues facing him in his new environment. As a result, he can remain hopelessly ignorant of a lot of things including the many odds that might arise against him. He is likely to remain so until such time as he becomes fully adjusted and integrated into the life and culture of his adopted country. This may take a considerable period of time. It may well be that years later, he will remember that particular early period and realise that after all much of his early ignorance was indeed bliss!

From the time I arrival from Lebanon, I did my utmost to conform to the college way of life. I complied with its harsh semi-Victorian rules and showed as much diligence in its active and devotional life as my fellow students. But I remained ignorant of much that was going on around me. In this new cultural atmosphere, I did not seem to feel in the least vulnerable. Why should I? I lived amidst the people of God and felt fully secure among them. As a matter of fact, I could only feel vulnerable to the goodness of the spiritual sphere in which I lived. For some, this may seem like an unconscious way of playing ostrich. If it seemed so, it certainly did me no harm even when, on one occasion and for the first time, the harm did actually come my way.

The occasion was a sunny afternoon. I was sitting on a bench outside the college dining room when a missionary lady, who shall remain nameless, walked towards me. She and her husband happened to be among a group of missionaries that the Moroccan government had recently asked to leave the country. As one who was well known to me, I stood up with a beaming smile to greet her. "What are you doing here?" she asked him with a straight face. "I'm enjoying a bit of sunshine," I replied innocently. "I don't mean that," she snapped back. "I mean, what are you doing in my own country? You ought to go back to Morocco where you belong. This is my country and you have no right to be here." Then she turned and walked away, whether angry or embarrassed, I could not really tell.

I was confused rather than stunned by that incident. I could not grasp the real implication of what that lady had just told me. Language at that moment in time was probably the reason for my confusion. But, I somehow managed to convince myself that no malice could have been intended by what she said. Missionaries, as I knew them, were the paragons of love and godliness and could not be spiteful or malevolent in any way. Most probably all that she might have implied was that as a Moroccan Christian I should be back in Morocco where the gospel was desperately needed.

After so many years in Britain, which is now my adopted country, and having become absorbed in its linguistic and cultural way of life, I am no longer confused about that lady's words, which I still remember quite vividly. What she implied was something that can mildly be described as totally out of order and out of character; but it was also something that could best be countered with love and forgiveness. Similarly, one day during dinner, someone told me something, which provoked laughter on the part of some but disapproval on the part of one or two. When I later asked one of my fellow students from London to explain to me what that person had said, he replied with a rather sad countenance, "You won't want to know, brother."

On another occasion I happened to have left the college to meet someone, and for some unknown reason I had forgotten to ask permission from the students' supervisor. On my return I went to him immediately and apologized profusely for my mistake. The supervisor muttered angrily as he walked away, "How dare you come to this country and think you can do anything you like." Fortunately, I did not pause to let these words sink in.

As time went on and my knowledge of the English language and culture improved, I moved from a state of genuine ignorance to an attitude of deliberately ignoring anything that was said or done to hurt me. For instance, a good number of vacant churches looked to Emmanuel College students for Sunday pulpit supply. Every Thursday, names of students assigned to take Sunday services in various churches were usually placed on the Board in the study hall. Yet, throughout my time at that college, my name was never on that Board once. Why? I did not know, and to this day I still do not exactly know the reason.

Of course, I had my own thoughts about this issue at the time, but through much prayer, I never allowed it to overwhelm me. True, the Lord would not allow His people to be tested beyond endurance. He would always *provide the way of escape*.[1] That way of escape was always there. When I felt that an act of hostility was about to overwhelm me, I would scurry to my safety zone of ignorance, and pretend that no harm was done or even intended. Looking back, I can neither regret nor resent that early stage of my ignorance. On the contrary, I am deeply grateful that in my case ignorance, real or pretended, was indeed bliss.

---

[1] 1 Cor. 10:13.

The Exception

I had been at college almost a year when the Arab-Israeli war, known as the Six-Day war, broke out. On June 5, 1967, Israel launched a pre-emptive attack against Egypt. Within six days (5th – 10th June) Egypt, Jordan and Syria (not to mention troops contributed by Iraq, Saudi Arabia, Sudan, Tunisia, Algeria and Morocco) suffered a crushing defeat. The news was a terrible shock to me. But more shocking was the attitude of the college staff and most of the students, which at first was one of a subdued sense of jubilation over the swift shattering defeat of the Arab armies. Soon however the pro-Israel and anti-Arab sentiments became more vocal, especially from the pulpit.

Until now I had been aware that since the establishment of the state of Israel in 1948, many Christians in the West viewed it as a fulfilment of Biblical prophecy. In fact, the Israeli victory over the Arabs in June 1967 was regarded by these same people as a classic illustration of God's will revealed in prophecy being fulfilled in the state of Israel. The Arabs were simply playing a demonic role. There were sermons in which Israel was compared with little David defeating the Arab Goliath, and the current conflict was seen in terms of a revival of the enmity that existed between Ishmael and Isaac.[2] At the Holiness Convention that was held shortly after the ceasefire was declared, a well-known Welsh guest preacher was so lost in wonder and praise of the state of Israel that a couple of ex-missionaries to Morocco looked quite embarrassed. He told the congregation that the recent Israeli victory and the rout of the Arabs reminded him of the alliance of the four eastern kings that were defeated by Abraham's small forces.[3] Israel, he said, must have learned this military exploit from their father Abraham, to the shouts of 'hallelujahs' from the spellbound congregation!

Sadly, the Arab-Israeli conflict at that time was (and still is) not seen in terms of Zionism and its corollary the state of Israel constantly clashing with Arab nationalism. It was rather seen from a purely religious and eschatological perspective. For them, the Middle East conflict was a conflict between Islam and God's chosen people, Israel – a conflict that is a pre-requisite to the return of Christ and end time. This was so in spite of the fact that Islam in the sixties was not

---

[2] Gen. 21:8-14.

[3] Gen. 14:1ff.

resurgent as today. Oddly enough, rejoicing over the triumph of one nation and the defeat of another seemed quite out of character. It was utterly inconsistent with the pacifist position that this college had championed since the days of its founder, J.D. Drysdale.

In this situation, I found it hard to scurry again to my comfort zone of ignorance. There are some things that one must confront head on. Meanwhile, a Jordanian Christian who had studied with me at the Beirut Bible School happened to be taking a theological course at the Manchester Nazarene Bible College. Unsurprisingly, he was having the same problem. According to him, the gloating over the Arabs' misfortune amongst the College staff and students was so disturbing that he contemplated returning to his own country of Jordan, which he eventually did. There he could feel very much at home with his fellow Christians in the Jordanian Church. As for me, the situation was different. I was cut off from my people, disinherited and had no native Christian Church in my country to return to. In brief, my position was such that all the bridges were burned behind him.

Both that Jordanian student and I were simply looking at the modern state of Israel from the Arab Christian theological perspective. What we were now hearing from our Western fellow Christians was at best a theological novelty and at worst an appalling heresy. For us, as for the Middle East churches (most of them are historic churches), the present secular state of Israel has existed since 1948 because of political action taken in history by man for man. This action is neither essentially related to Old Testament covenant or prophecy, nor is it ordained of God in the sense of a pending divine purpose yet to be fulfilled through secular Zionist Israel. Simply put: Zionist Israel today has no prophetic significance and is totally out of covenant continuity. The old covenant was done away with as God, in Christ, made a new covenant for the whole world and all humanity.[4]

The reaction to my view varied among the staff and the students. Some dismissed it as either a result of my serious ignorance of scriptures, or a deliberate distortion of clear prophecies that were being fulfilled in our day. There was at least one member of the staff who reportedly called my Christian faith into question. Obviously, for that gentleman, the current Middle East conflict was seen purely

---

[4] Heb. 8:6-13.

in terms of Islam versus Judaism. Any convert from Islam who believes that the state of Israel today has no prophetic significance or covenantal continuity, his faith must be dubious.

Although hurt by what had been said, I could not help thinking that some Christians may have a natural suspicion of converts from Islam – a suspicion that is connected with the myth that Muslims are unconvertible. But perhaps what that brother and those like him did not know was that my theological stance vis-à-vis Zionist Israel was the stance of millions of Arab Christians in the Middle East. Must their Christian faith also be called into question? In time, however, I discovered that not all Evangelicals in the West were cast into that Christian Zionist mould. Indeed, many of them were in full agreement with my theological position regarding the present state of Israel.

The tragedy of Christian Zionism is that it suffers from a terrible theological blind spot. For them, the Middle East conflict is not about justice, morality or human sufferings. It is rather about God favouring one nation over another, and blessing one people at the expense of another. It is about a pessimistic eschatology that sees the present state of Israel as a key player in a gruesome end time, which is likely to happen at any moment.

Years afterwards, I was able to lead many theological battles with a number of Christian Zionists. Such battles would not have been possible had I scurried as usual into my safety zone of ignorance. But in the event of the Six-Day War, and the triumphal reaction that it evoked in some fellow Christians, I thought it wise not to hide but to make an exception and come out to the open.

The Funny Side

Without a doubt the college was a good training Institute for men and women who felt the call of God to serve in the mission field overseas or in the ministry of the Church at home. The rules of discipline were tough. As students we rose up at 6.00 a.m. and our entire day's activity ranged from private devotions, to attending theological and Biblical lectures, to doing manual work. The training was certainly tough, and in spite of the difficulties I encountered, I remained hugely grateful for the countless benefits I derived from it. Doubtless, what I learned and experienced at Emmanuel College did much to sharpen my mind and squeeze me into the British cultural mould. For all this and much more, I remain eternally indebted to that Institution and its people. However, there were other people outside Emmanuel whose memory I will always cherish. Each Saturday a student or two would have a day off. It was on some of my Saturdays off that I had a chance to meet and establish contact with some Christians from other denominations. I shall never forget how greatly encouraged I was by their brotherly love, hospitality and prayerful support.

Now, being part of the Holiness Movement, the college's strict discipline governed the spiritual and practical life of all its students. But in spite of that, the funny side was by no means absent. One of its strict rules, for example, was 'no talking between men and women students'. It is said that this rule was even stricter during the time of its founder, J.D. Drysdale, which is hard to imagine.

A story is told that one morning, whilst the founder was across the Mersey in Liverpool on some business, he saw two of his male and female students holding hands and walking into a café. Unfortunately, they did not see him. After lunch, he made an announcement requesting the couple he had seen earlier that day in Liverpool to meet him at his office in thirty minutes. The story goes that when he entered his office he found three couples waiting for him! Just how true this story is, it is hard to tell. The funny thing is that according to some reliable sources a good number of missionaries and ministers happened to have met their married partners during training at Emmanuel! How could that happen in the face of such a strict rule? This question is never raised. The rule was so strict that male students sat at different tables from female students. When men or women students took turns to serve at dinner tables, no whisper could be heard from either of them.

The food served at mealtimes was simple and quite British. It often reminded me of what Principal Reed had once told him about British cooking, "If the Brits got confused about something they simply boiled it!" In any case, I shall never forget the variety of edible things that were served on toast. There were beans on toast, eggs on toast, tomatoes on toast, sardines on toast etc. . . . In brief, the only thing that was not served on toast was water! In that situation I could only long for those exotic dishes I used to enjoy in Lebanon. But, for me, those were *"the years that the locust has eaten"*![5] However, the most intriguing item in the dining room was an awesome portrait above the fireplace showing lions munching up the Christians in an ancient

---

[5] Joel 2:25.

Roman amphitheatre! It was easy for me to feel envious of those lions having steaks whilst I was struggling to finish my beans on toast!

During dinner, the college staff did not join the students, and male and female students had their meals in separate rooms. The meals on many occasions consisted mainly of what was left from lunch (i.e. '*hash*') and the rest was bread, margarine and jam. In saying grace, once an Irish student, who was then the head brother, prayed, "We thank you, Lord, for the food that is set before us. Grant us, we beseech you, adequate digestive systems to tackle it, Amen!" The students often preferred to sing the first verse of a hymn or a chorus of thanksgiving instead of saying grace. At a dinner, the head brother called on one student to choose a relevant hymn. The student, who looked far from pleased with the food before him that evening, broke out singing, accompanied by the rest, *"Nearer my God to thee . . ."*! The memory of the funny side of life at Emmanuel College still makes me laugh today.

During my first two years at Emmanuel, life was not easy. But, little did I know that in His wisdom God meant it to be a preparatory period for what lay ahead for me in a land which though a small island, is a land of great people. It is not for nothing that they call it 'Land of Hope and Glory'.

Chapter 14

BETWEEN TRIALS AND TRUST

*"Have courage for the great sorrows of life, and
patience for the small ones. And when you have
laboriously accomplished your daily task, go to
sleep. God is awake."*

(Victor Hugo)

Some Christians are possibly never as happy as when they are
walking through the valley of the shadow of death. If Eden looms on
the horizon they shy away from it. Perhaps for a non-Christian they
belong to the category of 'those who are not happy unless they are
miserable'. But faith is hardly ever pessimistic. Faith is optimistic. It is
almost always ready to believe that the best is just around the corner,
which, for the non-Christian, is too naïve for comfort.

Yet, St Paul mentions among the gifts of the Spirit *"the gift of faith"*.[1]
There are degrees of faith. There is, for example, the saving faith that
involves the reception of salvation through grace.[2] That was not what
the Apostle had in mind when he spoke of *"the gift of faith"*. Evidently,
when he spoke of this gift, he was referring to that particular kind of
faith that performs wonders and exploits.[3]

Now, this kind of faith is stronger, more robust, more contagious
and inspiring than that of others. The faith of a few, in varying
circumstances, has more than once been the living spring which has
nourished the morale of many. In some people this kind of faith is
a feeble and a flickering flame; in others it is a great beacon shining
through the darkness of every spiritual night. Indeed, this type of
Christian faith is almost always at its best when things are at their
worst. In this context optimism is one of the chief members of the

---

[1] 1 Cor. 12:9.

[2] Eph. 2:8.

[3] 1 Cor. 13:2; Mk. 5:34, 10:52.

faith family. It hardly ever fails to believe that the best is just around the corner, or that great things are yet to come. During this period also I was baptized.

In addition to being alone as a foreign student, my disadvantages and disabilities at that early stage were more than I could bear. The one thing that kept my spirit up was the fact that I was in a free country, thanks to Emmanuel College's sponsorship. As for the future, I had not the slightest idea what was in store for me. All that mattered to me then was to take a day at a time. But, in taking a day at a time, I was not unaware that each day I was groping in a terribly dark tunnel at the end of which there was no glimmer of light.

Yet, as I still remember quite vividly, there were moments of doubt, but hardly any sense of despair or despondency. Deep in my heart of hearts I had an incredible sense of resignation that the best was to follow. Such was my optimistic faith, though at that time I did not know what to call it. Today I have no hesitation in asking: if that was not 'the gift of faith', then what was it?

Trust and Smile

I had initially been admitted to Emmanuel College for a period of two years. The basic purpose for being there was not to obtain a theological diploma. I was in possession of one from Lebanon already. Rather I was there mainly to improve my English by taking part in college activities including attending all biblical and theological lectures etc. . . . As the days and the months rolled on, I was slightly disconcerted one day when I realised that the period of my stay at Emmanuel was going to expire in less than six months. But more disconcerting to me was the fact that in view of the short period that remained, none of the College officials had thought to ask me what my plan for the future was, or what my next step would be. Instead there was a wall of silence.

In that situation I requested to see Stanley Banks, the College Principal, in order to seek his counsel and help concerning this matter. When I met him in his study, I spoke first of my indebtedness to him personally and to all the staff for having me at Emmanuel College. I also spoke of my deep appreciation for being the recipient of so many spiritual benefits in that Institute. Then I expressed my deep concern over the fact that my last six months at College would soon expire, and I did not relish the prospect of leaving the College, which was my only home where I felt safe and secure. I had no idea what to do or where to go when the time expired. I certainly could not return to Lebanon as a worker without some reliable sponsorship from there. And there was no question of me returning to my native country of Morocco. "Above all," I added with a touch of humour, "I'm not sure that martyrdom is running in my veins at the moment! On my part I sincerely appreciate what our Lord meant when He said, '*when they persecute you in one city, flee to the next . . .'.*"[4]

The Principal sat motionless looking at me and listening in utter silence to all that I was saying. As a matter of fact, I could not help feeling a bit intimidated and discouraged by his posture. Then I plucked up courage and earnestly pleaded for his help as the Principal of Emmanuel College and as the head of its Mission with regard to this problem. I wondered if he, as the leader of this entire Christian Missionary organisation, could write and petition the Home Office to change my status and lift the restriction on me as a student.

I suggested that it should be explained that having previously suffered hostilities for my conversion (as missionaries resident in his hometown could readily testify), my return to a country where one is forbidden to change his religion would have serious repercussions. I thought it vital that his petition for a permanent stay in this country on religious grounds be presented and sponsored by the very mission that had led me to Christ and witnessed the hardship I endured for my newfound faith. In this way I was pretty sure that the likelihood of the Home Office turning me down would be very slim indeed.

When I finished speaking, the Principal briefly replied that he would write to the Home Office at the earliest possible opportunity, and let me know the outcome. As the weeks rolled on, I was not feeling in the least anxious. My trust in the Lord was being hugely encouraged and strengthened by that New Testament verse, which reads, "*Cast all your anxieties on Him, for He cares for you.*"[5] I was fully confident that in such a situation God Himself was my bond, and God's bond has always been His word, and in His word He says, "*I will not fail you nor forsake you.*"[6]

---

[4] Mt. 10:23.

[5] 1 Pet. 5:7.

[6] Jos. 1:5; Heb. 13:5.

One afternoon, the staff and the students had just finished lunch and were leaving the dining room, when the Principal drew near hastily and walked by my side. Then he took me aside and said to me abruptly, "Samuel, the reply from the Home Office has been negative." Having uttered this sentence, he walked to his office and closed the door.

As a student I had always held the Principal in the highest possible esteem for his godliness and his unique ministry as a holiness teacher. But my sense of being left in the lurch suddenly began to colour my view. For me, 'Holiness' as taught in the Wesleyan tradition can also be defined as 'Perfect Love'. How could I possibly reconcile this sublime message with what seemed perhaps like apathy towards a brother, who was also "a stranger in the land".[7] Although very grateful for the petition that the Principal had written to the Home Office, it remained a puzzle that I was never shown a copy of it, or even given a verbal resume of its content. By the same token, I never knew the content of the reply from the Home Office, or was even told briefly the basis on which I had been turned down. Naturally, I was unable to understand how a Christian mission could treat one of its sons so indifferently.

Suddenly, I felt conscience-stricken and turned on myself. Was I not being a little too judgmental? How could I possibly suspect someone of something without proof? The man representing the Mission had, in good faith, done what he could regardless of whether or not a written copy of the petition had been made available for my perusal. Was it his fault that the reply was negative? And what could he or anyone else have done after the die had been cast? As a Christian student I would do well to remember that there is nothing better than a charitable spirit. After all "love does not keep a record of wrongs".[8]

With such self-deprecation, I decided that by God's grace I was not going to allow the taint of evil thoughts to linger in my mind about the Principal or anybody else. Instead, I should learn that "whatsoever things are true, whatsoever things are honest, whatsoever things are just, whatsoever things are pure, whatsoever things are lovely, whatsoever things are of good report; if there be any virtue, and if there be any praise, think on these things".[9] I should also keep my eyes on Christ alone, and as long as I kept my eyes fixed on Him, I would not go wrong.

---

[7] Lev. 19:33-34; Deut. 10:19.

[8] 1 Cor. 13:5.

[9] Phil. 4:8.

In this way I was quickly brought back from the brink of pessimism into that optimistic faith that had so far sustained me. With my hope of asylum dashed, a door had been closed before me for the first time since my arrival in this country almost two years earlier. Yet, I was now not only passionately confident that when 'one door closes another opens', but that 'all doors open to the man with trust and a smile'.

Two Open Doors

Two weeks after I had been informed of the negative response from the Home Office, I received a letter from my brother in Morocco informing me that dear grandmother had passed away. It was a piece of news I could have done without under the circumstances. Yet, in the midst of my immense sadness and distress, I was confident that somehow a rift in the clouds would come and the sun would shine again. And that is precisely what happened. Among the friends I had informed of my grandmother's death was Mary Vaughan in Florida, USA. In her reply she graciously told me that she would be greatly honoured if I were to accept her as my spiritual grandmother. I was deeply touched by that request. In my response I heartily agreed addressing her as *"My grandmother in the Lord"*.

A couple of days later I received a letter from my former Principal, Donald Reed, who was then in Boston, Massachusetts. It was his first contact with me since he had left Beirut for the USA in the summer of 1966. The gracious content of that letter was overwhelmingly uplifting. In conclusion he wanted to know how I was settling in Britain and what I was planning to do when I finished at Emmanuel College. In my reply I told him in some detail of my experience in Britain generally and at Emmanuel College in particular. I even let him know that what he had told me once about British food was quite accurate! Nevertheless, I had no choice but to eat it otherwise I would not have lived to tell the tale! Finally, I informed him of my latest situation and requested his prayer that the Lord would guide me aright regarding the future.

The correspondence between us continued for about a month. I had only less than three months stay at College when Principal Reed wrote to tell me that he had secured a scholarship for me at Boston Nazarene Theological Seminary. I would take up my residence in the campus of the Seminary, and during vacations work would be provided to help me financially. He also instructed me to contact the Registrar Office of the Seminary and send a small amount of money (£16) as my registration fee. Finally, he informed me to expect my flight ticket to the USA to reach me in a couple of months. I was simply elated that the good Lord had opened a remarkable door for me.

Whilst still trying to come to terms with this joyful event, I was hardly aware that another door was opening. A friendly relationship was being formed between a lady and me. Miss Shirley Little was, as I knew her, a lady whose faith in the Lord and love for the Muslim people as a missionary were never called in question. She was unfortunately among those Emmanuel missionaries who had been asked by the Moroccan government to leave the country almost immediately after the Six Days War. It was something that she apparently could not get over. However, on returning home, she was assigned to Emmanuel Church in Skelmersdale as a Deaconess.

In a short time our friendly relationship turned into love. Now, for a foreign student in a Holiness Community to be in a love relationship with one of its ex-missionaries might possibly evoke strong disapproval. In that situation I had to watch my steps very carefully. On reflection, however, I dismissed that possibility believing that neither common sense nor spiritual norm could disapprove of a single Christian couple being sincerely in love with each other. Indeed, a little Christian approval and encouragement might be conducive to their future happy married life. In any case, I decided not to worry about this for the time being. I would cross that bridge when I come to it, as they say.

The immediate issue was to come to a decision regarding my future. Before me there were two open doors. On the one hand, there was the open door to the USA where my future would almost certainly be brighter than it had been in Birkenhead, England. Ample provision had been made for me to seize that golden opportunity and experience a bit of the 'American dream'. And with that I would be able to accomplish great things to the glory of God and the benefit of His cause. But on the other hand, there was the door of a sincere love relationship.

In my state of loneliness, disadvantage and vulnerability, being loved was an experience that made me feel I was highly valued. It somehow gave me a sense of triumph. Norman Cousins once wrote, "The eternal quest of the individual human being is to shatter his loneliness." Obviously, my loneliness was now being shattered. The burning question now was: how could I, in all good conscience, leave behind the woman I really loved? Real love is a dangerous and disturbing thing. It awakens a sense of unworthiness, and also creates the obligation of selfless and unwearied commitment.

There was another thing. I had for a while been like a ship sailing in a vast and troubled ocean with no harbour in sight. Then, one day I came upon one where I could find the warmth of love and security. How could I possibly pass it by? True, ever since my conversion I had tried to be as self-reliant as I possibly could. But as Herbert Hoover once put it, "At all times in history there have been many who sought escape into 'security' from self-reliance." And for me as a stranger there was no greater security, and indeed stability, than that which sincere love could offer. Therefore, after much prayer and consideration, I decided to write to Principal Reed and decline the invaluable opportunity he had offered me, on the basis that I could not find it in my heart to leave behind the woman I had so dearly loved.

God had thus put two open doors before me, and I had to choose one of them. It was the door I chose to go through which was to shape my destiny, albeit not without painful failures, bruising battles and deep-seated dilemmas that seemed at the time insurmountable and quite unsolvable.

The Reaction

It was the beginning of the summer of 1968, and some of my fellow students were looking forward to their graduation. I was then 27 years of age. About seven months earlier I had started a study correspondence for three GCE levels – Old Testament, New Testament and Spanish – with Wolsey Hall of Oxford. But due to a chain of unhappy reaction, which was triggered off soon after my engagement, my GCE study was temporarily interrupted.

As the news of our engagement became known, reaction was not long coming, and most of it was utterly negative. It was clear from the faces of some of the College staff that although saying nothing, they were in total disagreement with our engagement. Indeed, with the exception of two godly ladies of blessed memory everyone else was against it. And as memory recalls, the most ardent opponents in that situation were Shirley's family and almost all those in the upper echelons of Emmanuel Mission. But what was the reason for their opposition? At first, I could only think that the reason behind that opposition was 'racial prejudice'. But my judgement was simply wrong. I came to realise much later that the reason for that fierce opposition had more to do with fear than anything else. The opponents were of two kinds: those who were afraid of me, and those who were afraid for me. The undercurrent of opposition was so enormous that it seriously threatened to undermine our engagement.

In the light of this we both thought that marriage might be the solution to a number of problems. It would blunt the sharp edge of the opposition, keep our relationship intact and since both of us were spiritually part of the Emmanuel family, our opponents might eventually rally around us and become more supportive.

Having a complete trust in the goodness of the Christian heart, we naively wrote to inform the Emmanuel Council of our decision to get married. We also petitioned the Council to kindly consider admitting us to the work of Emmanuel Mission, pointing out that in our spiritual native element we were Emmanuelites after all.

On behalf of the Council, Principal Stanley Banks wrote back inviting me to come and meet with the Council members. When that meeting was held, only four or five Council members were present. The Principal was conspicuous by his absence. All along, the meeting did not touch on the issue of our engagement; nevertheless it was there in the background. Instead, it focussed entirely on the petition for future admission into Emmanuel work. It was clear from the atmosphere of the meeting that the idea was far from welcomed.

I vividly recall how intimidated I was by the harangue of two angry looking members of the council who wanted to know just what evidence I had that God wanted me personally in Emmanuel work. My trembling response that I was the fruit of Emmanuel Mission and that Emmanuel was my spiritual home did not seem relevant. But, of all those Council members, there was one from High Wycombe, who never uttered a word, but appeared full of sympathy with me. Whenever I made a nervously brief reply he nodded his head to me slightly and smiled. However, throughout that meeting there were moments when I felt that I was more preached at than questioned. When the meeting ended I felt embarrassed and utterly perplexed. The meeting was not only fruitless, but was also on the whole saturated with the absence of love. Under certain circumstances a Christian may not feel inclined to lend a helping hand to another; but charity must transcend all circumstances and all actions. In the words of Joseph Addison, "Charity is the virtue of the heart and not of the hands."

A few days later a letter arrived from Stanley Banks on behalf of Emmanuel Council. The content was addressed to us both. It briefly stated that the Council had unanimously agreed that we should postpone our marriage for year, and when the year is over our request would be re-considered. We did not know what to think of that statement. Was the Council playing for time in the hope that our planned marriage would eventually come to nothing? This and other questions did cross our minds. One thing however was clear; the Council's statement offered no guarantee whatsoever. In view of that we agreed not to pursue the matter any further. God must have had something else in store for us.

Having experienced such a hard knock, we decided just to grin and bear it. In sport the crowd admire the player who can take a knock and bounce up smiling. In business the people admire the man who can take a failure or a disappointment and come back still smiling and still wanting to go on. Should not Christians also, when disappointed, just take it on the chin and keep smiling? Indeed, that is precisely what we resolved to do. We had even gone further and asked Principal Stanley Banks in writing if he would be kind enough to officiate at their wedding ceremony when the date is fixed. The request was genuinely designed to demonstrate that there were no hard feelings on our part. His unequivocal reply was that he did not feel free in his own spirit to do so. It seemed as though nothing else could be done to alter the current reaction.

Going Up North

The date of our marriage was fixed. It was to take place on the 5th of July the following year (i.e. 1969). With my time at Emmanuel coming to an end, the Lord had providentially prepared another place for me. Through the mediation of my spiritual father, Dr Philip Rigby, Lebanon Missionary Bible College in Berwick-upon-Tweed offered me a one-year residential study to complete my GCE levels. The Principal was none other than Dr David Rigby, the brother of Dr Philip Rigby. As an ex-medical missionary to India and an excellent Biblical scholar, Dr David was a remarkable Christian gentleman.

His unfeigned humility and unique approachability were exemplary. He was particularly noted for his winsome smiles – smiles that were full of radiant love. And without a doubt, smiles are the reflection of kindness, which the deaf can hear and the dumb can understand.

Arriving at that College in the Northern English city of Berwick-upon-Tweed was certainly a new experience. The warmth with which I was welcomed at College on that first day of the first term touched me deeply. The atmosphere was very relaxed and friendly between staff and students. To my great surprise, there was no separation of men and women students in that College, and the rule of 'no talking between male and female students' did not exist.

Until then I had thought that such a rule was characteristic of all Evangelical and Missionary Colleges throughout Britain. Indeed, here male and female students simply mixed with each other, and shared together in Biblical discussions, acts of worship, open air meetings and prayer sessions of all sorts. From the day I arrived, I did not fail to savour almost daily the wonderful atmosphere of that Bible College. It was a place where brotherly love among its students prevailed and where the diligence and dedication of its teachers were both a challenge and an inspiration.

Ever since my conversion, I had never been in doubt that God had called me to His service. But until now I was far from certain as to the kind of work or sphere of service the Lord had marked out for me. With the failure of being admitted to Emmanuel work now behind me, the idea of returning to Beirut, Lebanon, to teach after finishing my education in Britain seemed first as something the Lord might well have chosen for me. But alas some months later the news broadcast indicated that things in that country were not conducive to peace. A few years later the civil war broke out and lasted for 15 years (1975–1990).

As a result I never returned to Lebanon. Obviously, it was not part of God's plan for me. Then I began to toy with the notion of becoming a lecturer one day. Oddly enough, that notion had been sown in my mind as a child. By whom or for what reason I cannot remember. And what could be a better time and place to develop this notion than during my time in Britain, a country, which could offer me the opportunity to realise my dream? I was now happy to conclude that education was precisely the sphere of service God had marked out for me. It would be a wonderful sphere in which I could serve the Lord. In that case I was determined to do my utmost to achieve that goal. The fact that I was doing my GCE levels meant that I was taking my first move forward in the right direction.

It was during my time in Berwick-upon-Tweed that I gradually felt as though God was putting His finger on me, so to speak. It was here where God's plan for my future began to crystallize. All my past notions about that future appeared to have been at best wishful thinking and perhaps at worst illusional. In the Lebanon Missionary College new conditions there were making me acutely aware of what providentially was in the pipeline for me. Life at that College was anything but repressive and its rules were far from draconian. On the contrary life there was relaxed, full of joy and harmony among staff and students.

I still remember with deep gratitude the enormous help and encouragement everybody had given me during my year stay there. But, my deepest appreciation would always be reserved for Dr Rigby, the principal. Coming to be part of this College for a year was wonderful, but it seemed that what I needed most was something to make me do what I could. And for me personally that 'something' was Dr David. He was instrumental in dispelling my last two years of inertia and bringing out the best in me. The thing that brings out the best in most people is encouragement. From the outset, I was made to feel part and parcel of the entire college community with all its activities. Most of all, Dr David made sure I took part in all preaching activities, such as open-air services and pulpit supplies on Sundays etc. . . .

As the weather was not always suitable for the open-air ministry, the pulpit was free from any climatic obstruction. Following my first few preaching engagements, I was soon in demand for pulpit supply by churches in town and its neighbouring areas. The reason for this was that I had, as they put it, a fascinating story to tell. It was the story of my conversion from Islam to Christianity, which both the devout and the nominal Churchgoers were quite keen to hear. Another reason was that my preaching tended to focus upon the ancient Middle Eastern culture of the Bible, which has not changed much. Telling people that the Bible was an eastern book sounded a very new thing to most of them, and even a romantic idea. In my Sunday sermons, the words of the Old Testament prophets, for example, or the words and actions of Jesus and His Apostles in the New Testament were almost always presented and explained against the cultural and civil practices of their Middle Eastern environment.

At first I was not aware that my style of preaching had been exciting and stimulating the interest of people in the Bible. But when it reached me, I was profoundly gratified and had to remember that this was not something I could be proud of. Pride of achievement can easily become self-conceit. Besides, as someone put it, "Pride is the sin of the man who is a moral and an intellectual fool." This was no achievement, it was simply and purely a gift from God. At that moment I was enabled to have a glimpse of what God had in the pipeline for me – He wanted me to be a preacher! At this point I was careful not to mistake my will for God's will.

Did God have to wait all that time, and then bring me all the way up north to give me a glimpse of His will? In point of fact, the purposes of God are sometimes delayed, but never abandoned. As a herdsman and dresser of sycamore trees from the Judean village of Tekoa, Amos was neither a prophet nor an apprentice of a prophet. Yet, his divine vocation was revealed to him only when he made his way to the kingdom of Israel up north.[10]

A Time to Laugh

There is a great deal of sense in the proverb which says, "All work and no play make Jack a dull boy". The Lebanon Missionary College, as I recall it, was by no mean some sort of a spiritual hot house, or a sombre ascetic community of theological students. Theological studies and witness activities were all taken with the utmost diligence and dedication. Yet, life at the college was almost always seasoned with humour and laughter. It was that supremely lovable soul, Haydn, who said: "God will forgive me, if I serve Him cheerfully!"

Unfortunately, there was a time in the history of Scotland when laughter was forbidden in Church, and it was even a heresy to make a congregation smile. But Jesus was not cast into this mould. We can imagine Him teaching with a smile during His earthly days. What a humorous picture he drew when he talked about the man with a plank in his own eye desperately trying to remove the speck of dust from someone else's eye![11] How the disciples must have appreciated it

---

[10] Amos 7:10-15.

[11] Mt. 7:3-5.

when He attached the nickname *"sons of thunder"* to that tempestuous pair, James and John![12] It is quite healthy to laugh. There is a maxim which says, 'We never stop laughing because we are old. We grow old because we stop laughing.'

Both staff and students quite often engaged in raillery, or good-humoured teasing with each other and I was quite happy to join in. Sometimes they teased me about some of my malapropisms, or about the occasion when instead of saying of an elusive guy, "I really want to get to the bottom of him," I said, "I really want to get to his bottom"! After the guffaw had subsided they tried to correct me. But far from admitting I had made a gaffe, I insisted, as my audience were in fits of laughter, that I saw no real difference between "the bottom of him" and "his bottom"! English, I argued, was far less awkward than what they thought.

Yet, with the passing of time I came to realise that to master English was a miracle second only to the crossing of the Red Sea! Of course English, like any other language, is not only words and sentences, in which a spade is called a spade, but a language in which a spade may technically be used to imply something else altogether different. There are idioms which have meanings other than their literal ones, such as *'He is over the moon'* or *'It's raining cats and dogs'* etc. . . .

A fine English family had once invited me, and a number of other people, for dinner. After the meal the guests retired to the lounge for a cup of tea and a chinwag. Soon the conversation between couples and groups became difficult for me to follow. And with my English not half as good as that of a British born person, the various talks and cross talks sounded cacophonous to me. I was beginning to feel uncomfortably out of place. This was compounded by the fact that the lounge was hot, and I longed for a chance to go out for a walk and some fresh air. Then, I overheard a lady say to another next to her, "I need to spend a penny!"

Seeing that the chance had not come quick enough, I turned to her and said, "I'll come with you!" There was a hush as everyone looked at every one else in that lounge. I had no idea what that lady implied apart from simply wanting to pop into the shop around the corner to buy something, and I wanted to go with her as a way of killing the monotony. However, the guests, including the above-mentioned lady, soon recovered and resumed their noisy chats.

---

[12] Mk. 3:17.

Eager to get out of that stifling lounge, I kept trying to catch her eye to signal if she still intended to go out. But the lady would somehow bashfully look away and ignore me. At last a smiling gentleman came and sat beside me, and after a preliminary greeting he asked me who I was, where I came from originally and how long I had been in Britain. It was a brief but pleasant conversation. Then he tactfully referred to a lady in that lounge that needed "to spend a penny".

"Yes", I promptly replied, "and I desperately want to go with her!"

"No, you can't", he responded with a chuckle in his voice, "that lady meant she needed to go to the toilet".

"And what has the toilet to do with a penny?" I asked curiously. The gentleman simply burst into laughter and moved away. Left alone in my quandary, I could not help asking myself, "What in the world would she do with a penny in the toilet!?"

It took me a few weeks to unravel what was to me 'a mysterious phrase'. I happened to be at the central station when I went to the men's public convenience. Inside, I found myself having a tough struggle trying to open one of the doors when the voice of the caretaker rung out, "You've got to drop a penny, sir!" Indeed, the penny dropped immediately, and I cringed with embarrassment as I remembered that incident a few weeks back. However, though I was glad I learned a valuable lesson my only regret was that I learned it in a most inconvenient place!

I also learned in those days that free and persisting inquiry does not always pay off. Miss Margaret Hudson, a former missionary to South America, and her brother were extremely kind to me during my time in Berwick-upon-Tweed. One day, Margaret invited me to speak to her group of elderly ladies who met in St Abbs, a small fishing village in the county of Berwickshire. After the introduction and the Bible reading, the elderly ladies suggested that I should favour them with a solo, which I had never done in my life. They were quite insistent in spite of my repeated excuse that I was more of a gale in the night than a nightingale! In the end I had no choice but to sing them one of my favourites, which begins, "*I cannot breath enough of thee, thou gentle breeze of love . . .*" And God knows I could hardly breathe with nerves as I sang it. To cap it all, the organ was in one key and I was in another. In brief, the singing amounted to a glorious disorder!

After the meeting the good ladies were full of admiration and compliments, which made me suspicious. On the way back to college,

I repeatedly asked Margaret if my singing was all right. She tactfully tried to assure me that my singing was appreciated considering it was the first time. I was not convinced, but persisted in asking the same question, albeit in different ways, over and over again. I only became aware that the subject had reached a tedious stage when Margaret politely said to me, "I would not worry about it if I were you, Samuel. Most of those dear ladies are deaf!"

There are a number of other hilarious incidents I still recall, and to mention them all would be beyond the scope of this chapter. Suffice it to say that a spiritual journey is one where trials abound and where the traveller can only be sustained by his faith. God will not fail to watch over His people. Yet, in the midst of this journey, God does not forget to refresh His people with moments of pleasure, joy, and laughter.

Chapter 15

LEARNING FROM UNLIKELY EVENTS

"Experience is not what happens to a man;
it is what a man does with what happens to him."

(T.H. Huxley)

When God's plan for one's life is crystallized, the tendency is that one can often be carried to one extreme or another. Some get beside themselves, or rush about trying either to force God's hand or push ahead of His time. In the end they run the risk of over-reaching themselves. Others may try to work God's plan out into their own already made agenda, or perhaps try to hold on to them both separately. In other words, they wish to have it both ways. It is easy to fall into this particular category, and that is exactly where I was, although I was not aware of it. God had indeed put his finger on me and His plan for my future was crystallized. This was attested by the sudden realisation of my gift of preaching, more often without notes. But for me this did not mean that God was calling me to the ministry. Such an idea was too impossible to even cross my mind, and had it crossed my mind I might have taken it more as a nightmare than as a vision!

The expulsion from my Moroccan college because of my conversion to Christianity years earlier had left me with an aching void – a void, which I was forever trying to fill. My greatest desire was to pursue an academic career through which I could one day serve the Lord.

When God's plan for my life was crystallized through my gift of preaching, I took it on board merely as another separate item that could be useful in God's service. In that case, I would be happy to enjoy the best of both worlds. I was hardly aware at the time that the plan, which God had crystallized, had a far-reaching implication for my life. To that end the road before me was to be full of undreamed of events, some of them intricate, others simply dark and painful. But, all along the way I was quietly confident that if God had made my programme, He would undoubtedly carry it out. I was often fortified by the words of Martin Luther, who once wrote, "I know not the way God leads me, but well do I know my Guide."

Unfamiliar Path

Spring had begun and the students were getting ready for the Easter break. I was looking forward to spending the Easter break in Skelmersdale where Shirley worked. On both occasions I stayed with a fine middle age Christian couple that were great friends of her. Shortly before leaving for the break, Dr David Rigby tactfully asked me during a brief conversation what plans, if any, both Shirley and I had made for our married life in terms of housing and employment. It was a difficult question for me to answer. As a matter of fact, we were both in a precarious position at the time. On the one hand, I was in the country only as a student and until the restriction had been legally lifted I could not be employed. On the other hand, as a Church assistant in Skelmersdale, Shirley had no stipend whatsoever.

In my answer I tried to play down the difficulties facing us. Strangely enough, Dr Rigby seemed aware of the situation even before he asked me. He then brought to my notice something that was very interesting. He told me that according to the British law, following my marriage to my British born wife, the restriction would immediately be lifted. That came to me as a joyful surprise. Until then I had honestly never known that this law existed. There was another piece of news he wanted me to hear. He told me that Dr George Frame, the District Superintendent of the Church of the Nazarene, was coming to address the students on the first week after the Easter break, and that he had arranged for me and him to meet afterwards.

The last sentence surprised me for a moment. "To meet afterwards?" I asked with a forced smile. "Yes," replied Dr Rigby, "I want you to know that after much prayer and consideration, I felt led to speak to my friend, Dr Frame, about you as an ex-Nazarene Bible student. He is quite keen to meet you."

I quickly suspected that something was cooking, and from my curious look, Dr Rigby gathered that I was eager to know a bit more. "It's just like this, Samuel," he continued in a low voice, "in a few months you and Shirley are getting married, but have no job or home to go to. Having spoken to Dr Frame, he seemed keen to help in this matter. The Church of the Nazarene in Scotland has a few small churches without pastors. Should the Lord lead Dr Frame to put you in one of them, you will have a roof over your head and a weekly income however small it is. In this way you will be tidied up until God decides what to do with you next."

What I had just heard gave me a very mixed feeling. Was my life beginning to take a different direction? Was this a sign that my cherished dream of becoming a lecturer one day might not be realised after all? Was I really suitable as a foreigner to take a pastoral care of a British congregation however small? These and many other thoughts so overwhelmed me that I felt like a kid having a stage fright on facing an audience for the first time. On the other hand, could I not see the Lord in all this? Was I not now behaving like the disciples, who instead of realising the Lord walking on troubled waters could only see a terrifying ghost?[1] If I thought I was being thrown into the deep end, could I not see that God's provision would certainly be there to cushion my future wife and me?

Meeting Dr Frame a week later, I was impressed by his personality. He had a touch of autocracy about him, but underneath he was humane and very kind-hearted. From the outset, his determination to help was obvious. After listening to a brief account of my conversion, he asked how I got on with my theological studies in Beirut and in Birkenhead. He also wanted to know the date of my wedding day, and wondered if my fiancée and I could arrange to meet him before then in Glasgow.

The date was fixed to coincide with the Church of The Nazarene General Assembly at Parkhead, Glasgow. When that meeting took place as planned, the Revd Sydney Martin and another pastor from Ulster were present. Both Shirley and I were asked a few simple theological and spiritual questions. Afterwards Dr Frame informed us that we were to be assigned to a very small congregation in a small former mining village in East Dunbartonshire called 'Twechar'. The manse was described to us as small but adjacent to the church and quite comfortable. We were also informed of the meagre weekly salary that the tiny congregation could afford. Finally, a date was fixed for what Dr Frame called 'a service of *introduction* rather than *ordination*' which came as a sort of relief to me personally. Deep in my own heart I had always nursed the idea that a lifetime ministry was not for me.

---

[1] Mk. 6:47-50.

For this reason I never bothered to find out why it was a service of *introduction* and not *ordination*.

In time however I learned that some weeks before this meeting took place, Dr Frame had written to Principal Donald Reed in the USA and Revd Stanley Banks in Birkenhead seeking their recommendations. The former, like Dr David Rigby, was positively in favour. But in his reply, Stanley Banks stated quite clearly that whilst my life and conduct at college were above reproach, he was not prepared to recommend me for any pastoral or ecclesiastical work. Thus, Dr Frame appeared to have acted on the basis of two to one in favour. Hence I found myself set on an unfamiliar path.

The Wedding and After

Our wedding took place at Skelmersdale Emmanuel Church on the 5th of July 1969 and was conducted by a fine Methodist minister. Among the good number of friends present were my spiritual father, Dr Philip Rigby and his wife Dina, and also Aunty Lily Randle of blessed memory. Grandmother Vaughan was also there all the way from the USA. But sadly, no member of Emmanuel staff or council was present and no wedding card arrived from any of them. This was noted in silence and soon forgotten. My attention was rather focused on the joy of the occasion, and to some extent on the prospect of the post that awaited us a month hence. But I tried not to dwell too long on this particular matter, for much of it belonged to the unknown, and peering into the unknown longer than necessary could easily spoil the enjoyment of that unique day.

After a short honeymoon, we spent a couple of weeks in Chester with Shirley's aunt before heading for Twechar in Scotland. Shirley's aunt, Brenda, and her husband were warm and kindly disposed towards me personally, but the rest of the family were not. Sadly, they never changed in spite of serious efforts on my part to earn their love and goodwill. In time however this unfortunate attitude was to play a lamentable part in our married life. Meanwhile, I thought I had better look the other way. After all I would not be around them for long. They might soon be relieved when I was far away and out of sight, and hopefully when I was out of sight I would also be out of mind.

We arrived in Twechar in the summer of 1969 to begin work in the Church of the Nazarene. Its very small but devout congregation could not be kinder and more supportive towards us despite its financial circumstances. On our part we counted it a joy to serve such a good and godly congregation realising after all that *"man shall not live by bread alone"*.[2] We were grateful that as a newly married couple we had a home to live in. In hindsight, Twechar was a training ground for me personally in so far as preaching and teaching were concerned. But at the time, I was hoping that this post would be a temporary stepping-stone to something completely different. I was fairly convinced that I was not cut out to be a clergyman. Now, due to our meagre salary we often had to exercise austerity. But an austere life can be quite bearable when peace and happiness rule supreme. For one thing peace rules the day when Christ rules the mind, and that is where happiness lies. "Happiness," as Spurgeon put it, "consists in being happy with what we have got and with what we haven't."

Settling to a married life is not easy. For some it can be heaven on earth, and these may be rare among mortals. For others it is the beginning of a life that soon after the honeymoon turns into a most powerful engine of domestic tyranny, sometimes a lifelong tyranny! But there are others who through time learn to negotiate their way through many difficulties until they finally blend together. There is a sense in which all marriages are wonderful; it is living together afterwards that is tough!

No Lasting Joy

On the 13th of April 1970 Ruth was born. The gift of our beautiful first-born baby daughter brought us immense joy, and also did much to dispel the tension that had been developing between us. We named her Ruth, hoping that like Ruth of the Bible, she would grow up to be a lady of faith, dedication and godly endeavour in her life. In my own heart I decided on that occasion to do all I could to follow the dictum, which says, "Raise your daughter to know the Lord and she will have a built in chaperone."

A year later, Jonathan was born. His birth on the 10th of July 1971 was no less thrilling to us than that of his sister Ruth. The gift of these two lovely children had a particular significance for me personally. In 1966 I had arrived in this country alone as a total stranger. Five years later I had a home and a family of my own, not to mention the

---

[2] Mt. 4:4.

wider circle of my spiritual family in various parts of the country. For me, this was a plain fulfilment of Christ's promise that His followers will be more than compensated for the loss of home, family ties and possessions, and even for the persecutions that their new faith so often entailed.[3] Indeed, in the words of Samuel Rutherford, "They lose nothing who gain Christ." Yet, I never imagined that a few years later I would suffer a catastrophic loss. It is a kind of loss that leaves a scar upon one's soul for life.

In our human experience there is no such thing as an absolute joy. No doubt, as Christians we can be sure that in Christ we have *"joy unspeakable and full of glory"*.[4] But such a state is never meant to be a sealed area into which no grief or adversity can intrude. Indeed, in spite of our standing in Christ, we can still be vulnerable, and some can be more vulnerable than others. During this time the signs were that harmony in our marriage was evaporating pretty fast and an increasing level of mutual disagreement and verbal clashes were becoming almost a daily occurrence. Also, living in an isolated village with a very small income and no means of transportation perhaps did not help the situation.

In 1972 we moved to Glasgow where I acted as a preacher to a Baptist congregation, but not as an accredited minister. The change however made no difference to our domestic trouble and strife, which continued unabated. Strangely, even the joy of obtaining my British citizenship on the 11th of April the following year was entirely overshadowed by the current atmosphere. At this point one must confess that the very painful memory of that particular period forbids further detail. Suffice it to say that our five years together ended up in divorce, which took place on the grounds of an irretrievable breakdown in marriage. Admittedly, this was a situation in which we were both guilty and both innocent. We were guilty in that we miserably failed to solve our domestic conflict. But we were also innocent in that certain forces were at work behind the scene. As a matter of fact, some strong members of Shirley's family had a hand in it.

It took five years for this lonely stranger to be blessed with a home, a wife and a family, and precisely another five years to revert to square one. As a result, there were many tough questions to wrestle with. Life suddenly became very bewildering and full of pain during that

---

[3] See Mk.10:29-30; cf. e.g. Acts 2:44; 4:34; Phm.10.

[4] 1 Pet. 1:8.

time. What happened seemed to defy understanding, and seemed to have no explanation. Anyone in such a situation is bound to feel that his world was falling apart around him. That was my personal feeling. I was not sure if what happened was part of God's will. If it was, then I must have no choice but to accept it. After all, I knew in my heart of hearts that the name of the God whose will I must accept was 'Father'. And in spite of all my human failings, shortcomings and vulnerabilities, my 'Father' would not let me disappear into the abyss. With this thought a flicker of hope still remained alive underneath.

An Angelic Intervention

When a terrible calamity occurs in one's domestic life, it is easy to lose heart. In my case, I had lost heart and decided to relinquish my preaching post, which I did straightaway. I was however allowed to stay in the house until I found another accommodation. The house was empty of everything except a bed, a pan, a plate, a fork and a knife. The deathly silence of the place would often bring back the vivid memory of little Ruth and Jonathan quietly playing or noisily chasing each other. Even going upstairs, the third stair would be a living reminder that until a month ago the two little kids would take turns to jump from it and I would catch them. I could almost hear them screaming with laughter. For me, life in that house was fast becoming as dark and as black as mid-night. On that summer day of 1974, I made a snap decision to leave the house in four days. I planned to put my suitcase with some of my belongings into my old Anglia car and just drive south, north or wherever the mood takes me. I was simply eager to leave come what may.

I had just finished making my decision when the telephone rang. When I picked it up the caller, who seemed to know me, said something that did not at first register with me. My mind was fully absorbed in my tragedy. I assumed someone was phoning to book me for a preaching engagement. I interrupted the caller and politely told him that I had stopped taking any preaching engagements. I was about to put the phone down when he said, "Sam, this is Stewart Frizzell. I'm just phoning to see if I can come and see you as soon as possible."

It was a joyful surprise to hear Stewart's voice. We had been friends some years back and due to circumstances we lost contact. I asked him when he wanted to come. He suggested that he would like to do so that very morning if possible. I agreed, and looked forward to seeing him. As I put the phone down I wondered why he wanted to see me so urgently. Apparently, the joyful surprise of finding a long lost friend made me forget to ask him, at least diplomatically, why he was so eager to see me. Then I began to suspect if he had got wind of my domestic misfortune and was now coming to see me out of curiosity or to commiserate with me.

About an hour later Stewart arrived. I greeted him with a mixed sense of warmth and concealed suspicion. The house was noticeably empty almost of everything, which Stewart either noticed or pretended not to notice. In any case, I was careful not to ask him about his family in case he would ask me about mine. Instead, I asked how his Parish Church was doing.

After our very brief conversation he said, "Sam, I've got a piece of good news for you." "And what's that"? I asked. "The Divinity Department of Glasgow University has a shortage of applicants this year," he told me, "and I strongly urge you to apply as soon as possible." Being in a state where I had already lost heart, my lack of enthusiasm did not escape him. But he refused to give up. "I beg of you, Sam," he pleaded, "don't miss this golden opportunity. If you want me to fix you an appointment with Professor Alan Galloway, the Principal of the Divinity Department, I'll be happy to do so."

Stewart's desperate effort not to let me throw this excellent opportunity to the wind seemed extraordinary to me at the time. Looking back, he seemed like one who was desperately trying to save a drowning man out of a very troubled sea. I finally gave in and kindly asked him to arrange for me to see the Principal, which he did that very day. The meeting was scheduled for the following morning.

Next day in the morning I met Professor Galloway at his office. The University then was on its summer vacation and its active life was at a low key. This perhaps helped to make our meeting reasonably longer and more relaxed. Having introduced myself, I expressed my sincere desire to do a Bachelor of Divinity course as a full time student at the University. He asked if I had any educational qualifications. I mentioned the theological Diploma I had obtained from the American theological school of Beirut after three years study. I also referred to the GCE level studies which I did in this country, and which I sadly failed to finish due to some difficult circumstances. There was a time, I pointed out, when I had just a little over a year to go to obtain a

BA from my Moroccan seminary, but was unfortunately dismissed because of my conversion to Christianity.

As a former University lecturer in Nigeria where he apparently rubbed shoulders with many Muslims, the Principal was visibly surprised that I was a convert from Islam. He then asked me to tell him briefly what attracted me to Christianity for which I lost my education and perhaps much more. After doing so, we talked a little more about the theological differences between Christianity and Islam. In the end he seemed to have been pretty impressed by his interviewee, and was subsequently pleased to do all he could to help me. Meanwhile, he asked me to accompany him to the Dean's office. On arrival he introduced me to Professor W.H.C. Frend who was the Dean of the Divinity Faculty that year. During our short meeting, Professor Frend also seemed quite keen to help in any way he could.

Returning to the Principal's office, he informed me that as a mature student intending to do a BD course, I must agree to do one-year preparatory course in the Art Faculty. During that year I would be expected to study and pass two subjects of my own choice. After that I would enter the Divinity Faculty to begin a three-year study for a Bachelor of Divinity Degree. If I agreed to that and received a written acceptance from the Faculty, then I could apply for a government grant on the basis of that written document. I told Professor Galloway that I wholeheartedly agreed, and thereupon I signed a paper that was to go before the Faculty in a couple of days. I left the Principal's office feeling as if the hand of providence that morning had reached out and caught me half way down the abyss. I really felt I was walking on air with joy.

When I met Stewart afterward for lunch as planned, I gave him the exciting news. He was gratified that I was now on the right course. We simply could not believe how things worked out so well and so quickly. However, in the course of our conversation, I asked him if he knew of a small accommodation where I could lodge because the house where I was now must be vacated in a few days. Stewart asked no question about my wife and family. Rather he told me with a sympathetic smile that he would make some enquiries and let me know next day.

I could not but conclude that Stewart was fully aware of my situation. He simply preferred to ignore it so completely as if he knew nothing about it, and he did an excellent job of it. True to his word, the following day Stewart came to inform me that a bed sitting room was available for me at 10 Park Grove terrace, Glasgow, at the price of £3.50 per week. The house, which had similar rooms to let to students, belonged to a lady who was a member of his Church. The following day I moved in. My new lodging was within a walking distant from the University.

The amazing way in which things fell into place so quickly was nothing short of a miracle. Indeed, after so many years, that particular divine intervention has remained indelibly stamped on my mind, and so has the angelic intervention of Stewart Frizzell.

Gratefully Restored

It was obvious from what followed that the work, which God had recently begun, would proceed somewhat rapidly to a successful end. A few days later, I received a letter from the Divinity Faculty accepting me as a student. Shortly thereafter I presented this letter together with my application for a government grant to an office in Edinburgh and was accepted within a week. The grant covered my tuition, my upkeep and my children's maintenance for the next four years of study.

The amazing way in which God's timely care and intervention occurred has since served to reinforce my faith whenever an adversity reared its ugly head. For me, the words of St Peter were true to my experience: *"In His kindness God called you to His eternal glory by means of Jesus Christ. After you have suffered a little while, He will restore, support, and strengthen you, and He will place you on a firm foundation."*[5]

In all this there were lessons to be learned. Before the miracle happened, the situation had been one of chaos and utter darkness. And in that situation however strong one's faith and hope may be, the ravages of doubts and uncertainties would inevitably come rushing in like armed men. Having gone through that experience, I learned never to denounce honest doubts or run away from them. It was Tennyson who once said that there was "more faith in honest doubt . . . than in half the creeds".[6]

---

[5] 1 Pet. 5:10 NLT.

[6] A. Tennyson, *In Memoriam.*

I also came to realize that it is not doubts that I should be ashamed of. What I should really be ashamed of is the failure to face my doubts. There is a sense in which nothing is reliable until it is tested, and neither is our faith. For many of us, Thomas, the disciple, has come to be known as 'doubting Thomas', but he was not really any more doubting than his fellow-disciples.[7] Perhaps he was more honestly vocal with his doubts than them. He was faced with a critical and unexpected dilemma, and it must have been his flicker of faith and hope that perhaps kept him within the circle of his fellow-disciples. Moreover, Thomas might have been slower than his fellow-disciples to believe in the resurrection of Christ. But when he did so, his faith was expressed in language that went beyond any that they had used: *"My Lord and my God!"*[8]

Critical and unexpected dilemmas do occur in many of our lives, and as a result floods of doubt and inner struggle can be overwhelming. Yet, at a moment that we least expect, the hand of providence can reach out and transform our dark and murky situation into a bright and glorious one. It happened to me. It was an unforgettable event. There is nothing like learning from unlikely events.

---

[7] Lk. 24:11.

[8] Jn. 20:28.

Chapter 16

TOWARDS NEW HORIZONS

"I lift up my eyes to the hills.
From whence does my help come?
My help comes from the Lord,
who made heaven and earth."

(Psalm 121:1-2)

Change is hardly ever an easy process. In the words of a 16th century English theologian, "Change is not made without inconvenience, even from worse to better."[1] I must have been an exception. The speed with which I was shocked out of a worse situation into a better one seemed to cause me no inconvenience whatsoever.

This joyful event might have largely been overshadowed by the sad and lingering memory of the recent dissolution of my home and family. The impact of that incident would frequently evoke some vexing questions. What if Stewart had never phoned that day? Knowing the state I was in, what if I had simply refused to pick up the phone when it rung that morning? What if I had been out when he phoned? Where would I have been by now had any of these things happened? And what would have become of me? These and other questions would so bombard my mind that a combination of depression and grief would grip me for a time. Then I soon realized that I was becoming a victim of my recent painful past. It was as though there was no post-crisis period. That was a form of ingratitude to God who had just pulled me back from the precipice.

The lesson for me was clear. As a Christian I should, by God's help, have the ability to learn to pass through the hard and painful experiences of life and not remain stuck in them. One of the tragedies in life is a life that is forever lingering in the past. There are people who are so gripped by the memory of past disappointments, past failures, past griefs or sorrows that they subsequently become

[1] Richard Hooker (c. 1554 – 1600). See *English Dictionary* (Johnson), Preface.

resentful and bitter throughout their lives. I certainly did not want to go down that road.

I happened to be reading Paul's letter to the Philippians when his words hit me, *"Forgetting the things which are behind,"* he wrote, *"and reaching forth unto those things which are before."*[2] From then on I learned not to let my mind linger on any past failure. I also decided not to trust states of mind that would allow the past to overshadow or eclipse the present blessing however small it may be. Even when I remember a serious past blunder, I should reflect no longer than is necessary to know and to repent it. It was time to rise, open my eyes wider and look towards distant horizons.

Dream and Reality

Now that the Divinity Faculty of Glasgow University had accepted me as a student, I was pretty sure the stage for a future academic career was being set. That was exactly what I had always dreamed of. I was somehow upbeat that my dream would more likely be realized within a decade at most. Time would show that this was not an initial step towards the realization of my dream. In fact, as I toyed with that dream I was oblivious to the reality which God had wanted me to see, and which oddly enough had been near at hand. In this respect I was no different from many others. We live in a world where the far-away has frequently made people forget the near at hand. But, little did I know that the Lord I belonged to was not going to allow His purpose for my life to be thwarted.

Unaware of my far-away dream, Professor Galloway, Stewart Frizzell and a few other friends were urging me at this particular stage to consider ministry in the Church of Scotland. With some reluctance I did respond positively to the idea, with the thought that a future academic career could not possibly conflict with an ordained ministry. Shortly thereafter my application for the ministry was accepted on the understanding that I should complete my university study and obtain my Bachelor of Divinity Degree.

The comparative ease with which my acceptance into the ministry took place is still a matter of astonishment and surprise to me today. Initially, I had been somehow doubtful if I would be accepted as a candidate for the ministry in the national Church. Being of a different

[2] Phil. 3:13.

origin, cultural and religious background, not to mention my recent marriage break down, I thought the prospect of success was slim.

Oddly, the possibility of being turned down did not concern me much. As long as my dream of a future academic career remained alive I was happy to pursue it patiently. Dreams are wonderful while they last, but with the light of day those dreams evaporate and one is faced with reality at hand. I had my own dream and I revelled in it. Then almost unexpectedly something undreamed of happened. God in His unfathomable way put His finger on me and called me to an already reserved place for me in the holy ministry. The reality of that divine action could best be described as a clear realisation of His purpose instead of a realisation of my own dream.

It is not a bad thing to have our dreams provided we are awake when we dream. In spite of that we cannot dream ourselves into what we could be. To some extent dreaming has its values, but never should it become a substitute for work that needs to be done. And God had a real work for me to do. There is a clear difference between a dream and a reality. In the words of C.S. Lewis, "Nothing which is at all times and in every way agreeable to us can have objective reality. It is of the very nature of the real that it should have sharp corners and rough edges, that it should be resistant, and should be itself. Dream furniture is the only kind on which you never stub your toes or bang your knees."

Newfound Friends

Weeks before the University started I looked for a job to supplement my grant. In this way I could adequately support myself and pay my children's maintenance. My first choice was to be a bus conductor. I soon discovered that life in the buses was a little too rough for me. I must confess that in my short time there I learnt a number of things I had never known before. Among them was a wealth of unrepeatable and unprintable adjectives with which most of my driving colleagues punctuated their talks! Yet, with all their honest vulgarity, those Glaswegians were the kindest, the friendliest and the most generous crowd one could ever wish to meet.

Looking for another type of work required a bit of time and patience. Walking alone most of the day in the streets of Glasgow and returning to a cold and lonely Victorian bed-sitter was a difficult routine to cope with. This particular situation made me realise just how painfully sharp the edge of loneliness can be. It can have its impact in the silence of one's abode or even in the company of friends and neighbours. One can certainly be lonely in a crowd.

Parked at the door was my old Anglia car. It was so old one would think it was dropped out of Noah's Ark! I had seldom used it because I preferred walking for exercise, and in a way that helped me save on petrol. After all, I had to be careful with my pennies. But, one day I decided to jump into the car and go for a run somewhere. As I drove for a few miles I found myself in north Kelvinside area of Glasgow. A short distance on the right, a Baptist Church caught my eyes, and out of curiosity I went near to read its notice board. It contained the times of the weekly church services, and underneath the name of the church secretary, Mr Alexander Kirkwood. I had the feeling that the congregation met for worship in the church hall instead of the sanctuary. That was exactly what I discovered when I visited the church the following Sunday morning for the first time.

To my great surprise I found that though the congregation hardly amounted to a dozen, the sincerity of their love and the warmth of their welcome surpassed anything I had seen elsewhere. Mr Kirkwood, his wife and their daughter Betty were simply models of godliness, gentleness and good-heartedness. When the service (taken by a visiting speaker) was over they were the first to come and greet me warmly. We engaged in a pleasant conversation over a cup of tea, and in no time we got to know each other.

Before I left they cheerfully told me how pleased they were to have my acquaintance, and I replied that the feeling was mutual. They also reminded me that there was a Bible study and prayer fellowship on Wednesday, and that if I were free I would be most welcome. I nodded in agreement and left.

On Wednesday I was sitting in that church hall among only five or six worshippers. It was a warm fellowship. Instead of joining with them in Bible study I was asked to share with them my conversion experience, which I gladly did. My testimony that evening seemed to have deeply touched those present and particularly the Kirkwood family. Before leaving, they wondered if I could come home with them for lunch next Sunday. That came as a joyful surprise to me, and I readily accepted. The happy prospect of making new friends after all the afore-mentioned losses was a completely new surprise to me. Little did I know also that this friendship were to bring with it some other more remarkable surprises.

During my visit for lunch, the Kirkwoods' kind hospitality was so overwhelming that I felt I was being thoroughly wrapped around in their Christian love and affection. At first, I wondered if they had been aware of my recent domestic misfortune. I came to know much later that they had. Possibly, their treatment of me might have been one of trying to show me sympathy and understanding. It might have been a way of trying to nurse me back to comfort and ease and make me feel completely at home with them regardless of the past. Whatever their motive might have been, I felt completely at peace among them. A number of things occurred on that occasion which came as a very joyful surprise to me.

Mr Kirkwood asked if I would be willing to conduct morning services at the church for the entire period of my university study. My acceptance, he added, would save him the wearisome task of having to arrange for pulpit supply every week. I replied that I had no objection. In our conversation a little earlier, I had spoken of my desperate need of finding a job before the university starts. Betty then mentioned that she would talk to a friend who had a high position at the RHM (Rank, Hoovers & MacDougall) bakery in Glasgow and would ask if he could find me a job there. I was delighted when three days later a job was secured for me in that bakery. I was fortified and indeed amazed by the fact that such joyful surprises came quickly one after another. Most of all, it was obvious that the Good Lord was indeed undertaking me at every step of the way.

In the evening I accompanied the family to church for the evening service. And as there was no visiting speaker, I was courteously asked if I could conduct the worship that evening. I agreed if someone could choose a few hymns. Happily, Betty who was the official organist had a number of hymns ready to hand. At the end of the service the Kirkwoods handed me an honorarium, for which I thanked them heartily.

I also thanked them for the wonderful day I spent with them, which was a unique change from my virtual sphere of loneliness. Their response was deeply moving. From now on, they told me, I should consider myself as a member of their family. Therefore, I should not feel lonely any more. Their home was always open to me, and they saw no reason why I should not consider spending the weekends with them.

As I drove home that evening I felt that such new surprises were indeed God-sent. On that particular day, I felt that as a lonely man the Lord had come closer to me in the person of that godly family. But little did I know that the good Lord had yet some more new surprises in store for me.

Hard But Enjoyable

As long as one knows that a task assigned to him is part of God's will, then a sense of ease and contentment would be unmistakable however hard that task might be. As a divinity student, I had a load of things to do. I was studying as hard as I possibly could, quite often to the early hours of the morning. I was a bakery worker during almost every university vacation and also an acting preacher for almost every Sunday of the year. My position was far from easy. But at the same time, I was confident that that was precisely the position God had placed me in, and I was content. I even derived some encouragement from the verse in Lamentation, which says, *"It is good for a man that he bears the yoke in his youth."*[3] Yet, with the Lord's help, that yoke became gradually easy and its burden light.[4]

A month before the university started, I was working at the RHM bakery. All kinds of people worked in that company, and it was not long before I came to know most of them. Some were extremely humorous, others were quite free with their unrepeatable nouns and adjectives, but all of them were rough diamonds. When they got wind of the fact that I was studying to be a clergyman, almost every profane word uttered in my presence was promptly covered with "Sorry, minister!"

Meanwhile, the Managing Director of this huge bakery, Mr Baird, was an interesting figure. He was a serious looking no-nonsense gentleman. Both staff and ordinary workers had a healthy respect for him. Interestingly, I learned from some reliable sources that he was a Church elder. I also heard it through the grapevine that he knew I was a divinity student training for the ministry. If I happened to pass by him I would say good morning or good afternoon, and he would return the salutation with a kind smile. When my four weeks work finished and I was leaving to begin my studies, I called on him at his office and thanked him for giving me the opportunity to work

---

[3] Lam. 3:27.

[4] See Matt. 11:29-30.

at the bakery. He appreciated my kind words and told me that work at the bakery would always be available for me during my university vacations. He was true to his word. For the entire four years of my University studies, my employment at that bakery was guaranteed at every vacation. Curiously, during all that time, whilst knowing I was a divinity student, he never so much as hinted that he was a Church elder; and I never ventured to ask him.

On the first day of the first term at the University there was a special meeting of all new divinity students with Professor Robert Davidson and Professor Murdo Ewan MacDonald and a few other lecturers. A couple of brief speeches were followed by a question and answer session.

What was said and discussed at that meeting was an eye-opener and a foretaste of what awaited us as students. Personally, I left that meeting with a good deal of things to think about. We were certainly left in no doubt that 'at the University one is not taught what to think, but how to think'. That was precisely what I discovered throughout my four years of studies at the Divinity Department.

I also discovered that my passion and diligence in my studies lacked a very important ingredient. I realised this at my first term examination on the subject of Ancient Near East History under Professor John MacDonald. A dictum has it that 'a little knowledge is a dangerous thing'. I am convinced that the same could be said of 'too much knowledge'! Having studied the subject thoroughly, I entered the examination room that day feeling highly over-confident. Out of eight questions, a student could only answer four, and the time limit was two hours. Because of my grasp of the subject, I was carried away with giving long and detailed answers in my examination papers. However, I was about to address the third question when the two hours ran out! The shock was unbelievable.

Two days later, Professor MacDonald called me to his office for a little chat. He told me that I obviously took my lectures in Ancient Near East History with serious interest. And it was evident from my exam papers that I had a good grasp of the lessons regarding the subject. But, unfortunately, I failed to address the four questions. He pointed out that what happened was not a failure in my knowledge of the subject, but a failure in my discipline. He then reminded me that whilst there was some merit in what I had written, I will do well to remember that a study life at a University does not only consist in gaining knowledge, but also in practising discipline. In response I briefly expressed my sincere appreciation for his advice acknowledging that discipline is a vital ingredient I should add to all my studies. I wholeheartedly confess that Professor MacDonald's advice that day stood me in good stead throughout my four years at the University. In such a place, it is all very well to be intelligent, but it is far better and indeed safer to be alert, disciplined and in first-class fighting trim.

On a different front, I was conducting Sunday morning services week by week faithfully and diligently at the small Church. This helped me to take a break from my hard going studies and be in a place where I could be spiritually refreshed and renewed. There is also a sense in which this was an exercise whereby I was being equipped and fortified for the life-long ministry that lay ahead. For one who was completely foreign to all these things, the going was really hard, but at the same time quite enjoyable.

A Happy Family Life

It is not unusual for one to enjoy his work regardless of the hardship involved. The reason may be because he regards this type of work as an irresistible challenge, or because he finds it more lucrative and rewarding. There are other possible reasons why one can enjoy a particular task even if it is beset with difficulties. In my case, I was coping with the above-mentioned tasks with a deep sense of gratitude and enjoyment, being constantly amazed how the good Lord suddenly blessed me with a series of open doors. To crown it all, I was blessed by being lovingly adopted into the Kirkwood family after I had been alone *"like a pelican of the wilderness* (or) *like an owl of the waste places"*.[5] Their remarkable act of kindness and love has remained with me, and will remain with me for life. God alone knows how much I loved and cherished the loveliness of that happy home life, which I had not known since my arrival in this great country. Moreover, this delightful home had yet another great surprise in store for me in not too distant future.

With such God-given series of open doors culminating in becoming part of a good and godly family, my joy was beyond description. As a matter of fact, these were the motivating factors that made me enjoy my current tasks in spite of the hardships involved.

---

[5] Psalm 102:6 (NASV).

Such hardships simply dwarfed in the light of what Divine providence had recently bestowed upon me.

Apart from my bed sitting room where I lodged and studied, the Kirkwoods' home had an ever-open door for me. In fact, they never ceased to remind me that as a new member of their family, their home was my home. One day they kindly suggested that I should spend the weekends with them at home. It was unhealthy being on my own week after week with no company. Consequently, I did agree to join them at home for some weekends, and later on I stayed with them quite often during my university vacations.

This was one of the happiest periods of my life. It was the period in which I came to realise, among other things, the real difference between a 'house' and a 'home'. Anyone can have a house. Indeed, anyone with plenty of money is able to acquire the best house that an architect can design. Yet, that house may not necessarily be a *home*. A *home* is where love, joy, peace, unity, togetherness and understanding combine to create a heaven-like atmosphere. It is true to say that a house is built by human hands but a *home* is built by human hearts.

A story is told of a cute little girl who was sitting on a pile of luggage in a hotel lobby. Her parents were at the desk registering for their room. A sympathetic lady asked the little girl if they were visiting relatives in the city. "Oh no," the girl replied. "We're going to live at this hotel until we find a house. My Daddy has a new job and we had to sell our house and move." The lady said, "Oh, it's too bad you don't have a home." To which the girl replied, "Oh we have a *home* – it's just that we don't have a house to put it in."

There was no greater joy for me than to know and experience at first hand and for the first time in this country the beauty of a happy home life. It was very clear to me that a happy *home* life could only have its true realisation in a happy *family* life.

A Very Huge Surprise

To be part of the Kirkwood's family was not only a privilege, but also a unique blessing. Alex and Annie Kirkwood were as much paragons of godliness as they were outstanding parents to their two sons and two daughters. With the exception of Betty who was single and always lived with them, the others had all been married and living elsewhere. I was often touched when the godly old couple remarked that the good Lord had blessed them with five kids – I was the fifth!

Now that I was the fifth kid in the family, I often affectionately called Betty 'my big sister'! The nickname did not bother her, probably because she was aware that I was younger than her. In fact, I was twelve years her junior. Betty's entire life revolved around her job as personnel officer for the disabled and her care for her elderly parents.

With me coming on the scene, life for her seemed to take a new turn. It was obvious that I was not only a new brother to her, but also a new friend with whom she had a lot in common. We shared many interesting subjects. We could, for example, discuss matters relating to current political or social events; and there were times when we agreed with each other and times when we agreed to disagree. On the whole, harmony, fellow feeling and good humour prevailed between the two of us. On her part, my big sister simply could not do enough for me. She washed and ironed my clothes, and she also typed for me. Her typing skill was a tremendous asset in presenting my academic assignments in a clear and orderly fashion and on time. Many who have gone through university would hardly deny or underestimate the academic pressures they often had to endure, and some of those pressures could be beyond endurance. Under such circumstances some students simply lose heart and call it a day.

As far I was concerned there was no question of giving up due to academic pressures. My only problem was my struggle with the type of academic biblical perspectives that were being taught. Contrary to the only orthodox evangelical method I knew, I was confronted with modern approaches to biblical studies. The Bible was being studied through the method of literary criticism, form criticism and redaction criticism.

At first, this plunged me into an academic and spiritual whirlwind. It took a considerable time for me to come to terms with this approach of Biblical study. Indeed, to reconcile this with my cherished faith was almost an insurmountable task. In time, however, I came to realise the value of this new study approach. I even discovered that in many ways my conservative perspective of scripture was greatly enhanced.

The credit for this outcome belonged almost entirely to Betty. During the period I was wrestling with this issue, she was constantly urging me to be patient, calm, diligent and objective. Some things, she would say, might not be to our liking. In this case, we must be careful not to throw the baby out with the bathwater! After all, we might be pleasantly surprised how much good can come out of something that we initially reject. Then, to reinforce her point she would use Samson's riddle, *"Out of the eater came forth meat; and out of the strong came forth sweetness . . ."*[6]

Although a devout and uncompromising Evangelical Christian, Betty was quite open-minded and by no means an obscurantist. As my University study progressed I discovered that what she said was true. The methods of literary and form criticism, through which most Biblical studies were currently taught, were not as dangerously destructive as I had thought. Indeed, apart from some things I could not subscribe to, I discovered that the benefits I could derive from this method of study by far outweighed the issues I disagreed with. Indeed, I found that some of my former Biblical perspectives were being corrected, some enhanced, and some wholly transformed.

Interestingly, this did not cause the slightest shift in my Evangelical stance. The reason for this, a friend of mine once jokingly told me, maybe because I was a convert; and according to some, converts tend to have a touch of fanaticism about them! This can undeniably be the case with some converts. But, so far as I know my own heart and mind fanaticism was never a characteristic feature of my newfound faith in Christ. To be of such disposition would be contrary to the character of Christ, who Himself was a victim of religious fanaticism. After all, "A fanatic" said Aldous Huxley "is a man who consciously over-compensates a secret doubt."[7] I have had many doubts about many things in life. But I could never doubt in the dark what God has done for me in the 'Light'.[8]

Doubtless, the credit for this immediate help belonged to God in the first place. In His loving-kindness He made Betty His instrument of wise counsel to address the huge concern that had suddenly hit me. Throughout my university study she continued to be a source of unremitting support and encouragement. In my view, she was simply rare among mortals. As a result, I was becoming unconsciously attached to her as well as fond of her. Perhaps if someone at the time had confronted me with this fact, I would have unhesitatingly denied it. The reason was that the shadows of my past domestic misfortune

---

[6] Jdg. 14:14.

[7] See his *Vulgarity in Literature*, Ch. 4.

[8] Jesus said, *"I am the light of the world"*, see Jn. 8:12; 9:5.

were still hanging over me. And I was shut in on myself in case history repeats itself. But it was not long before I became fully conscious of what lurked deep inside me.

Mrs Kirkwood had an elderly brother in Canada whom she had not seen for a long time. So, together with Betty and her father she flew to Toronto to visit him for a couple of weeks. It was during that period that for the first time I felt terribly desolate. I sensed that Betty's absence had left a painful void in my life and I really missed her. As a matter of fact, this came to me personally as a huge surprise.

Back on Course

The huge surprise turned into a strange combination of exuberance and fear. On one hand, as a gregarious person I imagined that the sun looks down on nothing half so good as a couple with a mutual appreciation for each other, enjoying each other's company and bearing each other's burden in life. In our case, Betty seemed to bear more of my burden than I did hers. On the other hand, the ghosts of my past domestic catastrophe would not lie dormant. They came to haunt me at that moment of my exuberance. This poignant assault brought with it a wave of doubts and pessimism. In the end, I decided that the way I was feeling looked like the beginning of a drift towards romance. So, I determined not to allow myself to be tainted by any form of romance that might result in another devastating heartbreak. I was certain that there was no insurance against that sort of heartbreak. In this way I managed to rid myself of this temporary sensation and turn to my study.

What happened so far had to do with my own personal feeling. It was one-way traffic. I strongly doubted if Betty had in any way missed my company. In my opinion, she had more sense to enjoy the company of a long lost member of her family than to even think of one she had known just recently. Then something transpired which was beyond my wildest dream. On her return from Canada with her parents, Betty told me in the kitchen, with what seemed like a twinkle in her eyes, "I thought of you a lot, Sam," she said, "and wondered how you were getting on."

I quickly wondered if what she had just told me was the same as saying "I missed you". I almost said it to her in response! Instead I bit my tongue, nodded my head nervously and went into the sitting room to chat with her parents. As they talked, I was not paying attention to what they were saying. My mind was side-tracked, completely captivated by those few words that Betty had just said to me. Then, I suddenly realised that I was beginning to renege on my already made decision not to allow myself to be dragged into a romance that might turn into a calamity. As a remarkable lady of outstanding moral and spiritual characteristics, I resolved to adopt Betty as no more than a dear and caring sister. Any romance that might lead to another misfortune must be ruled out. I had already recovered from one, but the scar remained. Fortunately, that scar seemed to have acted as a wake-up call. I was back on course. Nothing would distract me from pressing towards my goal.

Chapter 17

CHANGES AND TRANSITIONS

"Everything flows and nothing stays.
You can't step into the same river twice."

(Heraclitus, Greek philosopher (c.535–475 BC))

"One must never lose time in vainly regretting the past," wrote Anatole France, "nor in complaining about the changes which cause us discomfort, for change is the very essence of life." Yet, there are changes that we ourselves create regardless whether they are necessary or not. There are also changes that are circumstantially imposed upon us regardless whether we like them or not. But there are changes that occur unforeseeably and suddenly for the good of certain people who might simply describe them as accidental strokes of luck. For many it is better to be born lucky than rich.

I confess that I am not quite susceptible to the idea of 'luck'. As a Christian, I am very well at home with the concept of *'providence'*, which is presumably little understood. *'Providence'* is that activity of God by which He protects and cares for the world as a whole and everything in it. Broadly speaking this is known as *'General Providence'*. Then, there is *'Special Providence'* which points more particularly to God's care for humankind in the world. Some theologians speak of *'Ordinary Providence'* by which they refer to the general exercise of God's care through established principles and laws. They also speak of *'Extraordinary Providence'* by which they mean God's miraculous intervention in the ordinary course of nature and history.[1]

Personally, I know that the hand of *Providence* has been active and creative of so many remarkable things in my life. Indeed, even when I am touched by setbacks and adversities (as I have so often

---

[1] H.O. Wiley, *Christian Theology*, Kansas City, Mo. 1940, Vol. 1, pp. 477ff.; Louis Berkhof, *Systematic Theology*, London, Banner of Truth, 1974, pp. 165ff.

been in the past), I know that ultimately God causes *"everything to work together for the good of those who love Him . . ."*[2]

First Trip to America

It was my second year at the University and the year was 1976. Until now I had been well adjusted to my routine. I had been studying hard throughout the week and staying weekends with the Kirkwoods. During University vacations a job had always been available for me at RHM bakery to earn some extra money. Last but not least, I had been faithful in conducting worship for the small congregation of North Kelvinside every Sunday. So far I had not had a holiday break of any sort from my routine. Apart from my occasional trips to Chester, England, to visit Ruth and Jonathan, I had gone nowhere else. In fact, since coming to Britain in 1966 I had never visited any other country.

Among the tiny congregation I was ministering to, there was a Mr Olsen, a Norwegian gentleman, who had recently joined the little congregation. As I got to know him I learned that he had lived in the USA for a time. And owing to his type of job he had worked in a number of States and attended a number of churches and Christian fellowships. He very often urged me to consider visiting the USA one day. He was quite sure the Christians there would greatly appreciate my testimony and my teaching ministry. He told me that he had a good couple of friends in Denver, Colorado, who were in full time ministry. Should I decide to make a trip to the USA one day, he would contact them and they would be happy to welcome me. Every time he raised this subject I listened to him courteously but showed no interest in a trip to the USA.

One day, however, I thought that a trip to that great country might not be such a bad idea. At one time I had almost gone to the USA for good, but circumstances dictated otherwise, as I previously explained in some detail. After all, I already had some dear friends in the USA who had faithfully kept in touch with me. People like Principal Reed in Boston, my Syrian fellow-student Waheeb Antakly in Washington and Grandmother Vaughan in Sarasota, Florida, might very be delighted to see me again after a long time.

A few days later I told Mr Olsen that I was seriously thinking of a trip to the USA in the summer of that year, which prompted him to

---

[2] Rom. 8:28 (NLT).

contact his friends in Denver about me. Meanwhile, however, I wrote to my above-mentioned American friends telling him of my intention to visit their great country for a month, possibly beginning from late July of that year.

By the end of May the arrangement for my trip to the USA was complete. Mr Olsen's friends from Denver had sent me a warm invitation. His friends were none other than Pastor Wallace Hickey and his tele-evangelist wife Marilyn. Principal Reed in Boston and Waheeb Antakly in Washington had planned to host me in their homes and take me round to show me some interesting places. As for Grandmother Vaughan, she had sent me a month Greyhound bus ticket suggesting that as I travel in the USA I must not forget to visit her in Sarasota.

As I recall, on July 27th 1976, I flew from Glasgow to New York arriving at JFK Airport about late morning. Compared to the extremely tight security check up, which passengers experience today in USA airports, the situation then was far more relaxed. Customs officials were on the whole courteous and polite, but New Yorkers left a very bad impression on me as a new visitor in the USA. I was surprised to find a huge number of them loud, aggressive, intimidating and gravely lacking in patience and civility. Within my two hours transfer from Kennedy Airport to Port Authority Bus station in Manhattan I was snapped at, at least twice or three times. At the bus station, I politely asked a heavy browed cheerless Police officer where the ticket office was. He stared at me as though I had just robbed a bank, then turned round and walked away without saying a word.

It seemed as if the whole city of New York was on the verge of a nervous breakdown on that hot summer day! Surely, I thought, this is not the country that all the good and godly American missionaries I knew came from. Being apprehensive and somehow insecure, I was now judging all America by the city of New York. I soon discovered that I was profoundly mistaken.

To my joyful surprise I found that the bus for Boston was scheduled to leave in one hour. When the time came for boarding, one could not find a more eager man to sit comfortably in an air-conditioned bus than myself. Most of the passengers were apparently Bostonians returning home, and their attitude obviously stood in glaring contrast to that of the New Yorkers I had just encountered. As the bus pulled out of the station and I began to relax, I realised that my reaction as a new visitor to that country was downright negative and out of order. I could perhaps have been a little more understanding that all cultures are not the same, not even among Anglo-Saxon people. Perhaps the fault was not in the people but in me. Rightly or wrongly, I was being judgmental towards them.

Absorbed in my quiet self-criticism, I was suddenly interrupted by the voice of the person sitting next to me wanting to know if I was a Bostonian. I replied that I was probably the only non-Bostonians in that bus. I further told him about where I came from and about my arrival in the USA that day as a visitor for the first time.

He was a fine gentleman and I was pleased to make his acquaintance. In the course of our conversation, I shared with him my experience in New York that day describing it as a culture shock. I burst out laughing when he replied, "I am a born American, and I have a culture shock every time I visit New York!" He went on to explain that what makes New York peculiar was the fact that it consisted of all sorts and conditions of people from all over the world. In this kind of situation suspicion and fear become prevalent. So, aggressive and intimidating talk as a defence mechanism tends to become almost second nature to people in such a cosmopolitan environment. "But," he added with a giggle "they tend to change completely when they are outside New York city!"

His assessment of New York and its people sounded quite reasonable. I therefore had no reason to feel annoyed just because I was snapped at twice that day. If the people of that cosmopolitan city had no qualms rubbing each other the wrong way on daily basis, they would equally have no qualms if a newly arrived foreigner got the same. But I want to be on the safe side and assume that perhaps they did not mean to be snappy. Probably the atmosphere of that city made them act the way they did, as that gentleman had told me. I had no reason to doubt that in their heart of hearts they were normally good American people. As a matter of fact, the New Yorkers I had met on various occasions prior to my trip can only be described as the best that one could wish to meet.

As I moved from state to state and from city to city, it became obvious to me that New York City was uniquely peculiar of all places in that great continent. Most people must have experienced the same thing when they first landed in that city.

Old and New Friends

On my arrival in Boston I was exuberantly happy to see Principal and Mrs Reed again after ten years. I stayed with them for nearly a week during which Principal Reed took me to visit the well-known Nazarene Seminary and meet some of his colleagues and friends there. On the Sunday of that week, he and his wife took me to one of the churches of the Nazarene where I had the privilege of teaching adult Sunday school and afterwards preaching at the Church service. On the evening I preached at another church of the Nazarene in the city.

In both of those services the Lord's presence was real in our midst. Indeed, during my preaching on those two occasions it was not difficult for me to catch sight of the Reeds' remarkable facial expression. They simply seemed elated to be listening to one of their former students preaching in fluent English – a language he hardly knew over a decade earlier when he arrived in Beirut. I was aware meantime that the credit for that achievement did not belong to me. It belonged to them for their unwavering dedication to the work of the Bible School in Beirut. I have not seen them since that visit, but we have always kept in touch. Sadly, however, on the 1st December 2006, I received an email from Principal Reed informing me that his dear wife, Elva, had passed away the week before. She undoubtedly was a very godly lady. I shall always remember her enormous kindness to me during my time at the Bible school.

From Boston I travelled to Washington DC to visit my friend and former fellow-student Waheeb Antakly. It was a joy to see him in good health, happy and enjoying his high-ranking job. After more than a week of fellowship with him, it was time for me to head for Denver, Colorado. Instead of using my month Greyhound Bus ticket, Waheeb kindly bought me a plane ticket from Washington to Denver. I did not see him again until the winter of 1979 when he visited me in Scotland on his way to the USA. Needless to say, Waheeb and I have always been close friends and good brothers in Christ. Interestingly, of all the fellow-students I knew at the Beirut Bible School, Waheeb is the only one I have never lost touch with. I had every intention to visit him in Syria in the autumn of 2011, but unfortunately that did not happen due to the start of the uprising.

Arriving at Denver airport, I found Pastor Wallace Hickey waiting for me. He greeted me warmly and drove me home where I met his wife Marilyn, a lady of profound love for scripture and remarkable zeal for sharing it with others. Whether she was at the time already involved in the ministry of tele-evangelism or about to move into it I am not sure. The fact of the matter is that Marilyn seemed divinely fitted for that high calling.

Both Wallace and Marilyn were remarkable hosts. They simply could not do enough for me during the few days I spent with them. Pastor Wallace very kindly drove me to some parts of the Rocky Mountains, which apart from their awesome beauty, are known for their significant deposits of minerals including gold. As we drove along the eastern edge of the Rocky Mountains, I was told that it was the area which had attracted very many prospectors during what is historically known as the Colorado Gold Rush of the mid-19th century. In point of fact, we could see a number of people at various streams still looking for bits of gold. One of them who knew I came all the way from the UK handed me a tiny little piece of what he called 'Fools' Gold'. When I wanted to know its worth, I was told that it was worth nothing! Was that probably the reason why they called it 'Fools' Gold'!? At any rate, I was more than happy to keep it as a souvenir. On Sunday I accompanied Wallace and Marilyn to their church, which was full to capacity, and was invited to share my testimony with their congregation. The worshippers were apparently blessed by my testimony that morning, and that was a humbling experience for me.

Next day in the evening, Pastor Wallace drove me to the Greyhound Bus station where I boarded the bus heading for Atlanta, Georgia. It was the longest bus trip I have ever had in my life. With several stoppages and changes to other buses, the journey to Atlanta took two full days and was quite exhausting. When I arrived in Atlanta about sunset I phoned two people I had long been in correspondence with as Christian pen pals. These were Mrs Lois Chandler and Pastor Gordon White who was of Welsh origin. They had already arranged for me to stay with Don Van Hoozier, a Pastor of a very small independent congregation. I stayed with him for three days before pushing on to Florida.

Don was a remarkable gentleman. At first, I was struck by his very quiet manner, which often made him look quite pensive. I soon discovered that the poor gentleman was suffering from a relentless state of heartache. A day before leaving, he told me with tears in his eyes of his tragic involvement in a driving accident. A little child had suddenly run in front of him and was killed instantly. For him, time was no healer and the passing of years seemed to make no difference. Although it was not his fault he was still being relentlessly haunted by that dreadful experience.

As I listened to him, I did not know what to say. I realised that had I been in his position my inner torment would have been unbearable. I might never have wanted to drive again. I sincerely felt very sorry for him. I simply could not be aloof, blind or insensitive to his incessant agony of conscience. Meanwhile, it showed me just how vulnerable we humans are. Our conscience can be crushed not only by the wrong we have done deliberately, but quite often even by the wrong we have done unintentionally. The following day I left for Florida with Don Van Hoozier very much in my thoughts and prayers.

Next day I travelled to Sarasota, Florida, to visit Grandmother Vaughan. It was a real joy to see her, and on Sunday her Methodist Pastor introduced me in the Church as Mary Vaughan's spiritual grandson. Moreover, as a token of welcome, the Pastor asked me to take part in the morning service by reading a passage from the Bible followed by a brief homily. In the course of the service I read Psalm 92 and then gave an exposition on verse 12 where the Psalmist says, *"The righteous shall flourish like the palm tree: He shall grow like a cedar in Lebanon."* To my great encouragement that short address received a warm appreciation from the congregation.

I also visited the Christian Retreat Centre in Sarasota where I met the Revd Gerald Derstein and a number of interesting evangelical preachers, among them the Revd Costa Deir. Originally a Palestinian Arab Christian, Mr Deir was very delighted to learn that I was a close friend of his compatriot and former colleague, the Revd Bishara Zabaneh. He further urged me to visit him at the place of his ministry in Lima, NY, which I did a couple of years later.

Time had now come for me to return to New York in order to fly home. It was my greatest joy to see my dear old friends and renew my fellowship with them. It was also my happiest experience to have met and made new friends. Without distinction, they were all very nice. They were not merely nice people, but there was something uniquely kind and generous about them. There is a sense in which it is somehow incorrect to speak of them as 'old and new friends'. I am happy to describe them all as 'the new friends' whose utter and unimpeachable sincerity rested on the fact that each one of them, being in Christ, was "a *new creation*".[3] There is a grace that makes all things new.

A Degree with Honours

Back in Scotland, I was ready to begin my third year study at the Divinity Department of Glasgow University. Third year students were given the choice of doing '*Junior Honours*', after which, if they did well, they could go on to do '*Senior Honours*' in their fourth and final year. I immediately jumped at the opportunity and decided to do junior honours in the Old Testament that year, and senior honours in Ecclesiastical History on the final year. The study on these two subjects involved the writing of a good deal of essays. In short, the task was by no means smooth running, but in the end it proved most rewarding, thanks to the supervision and advice of Professor Davidson of the Old Testament Department and Professor Frend of the Ecclesiastical History Department.

The beginning of 1978 showed the earliest symptoms of the rise of temperature in many students, including myself! The degree exams had been scheduled to take place in the middle of May that year, and set to last for about a week. Every student had frantically been studying and getting ready for what we all dubbed 'D. Day'! True, "studies," as Francis Bacon put it, "serve for delight, for ornament and for ability" – yet, most of us knew that exams are formidable even to those who are best prepared.

On the eve of the first day of the exams, I had decided to go to bed early so that in the morning I would wake up in good time to go over some papers before going to the University. But, alas, I could not sleep. The tense anxiety about the possibility of failing, in some if not in all of my degree exams, was so dreadful that I suffered a wave of violent shivers in bed that night. Then about 2:30 a.m., I realized to my utter surprise that being strained and intensely focused on next day's exams, I had forgotten to offer my prayerful thanks to God and commit to His care all the exams ahead of me. I immediately slipped out of bed and knelt in prayer. But no sooner had I began to pray than I fell asleep on my knees and did not wake up until my alarm clock went off at 7:00 a.m. I felt that Monday morning enormously tired, drained of energy and barely able to marshal my thoughts. I

---

[3] 2 Cor. 5:17; Gal. 6:15 (RSV).

walked about with my shoulders drooped. Then after breakfast and a brief time of devotion, I shook myself and squared my shoulders and whispered as I stood up to leave, "I'm ready to go, Lord, please let your presence go with me."

Arriving at Gilmourhill Centre at 8:40 a.m., I waited with my fellow Divinity students to be ushered into the examination room at 9:00 a.m. for our first exam in the Old Testament. During that short period of waiting, something extraordinary happened. I felt suddenly energized, my mind quickened and every trace of tiredness gone. By the time we entered the examination room, took our seats and began answering our Old Testament questions I was on the trot, so to speak. Out of a set of eight or nine questions, four questions were to be answered within two hours.

I had just finished the two questions and began on the third when my pen ran out of ink. I searched my pockets slowly and diligently for another pen, but found none. My annoyance soon turned into a touch of alarm that running out of ink might soon lead to running out of time, and time was of the essence. Rabbi Dr Jeffrey Cohen, the exam supervisor, had noticed my agitation and came to see me. When he knew what had happened he cheerfully gave me his pen, which thankfully enabled me to answer the remaining two questions and finish exactly on time.

During the next four days, the exams passed smoothly and no dramatic event occurred. The last exam on Pastoral Theology took place on Friday morning. At the end of exam, almost at my last written sentence in the exam paper, the words of the prophet Samuel echoed spontaneously through my mind, *"Hitherto hath the Lord helped us"*.[4]

Over a week later the exam results came out. I very well remember that morning when accompanied by my divinity student friend, John Faris, we walked to the University to see if our names were among those who had successfully passed the degree exam. As we walked up the hill towards the University, each of us barely managed to conceal his apprehension of the unexpected. Arriving at the University gate, we anxiously walked to the Graduation Notice Board just over .twenty yards to the right. Today, I still cannot describe how exuberantly happy I was when I saw my own name among those who successfully passed the degree exam. My friend John was also overjoyed when he saw his name. For me, that was not only a time to rejoice, but also a

---

[4] 1 Sam. 7:12.

time to recall the event of nearly two decades earlier. With only a year and a few months to graduate, my dismissal from Islamic college on the basis of my conversion had been a shattering blow and a huge loss. But, in Christ I was now compensated for my former loss with credit – I had gained a Bachelor of Divinity degree with honours.

The Inevitable Move

The graduation took place on the 11th of July 1978. It was a highly joyful occasion. The celebration that same day in the afternoon took place at Alex and Annie Kirkwood's home. Their happiness for me as their adopted son could not be underestimated. On the other hand Betty was equally elated on that occasion. And, for anyone with a quick eye, she seemed slightly over-elated, which was contrary to her restrained and reserved nature. Was she perhaps trying to hide something? When I told her that she looked unusually in very high spirits, she replied with an emotional touch in her voice as she turned away, "Just ignore me, Sam. I'm OK!" But the tone of her voice suggested she was not alright.

At first, I did not know what the problem was. It soon struck me that Betty may well have been wrestling with the prospect of my inevitable departure from Glasgow soon after my graduation. She had been a very close friend to me during the previous four years. Shortly afterwards I was credibly informed that in all her life I was the only man she had ever become affectionately attached to outside her family. It was a staggering piece of information, because until then, I had never thought that this affectionate attachment was a two-way traffic!

A couple of weeks later, I was assigned by the Church of Scotland Offices in Edinburgh to Fullarton Parish Church in Irvine, Ayrshire. I was to serve there for one year as assistant to the incumbent minister, the Revd P.G. Thomson of happy memory. The procedure was designed, with the help of the minister, to familiarize the graduate student like me with the life and work of the parish church, and thus prepare him for his future charge. The news apparently did not go down well with Betty who tried to hide her feeling with a smile and a nod. On my part, it was extremely hard to think that I would soon say good bye to one I had come to love and value so much. And for the first time I had come to realize that I simply could not do without her. Therefore, I decided that my goodbye to Betty would not be a goodbye of detachment, but a goodbye of continued affinity and loving relationship. To put this resolve into action, a week before leaving for Irvine I tactfully asked her parents if I could still continue to see them at weekends. The response was absolutely positive. Betty's face simply beamed with immense joy and I was deeply gratified.

During the past four years there had been a good number of changes and transitions, some of them have already been mentioned in this chapter. It is said that 'change is as good as a rest'. Yet, I would not characterize any of those changes and transitions as 'rest'. Rather, I would characterize them as a 'driving force' that kept my mind focused and my heart in the right place. In this way, I was well protected from any form of apathy or stagnation. And the credit for this belongs to the good hand of Providence. As Alfred Tennyson put it:

> *The old order changeth, yielding place to new*
> *and God fulfils Himself in many ways,*
> *lest one good custom should corrupt the world.*

Chapter 18

A PROBATIONARY PERIOD

"The great cry of our heart is that God will
help us to be ready for whatever He has for us."
(Bob Pierce)

In July 1978 I began as a Probationer Assistant under Mr Thomson at Fullarton Parish Church, Irvine. I took up my residence in a council house at Dalrymple Crescent. It was the beginning of learning a number of new ideas including, *inter alia,* how to conduct the affairs of my future parish church. If there ever was a real honour, this was it.

It is not always easy to realise the tremendous value of the ministry. It was not for nothing that St Paul declared, *"I magnify my ministry".*[1] Yet, our focus ought to be on the task at hand and not on the honour that goes with it. Indeed, when we have discharged our God-given task, we should humbly acknowledge that *"We are unworthy servants; we have only done what was our duty".*[2]

Moreover, in the performance of any task, our notion of achieving success is never too far away. The first lesson I learned under Mr Thomson was that in the service of God the primary goal is not to be *successful* but to be *faithful.* Self-discipline was another valuable lesson I had to learn. I became fully aware that whereas most people have to work for an employer, a superior or a master, the minister is his own master. There is no one to make him work but himself. Indeed, there is no job in the world in which it is so easy to put things off and to leave things undone and to waste time as it is in the ministry. To be an efficient minister in the service of God a person has to have the gift of diligence which comes with complete self-discipline.

In addition to this, I had had a number of misconceptions about the ministry which needed correction. One of these was the notion that the ministry is confined almost entirely to the pulpit. Too often the

---

[1] Rom. 11:13(RSV).
[2] Lk. 17:10 (RSV).

attraction of the ministry is the pulpit. The person's vision is the vision of himself or herself holding some congregation spellbound. During my assistantship I learned that the most important part of the work of the ministry is done out of the pulpit, and often no one ever hears of it or knows it except the man or the woman who is helped. As for the pulpit, the more a person draws attention to himself, the less he draws attention to the Lord Jesus Christ. All these and much more I learned during my assistantship period under the Revd P.G. Thomson of happy memory. I can truly say that what I owe him is beyond evaluation.

My Probationary Period

I still cherish the memory of my Probationary period at Fullarton Church. It was most instructive and exciting. The atmosphere was almost always joyful and seasoned with humour, and my part in that humour is still remembered by some today. Furthermore, I was credited of being the only assistant who succeeded to squeeze the solemn no-nonsense looking P.G. Thomson into my humorous mould. I was also the only one who openly called him 'the bishop'! And although a tough Presbyterian, he seemed to have quietly enjoyed the title! In response, he was quick to label me as the 'the curate'!

However, I shall never forget the remarkable encouragement I received as a probationary assistant from the congregation of Fullarton Church. Their extraordinary kindness has remained indelibly stamped upon my mind ever since. On Sundays I was always with 'the bishop' in the pulpit, either to conduct the worship or to preach. My turn to preach occurred about once a month, or when he was on vacation. Now, being in a semi-traditional Church, I was first worried in case my evangelical brand of preaching might not go down well with the congregation. I was soon gratified to learn that after all my sermons were greatly prized and even described as most informative.

I had been about a month in Fullarton Church when something quite funny happened at the start of a Sunday morning service. Mr Thomson and I were sitting in the pulpit whilst the choir sung the introit, when he suddenly whispered in my ear, "You have a sizable *band of hope* this morning!" I shook my head indicating I hadn't a clue what he meant. "Look up at the left side of the gallery", he said with a faint giggle. As I looked up I saw a bunch of single young ladies sending beaming smiles towards the pulpit. It was obvious who the object of those smiles was. There were two of us in the pulpit, and I was the single young guy. I leaned on the bishop and whispered, "With a good looking bunch of single young ladies like these, I ought to hire some bodyguards or buy an insurance policy!" He could hardly stop laughing as the choir was coming to the end of their introit.

My task as a probationer assistant was to attend the businesses and functions of the Church and take part in most of them under the supervision of Mr Thomson. I was present at every Session and Board meeting, including one annual general meeting which concluded with a joyful celebration. I watched carefully how he chaired each of those meetings with a remarkable sense of tact, wisdom and authority. I was, however, reminded that at such meetings I was not to speak except on request and by permission.

It was also my duty to accompany my 'bishop' to the monthly Presbytery meetings, which for a raw curate' like me, were most enlightening, and often quite electrifying! In addition, 'the bishop' had a weekly programme for me, which consisted of parish visitation and school chaplaincy and other duties. He often assigned to me the task of teaching the communicants class which I thoroughly enjoyed.

Monday was of course a day off for both of us. There were times also when we met in the manse for what I can only describe as 'Reassessment Meetings', although he never gave them a name. During those meetings he would touch on most of my activities, pointing to some that needed improvement and to others that met with his highest approval. Most of all, as one who was thoroughly versed in Church Law, he was enormously keen to have me follow in his footsteps. I remain eternally grateful for the way he made me familiar with a vast number of essential ecclesiastical issues in *Practice and Procedure in the Church of Scotland* by James Cox. Those lessons were undeniably of huge benefit to me in my future charges. In brief, I enjoyed being at Fullarton Parish Church so much that I would not have minded had I been allowed to remain permanently there as a probationer assistant!

During my time at Fullarton I had often been called upon to conduct funeral services in the absence of my 'bishop', or been sent by him to conduct Sunday worship in Churches which were either vacant or whose ministers for some reason or another were absent. However, on one occasion, something happened that has left a lasting and most blessed impression upon me. Monseigneur Murphy of St Mary's Catholic Church in Irvine had asked my 'bishop' if he could let me come to his midweek service (on Thursday evening March the 8th 1979), and tell his people the story of my conversion. In response he kindly allowed me to go. I had never before been asked to speak in a Roman Catholic Church in Britain. The Church hall where we met was full of people, and almost half of them were monks and nuns who presumably came from elsewhere.

That evening, as I told the story of my conversion and the subsequent hardships and adversities that I endured, the reaction on people's faces was a moving revelation to me. There were broad smiles on the faces of some as expressions of their outpouring of love. Others looked somewhat spellbound for they had never before heard the story of a convert from Islam to Christianity. Then the moment came when I said, "When everything I lived for and cherished in my home and country was lost, my sense of love and duty to Jesus has remained. It is a wealth which I've never lost." At these words, most of those monks and nuns, not to mention others, were visibly moved to tears. In the meantime, I too could hardly control my own tears.

With hindsight, those tears also happened to have been evoked by the memory of a painful old incident. But little did I know that I was in for treatment on that occasion. The process of removing the scar of an old wound had begun. Nearly twenty years earlier, Beatrice's staunchly Roman Catholic family had bitterly opposed her loving relationship with me on the basis that I was a Protestant, which for them I was not a Christian. As previously mentioned, having failed to stop our relationship they finally whisked her off to Spain for good. What happened was a sin against love, and we were both the main casualties. An enormous wound had been inflicted simply because I happened to have come to Christ through Protestantism. By contrast, here I was now standing in a Roman Catholic Church, before a sizable Roman Catholic group who were making me feel as if I were bathed in sunshine. Indeed, I was left in no doubt that I was among them as a beloved brother in Christ, and with that the scar vanished complete. My spiritual experience that evening will always be remembered as one of the highlights of my probationary period in Irvine, Ayrshire.

Two Exciting Events

I can truly say that 1979 was an eventful year for me. On Monday March 12th of that year I attended the Probationers' Conference at Carberry Tower in Musselburgh. It was a Conference that every probationer assistant had to attend shortly before his probationary period expired. The Conference lasted two days during which a number of lectures and group discussions relating to the Parish ministry were most instructive and edifying. It was also a joyful occasion to meet again a number of my fellow university students whom I had not seen since our graduation. During the breaks some of us would share our particular probationary experiences, and some of them were quite funny. But the funniest experience for all of us in that Conference was our encounter with a visiting chaplain, who seemed quite edgy and irrepressibly argumentative. So, we decided that in the course of any encounter with him two words, 'yes' and 'amen', should be strictly observed!

At the close of the conference, and in accordance with the rules, we were given the green light to apply for charges. Aware that there were plenty of vacant parish churches, a week later I started sending my applications together with my curriculum vitae as required. At first I applied to five vacant churches, but to my surprise none of them replied. Then I applied to four other vacant charges, and again there was no response from any of them. To think that not one of those nine vacancy committees had the common courtesy to reply to my application was, to say the least, most disconcerting.

I did share this matter with 'the bishop' who told me that I should not worry; some vacancy committees can be quite sluggish. Obviously, he was trying to dismiss any sense of concern on my part. A while later I applied to two other vacant charges, and again there was no sign of a response from either of them. After some weeks no acknowledgment was received from any of the eleven vacant churches I had approached.

By now I had become so anxious that I decided to take the bull by the horn and phone the conveners of at least two Vacancy Committees and ask if my applications had reached them. When I did so, I was told that they had already picked their sole nominees. In this situation I could not help having my own thoughts. The more persistent thought being the possibility that most, if not all, of those Vacancy Committees must have realised from my name that I was a foreigner (probably with a funny foreign accent!), and quietly passed me by.

I shared that idea with 'the bishop' who brushed it aside saying, "A parish church of God's choice is already reserved for you, Sam. Just be patient and remember the words of the prophet Habakkuk 2:3, 'If it *seems slow, wait for it; it will surely come, it will not delay*.'" I took what he had said as a mild rebuke from the Lord for my weak faith. We are often unaware when our faith goes weak, but the Lord has ways of making us aware of it.

On Friday April the 27th 1979 I applied to three more vacant churches. Time was running on. The following month (May) was going to be my last month as a probationer assistant at Fullarton Church. Just before I posted those applications, I did something I had not done before. I offered a short prayer and left the outcome to God. I felt perfectly at peace. On May the 3rd I received one response. It was from the vacant linked charge of Chapelhall and Calderbank in Lanarkshire. The Vacancy Committee asked if it would be possible for its members to come and hear me preach at Fullarton Parish Church in the morning of Sunday May the 20th. There was also a request for a possible interview after the service, which I welcomed in my immediate reply. My joy was simply indescribable. God was indeed at work. Also, the recently encouraging words of 'the bishop' seemed to be coming true. Now that the Vacancy Committee would be coming in about two weeks, I knew I had better seek the Lord for the right message for that Sunday.

Now, shortly after my return from the Probationers' Conference I decided on a very important move. Throughout my probationary period at Fullarton Church, thanks to 'the bishop', I had been allowed to spend the weekends with the Kirkwoods in Glasgow and return to Irvine early on Sunday to assist in the morning service. I had always looked forward to seeing Betty whom I used to miss dearly. By now I had been resigned to the fact that for me life would have no meaning without her. Furthermore, I had seriously been thinking of proposing to her one day, but was very reluctant in case she refused me. However, during the Probationers' Conference one of the speakers had pointed out *inter alia* that 'a parish minister's life can be a very lonely life'.

That statement had had a sobering impact upon me and eventually set me thinking. I had been alone too long and seemed to enjoy my independence. But how long would I be able to maintain a lonely and independent life? A lonely and independent life may be suitable for some people under certain circumstances, but hardly for one with a foreign cultural background like mine becoming a parish minister in Scotland. I would not be fit to shepherd half a dozen goats on my own, much less a parish congregation! In any case, no man needs to deal with life alone, especially a ministerial life which I was aiming for. A helpmate therefore was very important in the ministry, and to that end God seemed to have already prepared one for me. Besides being profoundly attached to her, Betty was born and brought up in a good and godly home and the impact of her spiritual life on me personally could not be remarkable. I simply could not find a better lady than her in the world, and I could only hope and indeed pray that when I propose to her she would not turn me down.

On Friday evening (May the 4th), I arrived at the Kirkwoods for my usual weekend. Over an hour after dinner, Betty's parents went to bed and we stayed up watching TV. Then, somewhat reluctantly I asked Betty if I could share with her one or two important points. She agreed and put the TV off. I started by deploring the fact that of all the fourteen applications I had submitted only one response arrived recently. That period of waiting had been most trying for me. But one dictum had sustained me, "Nothing will show more accurately what we are than the way we meet trials and difficulties." The Vacancy Committee of Chapelhall and Calderbank that had responded were coming to hear me on Sunday May the 20th, and I sincerely asked for her prayers on that day.

Betty's reply was one of unremitting support and encouragement. As she talked I could not hear what she was saying for thinking so intensely on how to phrase my next crucial point to her. She had still been talking when I unconsciously interrupted her. "Betty," I nervously said, "I have a question I want to ask you." She replied, "Yes, of course, go ahead."

Being so uptight, I turned speechless. I stared intensely down at the carpet wishing I had stayed away that weekend. But, I was there now and had no choice but to offer my proposal and get it over with. So, I squared up and said with an air of bravado, "What would you say if I asked you to marry me, Betty?"

She answered with a broad smile, "I thought you'd never ask. Go ahead, Sam, I'm listening!"

I thought for a moment that she was either joking or being sarcastic. In fact, she was pleasantly astounded, but was playing it cool. "My proposal to you, Betty," I said, "is quite simple. Will you marry me? I strongly believe that should you accept, you will be an ideal wife to me."

With tears in her eyes, she replied, "I gladly accept, Sam." I was so full of joy that I walked to her, thanked her wholeheartedly and kissed her for the first time, on her lips!

Thus, two exciting events had occurred within two days: a response from one Vacancy Committee, giving me the opportunity to prove God's faithfulness; and also God's gift of an invaluable companion and helpmate in life.

A Double Celebration

Next day in the morning (Saturday May the 5th) as we sat at the breakfast table, I did something Betty had suggested the night before. I asked her parents for their kind approval of our engagement, which they gladly gave. In the afternoon I bought Betty the engagement ring from a jeweller in Byres Road, Glasgow. It was the very place from which she had bought me a watch for my birthday three years earlier, and which I still wear today. The following day (Sunday 6th) I was back in Irvine to assist in the morning service at Fullarton Church.

Before going into the sanctuary I had informed 'the bishop' of my engagement to Betty, which came as a joyful surprise to him. During the worship he took time to announce the happy event. It was followed by a thunderous applause from the congregation. Meanwhile, anyone having a quick eye for anything unusual must have noticed that the mood among the band of hope on the left side of the gallery was not quite so cheerful! The following Sunday most of them were conspicuous by their absence, but the few that remained must have either been uninterested or simply still living in hope!

On Saturday May the 12th, Betty and I had a long discussion during which we decided on our wedding date. We agreed that the date should be Saturday June the 16th. We also agreed to approach 'the bishop' and ask him to officiate at our wedding ceremony at his Fullarton Parish Church. We were soon gratified that our request had been gladly approved by his lordship! We further decided that our wedding and reception afterwards should be quite simple. Finally, we were both fully assured that in the event of not having had a call to a church by the time we were married, we were expected to stay with Betty's parents until one became available. With the main points of our discussion over, I finished my delightful weekend with Betty and her parents and returned to Irvine on Sunday morning.

The following Sunday (May 20th) the Vacancy Committee of Chapelhall and Calderbank would be coming to hear me at Fullarton Parish Church. Obviously I had never preached before a Vacancy

Committee, and it would not be honest to say that I was looking forward to that day. In fact, I was feeling slightly more anxious as that day drew near. Nevertheless, I was being greatly fortified and sustained through much prayer, study and meditation as I prepared for that day.

In the course of my preparation two things came to mind which made me feel more relaxed and encouraged. First, I was reminded that on Sunday May the 20th I should be entirely focused on preaching the Gospel to the whole congregation and not on giving a preaching performance to please the Vacancy Committee. Second, I had to remember that I would be there to glorify the Lord and not to sell myself.

Sunday morning May the 20th had arrived and the Church was packed as usual. Having been ushered to the pulpit by the church officer, all sense of nervousness on my part seemed to have suddenly gone. As I sat in the pulpit whilst the choir sang the introit, I could see and feel the overwhelming support and empathy of the congregation for me that morning. Indeed, some even looked a little anxiously nervous for me. The entire act of worship was conducted with a great sense of calm, dignity, confidence and a touch of humour. My sermon was preached *ex tempore* and was based on Luke 22:54b: "*. . . and Peter followed* (Jesus) *afar off*".

After the service a good number of people remarked that I preached with enthusiasm and deep conviction. Some even acknowledged that the sermon marked a turning point in their life. Unlike Peter, they would stop following Jesus at a distance. In any case, one thing I made sure not to do as long as I was in the pulpit that day. I was determined not to be as curious as to try and identify the members of the Vacancy Committee in the congregation, or find out how many they were. I would eventually meet them all after the service as planned. And meet them I certainly did.

The Vacancy Committee I met in the vestry afterwards consisted of about a dozen people. They were kind, respectful and complimentary about the service. An elder – most senior member of the Committee by the name William Hay – with tears in his eyes, graciously voiced his appreciation for what he described as a heart-searching message. I learned afterwards that he was among those who declared for Christ during the Billy Graham's campaign in Scotland in 1955.

The meeting was reasonably short and the atmosphere was quite relaxed. Among other things, they wanted to know a bit of my background, for some of them had thought I was of Italian origin!

They also asked if I was married, and were informed that I would be on Saturday June the 16th. As to their question regarding my 'likes and dislikes' as a minister in a Parish Church, my answer was brief and simple. I pointed out that I was against any form of games of chance as a way of raising funds for the Church. The Church is "*the household of faith*", and faith and chance do not mix. As for my 'likes', there was nothing I prized most than the full support of the office-bearers of the church for their minister. With their unwavering support for him great things can be accomplished.

At this point the old gentleman gently said, "That's all we needed to hear, sir". Everyone in that Committee enthusiastically agreed, and I closed the meeting with prayer. A week later, I was invited to preach as sole nominee for the above-mentioned linked charge on Sunday July the 8th. Betty and I were extremely delighted and had the feeling that from then on everything else would fall into place. Indeed, that was precisely what happened.

On Saturday June the 16th Betty and I were married at Fullarton Parish Church. Mr Thomson officiated at our wedding and the Revd Bob Leslie, minister of Bourtreehill Church, acted as my best man. It was a joyful occasion in which friends and relations were there to share in our wedding ceremony and in the reception thereafter at Stanecastle Hotel, Irvine. On Tuesday July the 3rd I was licensed by the Presbytery of Irvine and Kilmarnock. Five days later (Sunday the 8th), accompanied by Betty, I was at Chapelhall Parish Church preaching as sole nominee for the linked charge. I was greatly encouraged and heartened by Betty's presence with me on that occasion. After the service we were hugely gratified to learn that the vote was overwhelmingly in my favour.

A couple of weeks later the call was sustained by the Presbytery of Hamilton and the service of my ordination and induction was scheduled to take place in the Parish Church of Calderbank on Wednesday September the 26th. I shall never forget that awesome day as long as I live. The church was packed to capacity and the solemnity of the service was sublime. I was deeply and emotionally touched as I stood to take my ordination vows. At that moment the past with almost all its complexities, upheavals, hardships and bitter struggles (which I had endured since I left my native land as a convert) came back to mind vividly. But that past was like a coin. It had another side – the side of God's gracious benevolence that had restored to me *"the years that the locust has eaten"*.[2] And I was aware that the very act of my ordination at the time was the pinnacle of that divine benevolence.

A Gaelic speaking colleague of mine recently drew my attention to the fact that the Gaelic term for marriage is *'posadh'*. This same word is used for the induction of a clergyman to his charge. In other words, at his induction he is married to his church. The year 1979 was indeed an eventful year, and I shall always remember it for two very important events. It was the year in which I was married to Betty and shortly thereafter married to my first Parish charge of Chapelhall and Calderbank. As a matter of fact, it was the year in which I was abundantly blessed with a double celebration.

Friends Above Reproach

I had first visited the USA in the summer of 1976, and I have visited that great country every year since then. However, a year before my marriage and my call to the above-mentioned charge, I had been scheduled to conduct a teaching ministry at a church in Atlanta, Georgia, for a week beginning from August 20th 1979, approximately five weeks before my ordination and induction. Had this service been fixed to take place somewhere in the middle of September, my trip to the USA would have been cancelled. Time therefore was on my side, and with Betty's agreement I decided to honour my commitment and arrange my flight to Atlanta, Georgia.

Just as I was getting ready to do so I received a phone call from the pastor of the Church I was to visit. The pastor was my good and faithful friend the Revd Amos Holcombe. He told me that due to unforeseen circumstances, which he did not disclose, the church had regrettably decided to cancel my visit which was expected in fifteen days. He went on to say that if I had already purchased my flight ticket the Church was ready to reimburse me immediately. He was greatly relieved to know that his phone call that evening had spared me the trouble of purchasing my flight ticket to Atlanta, GA, the following day.

"Now, brother Sam," he said to me, "I'd like you to go ahead tomorrow and get a flight ticket to Charlotte, NC, instead of Atlanta, GA. I've just spoken to an excellent friend of mine who would be very happy to have you minister to his congregation in Charlotte for a few days. His name

---

[2] Joel 2.25.

is Pastor Edward Chidester. You will find him and his family after your own heart," he assured me. "And who knows, brother," he concluded, "this might be the beginning of a long and blessed relationship between you." Then, he gave me Ed Chidester's phone number and urged me to call him immediately. I phoned him half an hour later. His gentle tone of voice, his amiable and warm manner suggested that here was a man who seemed, in the words of Dr Samuel Johnson, to have "always set a high value on spontaneous kindness". He assured me that he, his family and his congregation look forward to seeing me on August 20th. He wanted to know as soon as possible the precise time of my arrival in Charlotte Airport so that he could arrange for somebody to meet me.

I did that two days later when I got my flight ticket to Charlotte, NC via New York. Twelve days later I landed at Charlotte Douglas Airport. Waiting for me at that Airport were Everett and Alva Sipe whose kindness and warm hospitality in their home I still cherish. The bond of Christian love and affection between us has remained intact ever since. Driven to the Church area, I was delighted to meet Hart and Anne Hutchison, a very good couple, whose acquaintance I was most honoured to make. In the evening I was driven to Sloan Drive to meet Pastor Chidester and his good wife Joann.

I shall never forget that day. The enormous respect and the joyful manner in which I was received can only be described as a humbling and moving experience. I felt absolutely at home with them. Having enjoyed a lavish dinner, we spent about a couple of hours in conversation during which a tremendous sense of affinity was firmly established between us. It was, as Pastor Holcombe had suggested, the beginning of our long friendly relationship. On the 10th November 1990 I was given the honour of officiating at the wedding service of Christie, pastor Ed. Chidester's daughter. She married Randolph McCurry, a fine Christian gentleman of high spiritual quality and unfaltering friendship. Fr me, this couple remain to this day among the best of my friends and associates who have enriched my own life.

Needless to say, through the Chidesters I later came to know Pastor Arlie Whitlaw, the founder of the Community Church in Ashburn, Virginia. My long acquaintance with him and his family has been remarkable. But my enormous affinity has been with Pastor Arlie's son and successor, Pastor Charles Whitlaw – a man of great gifts and profound spirituality. His enormous diligence in God's work is exemplary."

The year 1979 was my fourth annual trip to the USA. My first four trips happened during the heyday of that peculiar American phenomenon, coined by Time magazine as 'Televangelism'. At first, I was fascinated by the dazzling glamour of its production which could rival any major network. But I was soon dismayed to realize that the programmes were largely preoccupied with fundraising and constant appeals for money. Journalist Tim Dowling summed it all up when he wrote, "There was the prevailing notion that your money, if given in sufficiency, will buy you some sort of intercession."[3]

For me, Televangelism (including certain other forms of Evangelism) in the USA was and still remains predominantly a fundraising enterprise. In this context, I am reminded of someone who wrote, "Christianity began on Palestinian soil as a relationship with a person Jesus. But it moved on to Greek soil and became a philosophy. Then it moved on to Roman soil and became an institution. It moved on to British soil and became a card carrying church culture. It moved on to American soil and became an enterprise, something packaged and sold."

I returned home from that visit to the USA ready for my ordination and induction into my new charge, which were to take place at the parish church of Calderbank on Wednesday September the 26th 1979 as already mentioned. The lesson I learned from that important trip has remained with me ever since. The ministry is not a position where self-interest drives one to speak all sort of things and play all sort of games for self-gratification. Nor is it a sphere where relentless energy and gifts are employed more for self-aggrandizement than for the glory of God. God would prefer to be served differently, and John Milton could not have put it better:

> . . . *God doth not need*
> *either man's work or his own gifts.; who best*
> *bear his mild yoke, they serve him best. His state*
> *is kingly: thousands at his bidding speed,*
> *and post o'er land and ocean without rest;*
> *they also serve who only stand and wait.*

It is perhaps the noblest thought for all who are preparing for the service of God.

---

[3] Guardian, Friday 2, March 2007.

Chapter 19

IN THE HOLY MINISTRY

"You do not do God a favour by serving Him.
He honours you by allowing you to serve Him."
(Victor Nyquist)

The end of September 1979 found me fully established as a minister of the Church of Scotland, in charge of two parish churches. I had heard that a linked charge is never an easy task for a clergyman. However, in trying to implement the linkage of my two parish churches, the Presbytery of Hamilton had promised the gift of a lay assistant. I had been a couple of months in my charge when the Church of Scotland Offices called me to say that the only available lay assistant they could recommend was Roy Copeland. The latter was a good and decent elderly gentleman. Although not in good health, which he obviously managed to play down, he honoured his obligation and carried out his duties to the best of his ability. He stayed with me about three years and then because of ill-heath he decided to call it a day. After him no replacement was made and I decided not to pursue the matter. Instead I resolved to continue on my own.

For the first time in my life I found myself in a position of leadership. The best that could be said about a leader is that he is an ordinary person with an extraordinary determination. To that end I had to work quite hard to come up to that level. Of course, there could be no determination without exercising a reasonable degree of power. I say a reasonable degree of power, with the words of Lord Acton very much in mind, "all power corrupts, and absolute power corrupts absolutely".

In my new linked charge I was expected to lead, and I was under no illusion that all leadership is open to criticism. In particular, the ministry is most liable to criticism more than other professions. The simple reason for this is that people expect a standard from the ministry that they do not expect from any other profession. I decided not to be over-sensitive when faced with positive criticism. I should accept it with all humility and lowliness of heart and mind. "We become," Chesterton said, "taller when we bow." The only criticism I needed to fear would be the criticism that finds an echo in my own conscience. Above all, I recall with deep gratitude the unremitting support and wise council that Betty gave me in that early stage of my ministry. One of her statements still echo in my mind today. "No man," she once told me "can lead who does not love the people he leads." Indeed, his leadership should primarily be a leadership of love.

A Time for Adjustment

In serving two parish churches one must exercise his balancing act as scrupulously as he possibly can. And that exactly what I did. I made sure that in my ministry the two churches would be treated with complete equality. I was careful not to lend more importance to the one church and not to the other. Indeed, this was so even when I felt sorely tempted to show favour to the more responsibly active and conscientious of the two. Through time the two congregations might certainly have found plenty of fault with some of my actions and decisions. It is nigh impossible to find incumbent clerics that have not been touched by one kind of unworthy criticism or another. Sometimes, however, we come across an incumbent priest or minister who is unjustly made so unpopular that his name becomes mud. This reminds me of an anecdote I heard long ago.

The story is told of a newly inducted young minister, who on his first week in the parish, decide to go out and meet his parishioners. Walking along a lonely street he saw two little girls sitting on the ground making mud pies. He stopped and with a broad smile watched them at work. Looking at his clerical collar they realised he was a clergyman, and immediately proceeded to make a church.

"What are you doing, little girls," he asked. "We're making a church, mister," they replied.

The young minister watched and waited patiently to see the outcome of their construction effort. When they had finished they proceeded to show him their handiwork.

"Here is the pulpit," they told him. "And here is the organ, and near it is the Communion table. Here are the choir in the chancel standing and singing. Over there are the congregation with the hymn books in their hands . . ."

In brief, they showed him everything one would expect to see in church on a Sunday service, but one important figure was missing. The young minister complemented the little girls for their work, and then gently asked, "And where is the minister?"

"Oh," said one of them, "we just haven't got enough mud to make one!"

Before reaching that stage prudence was necessary! I thought it best to exercise a good degree of receptiveness and open-mindedness towards my flock. Elders and members of the congregation are there to help their minister. On the other hand, the minister should not hesitate to seek their opinions in matters that are of paramount importance to the work and witness of Christ and His Church. No one can doubt or overlook the leadership and influence of the incumbent priest or minister in his parish church. He is there with his leadership to shape his flock, but he is also there to be shaped by them. I had to address myself to these issues in all seriousness.

It was not easy to work through these and other issues in the early stages of my ministry. The one thing I could handle so easily was preaching and teaching. I was entirely in my element both when I was preparing and when I was delivering my sermons extempore. I was even generally renowned for this particular gift. I could not help looking upon it as a remarkable ministerial asset. Meanwhile, I was aware that this could by no means supersede the ministry of *'helps'*.[1] In His desire to win men for the kingdom of God, Jesus proclaimed the gospel, but He also *"went about doing good"*.[2] The two things are closely and inseparably linked. I must indeed do the work of an evangelist, but I must equally be dedicated to the works of mercy, kindness, forgiveness and help to those in distress. It just happens that people will remember a minister's kindness in a time of trouble when they have forgotten every sermon he ever preached.

No One is Perfect

No doubt, one can make very good decisions and keenly implement them in life with satisfactory results. Yet, however

---

[1] 1 Cor. 12:28.

[2] Mk. 1:14-15; Acts 10:38.

immensely remarkable his achievement might be, somewhere along the way serious blunders and mistakes can occur.

It is always wonderful to do good. But why is it that our good can often misfire or backfire? Sometimes goodness can be spasmodic. The chart of our goodness is like the temperature chart of a person with a high fever. We are capable of reaching the heights of goodness, and we are just as capable of taking a sudden nose dive into the depths. However hard one tries to do the right thing and sticks to it, in an unguarded moment something goes wrong. Often our rigid stance on self-made rules (or man-made rules), which we adopt as golden rules, can have unexpected repercussions. George Bernard Shaw wrote once, "The golden rule is that there are no golden rules." This is so especially if those rules are not conducive to the good and happiness of the individual whom God loves.

I had been in my first charge for over two years and had so far been a stickler for the rules of the Church in addition to my own rules as mentioned above. In that way I presumed one could avoid a great deal of problems and keep things rolling smoothly. Then something happened that has left a lasting and devastating impact upon me. I had been in my study one afternoon when the doorbell rang. At the door there stood a lady in her twenties. She looked pale, pretty run down and her arms were covered in tattoos. I thought first she might have been an alcoholic or a drug addict scrounging for some money to feed the habit. The clergy often do have this kind of people landing on their door step. I was wrong. The lady smiled and politely asked me if I would kindly baptize her recently born baby. I replied by asking her a number of questions. I asked her if she was a member of the church, and if she herself was baptized. I also asked if she had ever attended a church in her life, and whether she had an idea what a child's baptism was all about. Meanwhile, I was unaware of the prideful tone of voice and clerical pomposity with which I spoke to her.

When that lady answered 'no' to all my questions, I told her with a silly smile that I simply could not baptize her child. I never realised at the time that the natural result of pride is contempt for other people. Indeed, there is no sin quite so unchristian as contempt. This and what followed shortly afterwards have come to haunt me for many years to come.

On my vestry day over a week later the same lady came to see me. I immediately thought she might have returned with a deal that could persuade me to change my mind and baptize her child. To say the least, I was not ready for what she came to see me for.

"Minister," she softly said, "can you please take my baby's funeral?" The news of the baby's death so soon, came down upon me like a bolt from the blue. I was simply so dumbstruck that she had to ask me the same question twice.

A combined sense of grief and guilt had immediately set in. My grief for that lady's loss of her baby was beyond endurance. I could not say a word for a couple minutes; and she could only look at me as my eyes filled with tears. At last I pulled myself together and told her that I was willing to take baby Alex's funeral.

But there was also a surge of guilt that has left its scar on me long after it had receded. At the time I could only figure myself out as being more of a minister of death than of life – more instrumental in burying the dead than bringing them to the prince of life. I could clearly count myself among those who prevented the little *'infants'* from coming to Jesus.[3]

I realised that there were things I could have done to win that lady and her partner and so pave the way for that child's baptism. I could have at least visited them at home or invited them to my vestry for a serious chat about their baptism and that of their child. Failing that I could have asked an elder or a faithful church member to stand as a sponsor for that child's baptism. Instead, I had dismissed that poor mother on the basis that ecclesiastical law allowed only children of church members to be baptized, forgetting our Lord's dictum that (the law of) *"the Sabbath was made for man, not man for the Sabbath".*[4]

A couple of days later I took baby Alex's funeral. It was the saddest and the most emotionally tearful funeral I have ever taken. I too was not ashamed to weep with those that wept, and also to weep in bitter regret for what I had done. And what could be more intensely remorseful than taking the funeral of an infant I had only a week before refused to baptize?

In that sad atmosphere and as a token of contrition I vowed to God in the silence of my own heart never again to refuse baptism to a child. I have honoured my vow until I retired a few years ago. I believed then and I still passionately believe that to receive a child in Jesus' name means to act as a true representative of Christ who loved

---

[3] Lk. 18:15-17.

[4] Mk. 2:27.

little children.[5] At any rate, during that agonizing experience, Betty was a tower of strength and consolation to me. Her prayerful support and wise counselling did much to help me pull through that painful period. Nevertheless, no man is ever safe from memory. After more than three decades I still recoil when I remember that unhappy incident.

John B. Gough, the great temperance orator, became a man of God. He always rejoiced in God's forgiveness, and he pleaded with others to accept it; and one of the things he used to say to young men was: "Watch what you are doing. God can forgive you, but the scars remain." God also knows that among mortals no one is perfect.

Unexpected Paradox

Life would be much easier if there were no such things as mistakes and regrets and remorse. Indeed, life would be much easier, if a man had no conscience, and God would just let him alone. But as a matter of fact, that never happens. God might sometimes, for our own good, put us in a highly difficult situation where we feel utterly alone, vulnerable and totally helpless. The sense of God's absence becomes all too real. But does God really forsake us in that situation?

A story is told of a Native American Indian tribe that had a peculiar way of initiating young boys into manhood. The father would simply pick his young boy up, take him to a far distant and dangerous forest and leave him there alone for the whole night. One day a father did just that with his young boy. The boy was simply dropped into a forest that was infested with all sorts of snakes, bears and what is known in the USA as mountain lions.

The boy was cold, terrified and panic stricken. He wept and cried out for his Dad all night but to no avail. At dawn, his father came and took him home. Hardly able to stop crying, the boy berated his father for what he had done to him. "I thought," said the boy, "that you were not only my Dad but also my friend. How could you leave me in a cold and deadly forest and return home without me?"

The father replied, "My boy, I did not forsake you in that dangerous forest alone. I did not return home. When I left you at the foot of that huge tree that evening, I went under cover of darkness and sat behind another tree a few yards from you. Yes, I heard your cries, but my eyes were on you all night so that no harm would come to you. You were

---

[5] Lk. 9:47-48; 18:15-17.

not alone, for I was with you throughout that dark and dreadful night, my son."

Sometimes, for our own spiritual growth, the Lord deals with us in a similar way. The ministry is not an easy life. It certainly has its dark and lonely moments. Yet, through all adversities we as Christians are bidden to be of good cheer and rejoice.[6] Russell Maltby once said that Jesus promised His people three things – that they would be in constant trouble, completely fearless and absurdly happy! A Christian should be enjoying life, and he should look as if he was! Sometimes even through grim and sad circumstances, God has ways of throwing in a bit of joy and laughter into the situation. I have known this by experience.

On my fourth year as minister of the linked charge an English lady came to see me one day. She was slightly over sixty, elegant and spoke with a lah-di-dah accent. She told me that her Scottish husband, Arthur, had just passed away. And as he was a Protestant, she wondered if I would kindly take the funeral. As the couple lived within the boundaries of my parish of Chapelhall, I agreed to take the funeral service, which was to be at Daldowie Crematorium in Glasgow a few days later.

At the Crematorium, prior to the service the lady handed me a sheet of music and asked if the organist could play that piece at the committal. As I could not read music, I had no idea what piece of music that was. However, I passed it on to the organist with the lady's request and went to the pulpit to begin the service. Glancing at the organist from the pulpit, I noticed him laughing quietly with his head down. I had no idea what was making him laugh on such a sad occasion. The funeral service was conducted satisfactorily right up to the committal. At the committal, as I intoned "Forasmuch as it hath pleased Almighty God to take unto Himself the soul *of our brother* here departed . . ." the organist at once played, *"Happy days are here again . . ."*! I was utterly flabbergasted, but fortunately not lost for words! I continued until the benediction. Inside me, however, I was astounded. "Dear Lord", I whispered to myself, "that wife couldn't wait to get rid of that poor man!"

At the door, that lady came and shook my hand and expressed her heartfelt thanks for what she described as a most comforting service. Then she nicely explained what that piece of music which the organist played had meant to her. It was, she said, the piece of music to

---

[6] Jn. 16:33; Rom. 5:1-5.

which she and Arthur danced at their first dinner dance about twenty seven years ago. That was a funny surprise to me, and I could hardly stop laughing when I was returning home. Maybe the laugh was on me, because I failed to see and even appreciate on that occasion the unexpected paradox.

Time for Change

Taking pastoral care of a linked charge is never an easy task for any clergyman. With the beginning of spring 1985, I was in my sixth year as minister of Chapelhall and Calderbank parish churches. After much prayer and consideration, Betty and I decided that the time had come to look for another charge, preferably a single parish church. I did not want to hang on in one place too long. After all, the man who hangs on too long can be a sad spectacle.

Meanwhile, I was worried in case history might repeat itself when I start applying to vacant churches. The immense difficulty I had experienced in seeking a charge some years earlier was very much on my mind. My concern about this matter did not escape Betty. One day she humoured me by saying, "I won't worry if I were you, Sam. You are now so well known that it might just be a matter of first come first served!" I laughed thinking how good Betty was at massaging my ego! What happened next showed that what she had said proved somehow prophetic.

The following day, my colleague, the Revd James Salmond, minister of Holytown parish church, phoned to give me an interesting piece of news. He informed me that the nearby charge of Fauldhouse St Andrew's parish church had recently become vacant. This West Lothian parish church is roughly nine miles from Chapelhall. My colleague was quite keen that I should apply for it at the earliest possible convenience.

A few days later, I sent my application together with my CV to the Vacancy Committee of Fauldhouse St Andrew's. In less than two weeks I received a positive reply from the Vacancy Committee. Unknown to me, however, some people from Airdrie who often attended my Sunday morning services at Calderbank, had already been recommending me to a couple of their friends on the Committee. Now I was being asked if it would be possible for the members of the Vacancy Committee to come and hear me on Sunday April 28th. They also wanted to meet me for an interview after that Sunday morning service.

On that day I took the morning service at Calderbank parish church. I made a point during the service not to try to scour the congregation to see who the Vacancy members were and where they were sitting. Instead I focused entirely upon the conduct of the worship. After the service, they discreetly introduced themselves to me, and then as planned, they made their way to the manse in Chapelhall for the scheduled interview. The members of the Vacancy Committee were a fine group of people, among them four church elders. The interview went very well with hardly any intricate question being asked. They did however ask me about my background and my conversion to the Christian faith. In the end they expressed their sincere appreciation for the conduct of the morning service and for what they described as a heart-searching message.

Ten days later, I was invited to preach as sole nominee for the vacant charge of Fauldhouse St Andrew's parish church on Sunday June 2nd. It was 'first come first served', just as Betty had suggested. In any case, she was hugely delighted with the news. On that particular date, I preached as sole nominee and afterwards was voted as minister of that parish church by an overwhelming majority of the congregation. Shortly thereafter the date for my induction was scheduled by the Presbytery of West Lothian to take place on Wednesday July 3rd 1985.

The induction service, as I recall, commenced in an atmosphere of expectancy and jubilation. Then something happened which obviously marred that sublime atmosphere. One of the church elders sitting with his colleagues in the chancel suddenly died with a massive heart-attack in the middle of the opening hymn. I was deeply shocked at what happened. Although not a superstitious man, I could not but hope and indeed pray that that might not be a bad omen. I looked and saw Betty sitting in the choir with her head down, presumably praying. Then she raised her head and looked at me with a gentle smile and a nod, as if to say, "Don't worry, Sam, all will be fine."

So oddly enough, my ministry in Fauldhouse began not with my first Sunday service, but with the funeral service of that poor elder. There is a sense in which the holy ministry can be an occupational hazard! I wondered for a moment what else my time in Fauldhouse had in store for us. But, on reflection, I was sure that come what may we could be certain of God's gracious presence with us in our new charge.[7]

---

[7] Ex. 33:14-15; Mt. 28:19-20.

Chapter 20

DILEMMAS, DOUBTS AND DEMANDS

"If you falter in times of trouble,
how small is your strength!"
(Proverbs 24: 10 NIV)

Not long before leaving the linked charge of Chapelhall and Calderbank we had been deeply saddened by the death of Betty's father, Mr Alex Kirkwood. In fact, he was the loving father of both of us. I remain eternally indebted to him for his unfaltering kindness to me personally from the day I met him until the day he left this scene of time.

He was survived by Annie, his dear wife, who was also mother of both of us. Sadly, her widowhood coincided with a serious eyesight problem, which consequently led to her blindness. This and the loss of a remarkable father had dealt a shattering blow to us as a family. Nevertheless, Betty seemed to have taken it harder than any of us; and that was perfectly understandable. She had been the only sibling to live with her parents until I came on the scene a few years earlier. I also gathered in the process that she had some lingering sense of guilt. She tended to blame herself for not remaining at home to take care of her aged parents. Did she regret marrying me after all? I refused to think that and kept completely silent. I believed that she was simply going through a very critical period of grief which might soon blow over. But it did not.

Meanwhile, mother's eyesight was failing quite fast. She was now living with her daughter, Christy, and her family. When we moved to Fauldhouse Betty often brought her to spend a day or a weekend with us.

One day, Betty somehow reluctantly asked me if it would be possible to bring Mum to stay with us for a week or ten days. "How dare you ask me such a question, Betty," I seriously told her. "You need no permission from me. She is as much your Mum as she is my Mum.

You can bring her here any time. She is welcome to stay with us for one week or one month if she wants. Indeed," I added, "If she wishes to stay with us for good, I would be more than delighted." I saw tears of joy on Betty's cheeks that day. "I'm very sorry, Sam," she said with her head on my shoulder, "I could not have married a better man." I knew immediately that her critical period of grief had blown over, at that very moment.

Zeal Not Fanaticism

Having served as minister of two parish churches for almost six years, I was now more than happy to be the incumbent of a single parish church, and it was the only parish church of Scotland in Fauldhouse. Then, I soon discovered that it was the only place in Scotland, if not in the whole of Britain, where the medical doctor and the parish clergyman were Arabs! Dr Camal al-Ubaid is a native of Iraq (the easternmost part of the Arab world), and I am a native of Morocco (the westernmost part of the Arab world). We consequently took him as our doctor and we soon became very close friends.

Besides being a good man, he was noted for his playfully mischievous sense of humour. "Sam," he asked me once, "don't you think the BBC ought to have an interview programme with us in Fauldhouse?" When I asked why, he replied, "As a small village, Fauldhouse will be world news. It's the only place where there are two prominent Arabs, one a doctor and the other a clergyman – one kills them and the other buries them!"

It had been over a month now since my induction. Apart from our huge Victorian manse with its intolerable draughts and a number of seriously needed repairs, we seemed happy enough to be in the place of God's perfect choice. The warm welcome shown to us by our new parishioners had been a source of great joy and encouragement. Meanwhile, now that I had only one parish church I decided to break the mould of formality and bring some spiritual excitement into the life of my new church.

I first resolved to start three services a week: Sunday morning and evening services, and a midweek service of Bible study and prayer fellowship on Wednesday evening. This was indeed a tough task to embark on. In my heart of hearts I knew that the Spirit of God is always looking for a mind to use, and I had a mind that was sufficiently equipped with a knowledge He could use. Of course, knowledge is not everything, but when that knowledge becomes what a famous evangelist called 'knowledge on fire', then things really begin to happen. Consequently, a number of people, mainly of the evangelical wing, gave their enthusiastic response to the idea. But others were somehow cynical. For them Sunday morning service was enough. Moreover, I was credibly informed that someone had not been surprised that a convert like me should embark on three services a week. "After all," he jokingly remarked, "converts can be a bit fanatical!"!

A colleague once told me a story of a Vacancy Committee that had gone to hear a minister. After the service they met him for an interview during which they spent most of the time asking him what his likes and dislikes were. When his turn came to speak, he asked them what they thought about preaching the Gospel and winning souls for Jesus. "Well, sir," replied one of them almost abruptly, "we are looking for a minister not for a fanatic!"!

It is quite easy to mistake spiritual zeal for fanaticism. But, in the words of Charles Haddon Spurgeon, "Even fanaticism is to be preferred to indifference. I had sooner risk the dangers of a tornado of religious excitement than see the air grow stagnant with a dead formality."

Nowhere Else to Go

We had been in Fauldhouse over six months, when one day Betty complained about tiredness, light-headedness and a slight pain across her chest. In spite of that next day she drove to Hillington Industrial Estate in Glasgow where she worked as Personnel Officer at Haven Products. At that moment I recalled what happened in the summer of the previous year when we were motoring in Spain. We had been travelling from Valencia to Alicante when Betty, sitting beside me as I drove, suddenly crouched in what seemed to be an excruciating pain. I was so worried I wanted to stop immediately to find out what was happening to her. But she insisted that I drive on and that she was merely having a severe stomach pain. When the pain had gradually subsided, she looked utterly pale and exhausted. For the rest of that Spanish holiday, Betty was not the same. Whatever the nature of the pain she had suffered in the car, the effect of it was obvious. It left her weak and lethargic despite making a brave show that she was all right. We were finally grateful to return safely home from that holiday.

However, three days after Betty's unfortunate pain across her chest, Dr al-Ubaid paid us a surprise visit during which Betty mentioned to him that incident. He immediately took her blood pressure and listened to her heart-beat. He then pointed out briefly that she had a kind of irregular heart-beat, and that he was going to send her for an Electro Cardiogram (ECG) as soon as possible. Betty did not like the sound of that and remarked that she did not think there was anything wrong with her heart. "Well, Betty," replied the doctor, "we just want to be on the safe side. It's better to be sure than sorry."

A week later, Betty received a letter from Bangour hospital asking her to report in a couple of days to the Electrocardiography Unit for a test. I was with her that afternoon when she was undergoing the test. The young doctor who was doing the test was carefully inspecting each of the ECG recordings. His careful inspection which seemed to take a long time gave us the impression that after all there might not be anything wrong. Betty's optimistic smile as she looked at me seemed to suggest that. Then, suddenly the doctor said, "Ah! There it is!" Our hearts sank as we heard that sentence. "Is it all right, doctor?" asked Betty in a relaxed tone of voice. "In point of fact", he replied calmly, "we are sending our finding to your doctor and he will explain everything to you."

The following week Doctor al-Ubaid came to see us with the outcome of the ECG. He explained to us in medical terms the nature of Betty's heart condition, which for me personally was extremely difficult to follow. But one thing was clear. The need for an operation was of paramount importance. He told us that he was going to contact an Edinburgh hospital immediately.

From this we were left under the impression that this operation was a matter of the utmost urgency. Yet, dauntless as always, Betty was still travelling to work every day despite my frequent attempts to dissuade her from doing so. However, the fact remained that we were both gravely concerned and down-hearted, yet we managed to hide it from each other. In the open, we were managing to play the whole thing down by reminding each other, among other things, that heart operations nowadays are simply plain sailing. But in private, the burden of worry weighed heavily upon me personally. In that situation, we were driven to our knees in prayer because we had nowhere else to go.

A Tragic Let Down

About the end of March 1986, Betty was called to Edinburgh hospital for what is known as a pre-operative assessment. After that the operation was scheduled to take place in the middle of April in the same hospital. But as a Glaswegian, Betty requested that her operation should take place at any hospital in Glasgow where she would be near her family. Edinburgh would be too far for them to travel to visit her. At her insistence, however, the venue was changed.

Her operation was now scheduled to be done in Glasgow two weeks later than it had been scheduled in Edinburgh. The reason for those two weeks delay was difficult to understand. It crossed my mind that the reason for the delay might have been due to Margaret Thatcher's policy at the time. Her opponents at the time were claiming that the health services had been cut back and that there had been an acute shortage of hospital beds. If so, then I had no idea what Betty and her family thought, for they were staunch Conservative supporters. Although I was no Conservative supporter, I really was not sure if Mrs Thatcher was somehow bent on destroying our National Health Service, which has been the envy of the world.

During the first week of April I began to notice some deterioration in Betty's health. If she walked up the stairs or was busy doing something at home she would easily be short of breath, and either had to slow down or stop and rest a bit. If I voiced my concern about it, her reply was simply, "There is nothing to worry about." To convince herself and convince me that there was no cause for worry, she still drove all the way to work daily, which was a matter of enormous concern to me.

On Friday morning the 25th of April, Betty told me that she was not leaving for work. I was partly happy but a bit ill at ease. It was not like her to do so all of a sudden. After all, driving to work daily was her way of saying that there was nothing serious to worry about. As I kept an eye on her that day I could not help noticing that she was not her usual self. She sat downstairs almost the whole day looking slightly pale and dozing off most of the time. I cooked some meal for us both which she managed to eat slowly. I offered a couple of times to call Dr al-Ubaid to have a look at her, but she dismissed the offer with the usual "there is nothing to worry about".

In the evening she slowly walked upstairs to the bedroom, and as she reached the top of the stairs she stopped for a moment holding on to the banister. I noticed poor Betty struggling to regain her breath. I pretended I was not looking in case she became agitated. She always played being brave, and I did not want her to feel robbed of the little confidence that she might have had.

She could hardly sleep that night and neither could I. In fact, I deliberately stayed wide awake feeling her every movement and listening attentively to the rhythm of her breathing. A sense of foreboding seemed to permeate my mind all the time. Just shortly before dawn I fell asleep, and in my sleep I had a nightmare. I dreamed I had lost a molar tooth.

The dream was so dreadfully vivid that I jumped out of bed and sat at the edge of it with my head down. Betty, who had apparently felt the impact of that jump, asked what was wrong. I told her that I had a nightmare. I dreamed I had lost a molar tooth. After a short pause she asked if that dream had any significance. I replied with a chuckle that I was no interpreter of dreams, and in any case that was just a passing nightmare. As I laid me down to sleep again, I recalled how in Morocco (and probably throughout the Arab world), dreaming of losing a member of one's body (like an ear, an eye or a tooth) is taken as a seriously bad omen. It suggests the possible loss of property, employment or even the loss of a loved one. Moreover, it was believed that if such a dream occurs at dawn or near it, the significance of that dream may be realized sooner than expected. For a moment I shuddered to think that such a thing could happen to me. I promptly dismissed that atrocious idea as purely superstitious and went to sleep.

On Saturday Betty was the same as the day before. I stayed at home the whole day partly preparing for my next day Sunday service, and partly keeping a watchful eye on her. The next day being Sunday Betty stayed at home owing to her state of health while I went to Church to take the morning worship. The congregation were aware of Betty's condition and kindly assured me after the service that she was very much in their thoughts and prayers.

After the service I returned home and stayed to take care of her the whole day. That day she looked more gravely ill and weaker than I had seen her before. Before going to sleep, she handed me a few vasodilator tablets saying that if anything happened to her during the night I should immediately put one of tablets under her tongue. At about two in the morning, Betty had a severe heart attack and was consequently writhing in pain. As she rolled herself about in severe pain, I could not possibly find a way to put one of those tablets under her tongue. I ran to the phone and called Dr al-Ubaid who happened to be in bed. He arrived in no time and quickly gave her a pain relief injection while I called the ambulance. She was rushed to Bangour Hospital where she was immediately attended to.

As she lay in her hospital bed she looked completely drained but not in pain. Before I left her, she quietly looked at me with a faintish smile, as if to say, "Sorry for this bother, Sam." "Never mind, Betty," I whispered to her, "you will be just fine." Then, I prayerfully committed her to the Lord and left. That was the early morning of Monday April 28th. Returning home I was able to sleep on the sofa for no more than a couple of hours.

At about ten that morning I went back to the hospital to see how she was. I found her asleep. The nurse on duty told me that her condition was stable and that it might be a good idea not to disturb her sleep. She suggested that I should return early in the evening, which I did. She looked tired and a somewhat drowsy. When I was leaving I told her that I would be seeing her next day in the morning. She suggested that as the doctors were usually busy doing their rounds in the morning it might be more convenient if I came in the afternoon or the evening. Then she slowly sat up, gave me a good-night kiss and lay down again.

On returning home that evening, I made myself something to eat and sat down to watch the TV. I was watching the ITN news when at the interval, which was precisely 10.15 p.m., the telephone rang. It was a nurse from the Bangour Hospital asking me in a gentle voice to come, for Betty had taken a bad turn. As I drove to the Hospital I fervently pleaded with the Lord that I might not lose Betty. When I arrived at the Coronary Care Unit a nurse escorted me to a small room and told me that a doctor was coming to see me shortly. I waited anxiously for about a few minutes which seemed intolerably long.

A young doctor came in and sat next to me. "Sir," he said in a low tone of voice, "we did everything we could and . . ." Before finishing his sentence I bitterly interrupted with my head down, "You've let me down!" I heard him say calmly, "No, sir, we haven't," putting his hand on my shoulder. "I'm sorry, doctor, I was not talking to you," I responded, "I was talking to someone else."

At that point he went quiet. I am not sure if he understood what I meant. He asked me if I wished to see her, and I agreed. A nurse then escorted me to the room where Betty lay. Traumatized and in deep anguish I looked at Betty as she lay there lifeless. I drew close to her, put my cheek close to her cold cheek and briefly gave vent to my grievance. "My world has just fallen apart around me, Betty," I sobbingly complained. "I'd frantically battered at the gate of heaven, pleading with God to spare you, but all to no avail. It's a tragic let down . . . !"

Picking Up the Pieces

I returned late that evening to an empty manse – a manse that would never again be brightened up by Betty's presence. The first thing I did was to phone Betty's mother and family who did not take long to arrive. I went to bed in the early hours of the morning nursing a double blow – my irretrievable loss of Betty, and my passionate pleas to God for her which went unanswered. Why should He take her away? It was a hard issue to come to terms with. In fact, any desire to come to terms with it was virtually absent. At that moment in time I was mainly focused on the negative aspect of what happened. In the silence of my own heart and mind I certainly had a serious bone to pick with God, both at that time and a while after Betty's funeral. There were many intricate and burning questions which were doubtless fuelled by my sense of loneliness and desolation. The answer was utter silence. But little did I know that, as Carlyle put it, "Silence is the element in which great things fashion themselves."

It was during that painful period of silence that something happened. A few days after returning to my church duties from a month leave of absence following Betty's funeral, the Harthill undertaker phoned to tell me that a tragic death of a young wife and mother of two children had just taken place in my parish. I could really have done without that piece of sad news for I was still under the painful impact of my own bereavement. I most certainly was not looking forward to taking any funeral so soon. In any case, as part of my parish ministerial duties I had to go and visit the bereaved family, which under the circumstances, was far from easy.

On arrival I was received by the bereaved father and his children with the utmost respect and courtesy. Then, before I could say a word, the grieving gentleman gave me his deepest sympathy for the recent loss of my own wife. "When Jennet, my wife, passed away," he said emotionally, "you were the first person to come to mind, minister. We could imagine how enormous your sense of grief and desolation must be." He went on, "Your situation is perhaps compounded by the fact that unlike me, you have no family to support and comfort you in your time of bereavement . . . However, Jennet has been the second wife to pass away after your wife in this village, and it's going to be the first funeral since that of your wife."

Then he leaned forward and calmly said, "I'm pretty much aware that it might be very tough on you conducting my wife's funeral service so soon after your wife's passing. If you wish to decline taking this service, we shall sympathetically understand your position. We don't mind if one of your colleagues steps into your place."

I appreciatively brushed aside his kind suggestion insisting that it was my bounden duty to take the funeral service. I thanked him for his kindest thoughts and words and profusely apologized for my virtual silence throughout my visit. He assured me that at a bereavement words can be quite inadequate. What mattered to him and his family was my presence which he described as most uplifting. Finally, I prayed with the family and promised to return the next day so that together we could draft a tribute to Jennet to be read at the funeral service in a few days.

I left the family with an extraordinary feeling. Here was a visit in which, as a parish minister, I was supposed to allay the people's grief and comfort their hearts. Instead I found myself being the recipient of all the sympathy and solace from the very people who were in the immediate need of them. At first, I was pleasantly uplifted by the warm sympathy and kindness of the bereaved husband and father of family, but shortly afterwards I was hit by a terrible sense of guilt as I recalled the first words of that gentleman: "When Jennet, my wife, passed way, you were the first person to come to mind, minister." By contrast, when Betty passed away, my egocentricity had no bounds. I was so gripped by my tragic loss of her that I never gave a thought to a couple of my parishioners who had of late suffered the loss of their husbands. Perhaps I was unconsciously seeking consolation myself, forgetting that my duty was 'not so much to be consoled as to console'.

A few days later Jennet's funeral service took place at which I officiated as the parish minister. At the end of that funeral service, and particularly before the benediction, I did something I had usually done at every funeral service. I concluded with two or three Biblical texts. Almost always one of them would be Job 1:21b "... *the Lord gave, and the Lord has taken away; blessed be the name of the Lord."* Interestingly, even today among the Arabs of the Middle East, the survivors of the dead person utter a liturgical formula, "His Lord gave him, and his Lord has taken him away."[1]

As at every funeral service, this was virtually the concept I expected the mourners to accept with some degree of meekness and resignation. But it was a different case when death came to my doorstep. As I uttered those words at that funeral, I realized for the first time that in the dark loneliness of my bleak affliction, I was nursing a quiet resentment against God. I regarded myself a victim – and a silent victim at that. In that case I was oblivious to others' grief and resentful of the silent and inscrutable heaven.

After that funeral service it was time to take stock of myself, my life and my attitude. From Betty's death until then my life had become characterized by prayerlessness. But now, I was the man for whom there was nothing left to say but: "God help me! God help me!" I gradually became acutely aware that there are sorrows which none but God can comfort. There are problems which none but God can solve. There is a strength which none but God can give. Indeed, there are times when every man reaches the limit of human effort and human endurance. At that moment he can only stretch out his hand to God and ask Him for the strength to pass the breaking point and not break. With this remarkable change, I was becoming conscious of God's gracious intervention in my situation. That was also the time in which I was getting enough strength to start picking up the pieces.

A Puzzling Issue

After almost seven years marriage to Betty I was now back on my own. I have carried her memory with me ever since she passed away on the 28th April 1986. With her memory indelibly stamped on my mind, I decided the time had come for me to move on. I was now a single man again with no choice but to soldier on alone – and yet not alone. I made sure that I would keep myself as vigorously active as I possibly could. Besides my steadfast commitment to my daily parish

---

[1] See E.G. Kraeling, *The Book of the Wars of God* (New York 1939), p. 184.

work, I had a rekindled desire to return to my Biblical research study, and to that end I already had an excellent library.

My attention was particularly focused on the Old Testament which I had already done in my BD course at Glasgow University. My interest in this subject happened to have been mainly renewed by Ronald De Vaux's exciting book *Ancient Israel: Its Life and Institutions*. Within the next two years I had enthusiastically covered wide areas of Old Testament history and theology. During this period I had also become keenly interested in the study of the inter-testamental period, and in the history of the rise of what is known as 'Normative Judaism'.[2]

On the 19th March 1986, almost a month before Betty passed away, I (among two others), was appointed to the Board of World Mission and Unity by the Nomination Committee. But, owing to Betty's grave illness and subsequent death I attended the Board in Edinburgh only once. Therefore, my knowledge of what the Board was all about was nil. In November that year I was appointed by the Board of World Mission and Unity to the 'Relations with Israel and with People of Other Faiths Committee'. Now, having recovered from the ravages of my bereavement, I decided to honour my obligation and start attending that Committee.

At the start of the first meeting which I attended, the atmosphere seemed full of cordiality among all the members present. But when the report of a recent meeting of some of the Committee members with the representatives of the Jewish Community in Glasgow was given, the atmosphere began to change. It became obvious from the discussion which followed that neutrality among most of the Committee members vis-a-vis the Arab-Israeli dispute was terribly lacking. The balance was noticeably in favour of the Jewish people,[3] and their support for the Zionist state of Israel was a forgone conclusion.

---

[2] "The Judaism which predominated the early centuries of our common Era to the present time (is) called '*Rabbinic*' or '*Talmudic*' or simply '*Normative* . . .*'* See Jacob Neusner, *The Description of Formative Judaism: The Social Perspective of the Mishnah's System of Civil Law and Government*, Cambridge University Press, Vol. 5, (1980), p. 63.

[3] It was emphasized that Western Christendom owe the Jewish people unequivocal and unceasing apology for the appalling suffering they had historically endured at its hand, ranging from Medieval pogroms to the Nazi Holocaust.

At that point I felt somehow irked. I was about to ask where the Christian sense of justice for the dispossessed Palestinians comes in when a female colleague spoke out. She briefly reported that a member of the Jewish representatives had told her after a recently held meeting in Glasgow that "all the Arabs should be kicked out of the land. Palestine belongs only to the Jewish People by divine right". The report was noticeably most disconcerting to the Committee. However, that colleague and I asked whether, like their comrade, the rest of Jewish representatives were also in favour of mass Palestinian expulsion. If so, then should our dialogue with them continue?

One colleague, who has long passed away, responded rather sharply that we should be careful not to say or do anything that might be construed as anti-Semitic. I calmly replied that there seems to be no problem today in the West to vilify and demonize the Arabs generally and the Palestinians in particular. It may be fashionable to be anti-Semitic provided the Semites are Arabs!

At this point the chairman decided that we drop this subject and move on to the next item in the agenda. In this way he made sure that our different point of views on such a thorny subject would not lead to acrimony. However, in 1987 the 'Relations with Israel and with People of Other Faiths Committee' changed to the 'Middle East and North Africa Committee'. Under the leadership of Revd Robin Ross and others this Committee did much to champion the just cause of the Palestinians in the Church of Scotland. This was further enhanced by the already existing relations between the Church of Scotland and the Palestinian Churches, not to mention other Middle Eastern and Egyptian Churches. There was nothing more gratifying to me than to see this relationship being consolidated between the Church in Scotland and the Church in the Arab world.

However, to this day there has remained a burning question to which I have not been able to find an answer. In the 'Middle East and North Africa Committee' I was the only Arab with the full knowledge of the Arab world, its language, its history, its culture and its current politics. Yet, for over six years as a member of that Committee no active role had ever been assigned to me. Almost all members of that Committee had at one time or another been sent as delegates to visit partner churches in the Middle East and Egypt, but I was never once included among them. I had often offered to pay my own way if the Committee would allow me to accompany a future delegation, but all to no avail. When meeting with clerical Arab delegates in the General Assembly, they would obviously be surprised to see me as the only ordained Arab clergyman in the Church of Scotland. Indeed, they would be even astounded when they discovered my current position as a member of the 'Middle East and North Africa Committee'.

Apparently, during their visits to the region no delegation had ever mentioned that the Committee they represented had an Arab member. Men like the Revd Bayadi of the Synod of the Nile and Riyah Abu al-Asal, the former Anglican bishop of Jerusalem (not to mention a former Moderator), had pleaded with the officials to involve me in the work of this Committee. For then, as they pointed out, by virtue of my linguistic and cultural background I could be a great asset to the Committee. Sadly, their plea fell on deaf ears.

My term as a member of this Committee came to an end by the summer of 1992. That was a tremendous relief for me! During my entire term in this Committee I had done no more than attend meetings. I might as well have been a silent observer! To date I am still grappling with what may seem to some as a form of marginalisation. I have not found an answer to it yet. This has indeed been a puzzling issue.

Brotherly Disagreements

I had not been a year in the 'Middle East and North Africa Committee', when the Handsel Press published a series of five booklets on 'Church and Israel'.[4] At least four of the authors were my friends and colleagues, and to this day I still hold them in the highest possible respect for their spiritual calibre and zeal for the gospel. In terms of our Biblical and theological stance we have always been of the evangelical wing and of the same mind in the Lord. But when it came to Israel and Zionism we were simply poles apart. The common theme that runs through all the above mentioned booklets is the

---

[4] D.W. Torrance, *The Mission of Christians and Jews*, Handsel Press Edinburgh 1986; D.W. Torrance and A.F. Lamont, *Anti-Semitism and Christian Responsibility*, Handsel Press, Edinburgh 1986; J. Walker, *Israel – Covenant and Land*, Handsel Press Edinburgh 1986; H. Taylor, *World Hope in the Middle East*, Handsel Press 1986; W. Riggans, *Israel and Zionism*, Handsel Press Edinburgh 1986.

glorification of the Jewish people and the secular Zionist state of Israel. This glorification rests on the unwarranted idea which views world Jewry, including the state of Israel and its claim to Palestine, as having covenantal and prophetic significance. In response I wrote my *Israel Reassessed: A Christian Arab View*, which became the sixth booklet in the so-called 'Church and Israel Series'.

The subject of this booklet stood in glaring contrast to the theme of the other five booklets. It was a totally new thing to many a Christian reader. As a result it was rumoured that it had sold more than the others. My argument in this booklet is that both the Torah and the prophets are emphatic that the Abrahamic covenant promise of land is conditional upon continuing obedience and faithfulness to the terms of that covenant. To argue otherwise does not only ignore covenant conditionality, but is also a reversal of the covenant order. I further argue that covenantal details such as sacrifices, land and circumcision were temporal and conditional in nature. Once their purpose was realized in Jesus Christ, there remained no further need for them in God's redemptive purpose (see Heb. 8:13).

Admittedly, I have always been averse to that form of eschatology which views the current Israeli/Palestinian conflict in pre-millennial-dispensationalist terms. For this and other related Christian eschatological schools, the Arabs generally and the Palestinians in particular are almost always villains of choice. Conversely, Israel is viewed as the elect and Jewish history is predestined by God and foretold by prophecy. Therefore, ordinary rules of international law of morality do not apply to God's chosen people; and there is no absolute standard by which they can be judged. In that case the entire sublime attribute of God's justice is called into question.

However, I believe, as does the bulk of Christendom, that Old Testament prophecies are fulfilled only in the Spirit-filled Church of Christ. Such a theological perspective must not be construed as anti-Jewish. I harbour no animosity towards the Jewish people nor will I ever do so. In Morocco, the country of my origin, Moroccan Jews lived side by side with us in peace and harmony. I had a good number of close friends among them since childhood, and I still cherish their memory. I even recognise the right of the state of Israel to exist – a nation like all other nations, as Israel's Declaration of Independence clearly implies. I am most decidedly against its dissolution or dismantlement. But I also solemnly believe that

Palestine is a land for two peoples. And sooner or later there will be a Palestinian state existing peacefully side by side with the state of Israel. There are signs that politically things are moving to that end, and the bulk of the Israelis believe that a Palestinian state is inevitable.

In reality I have no problem with the state of Israel. My real problem is with that branch of Christian eschatology which vests one party in the current Arab/Israeli conflict with the mantle of divine approval and absolute territorial ownership to the exclusion of the other. This type of Christian, with all their evangelical zeal, cannot hope to succeed in evangelizing the Arabs and Muslims when on one hand they tell them that Jesus loves them and has a wonderful plan for their lives, and on the other they believe that the plan necessitates removing them from their homeland and destroying their dignity. How can they convince them that the Bible is 'Good News' when their interpretation of the scriptures calls for the end of their right to the land of their fathers? They simply cannot win them for Christ in this way. Indeed, to do so is tantamount to trying to evangelize them in the context of injustice.

It is high time that we as Christians, with our many and varied theological perspectives, should pay close attention to St Paul's golden principle: *"Give none offence, neither to the Jews, nor to the Gentiles, nor to the Church of God. Even as I please all men in all things, not seeking mine own profit, but the profit of many, that they may be saved"* (1 Cor. 10:32-33). This should help us to re-cast our Christian image so that our witness may be worthy of Christ who championed the cause of the oppressed. It should also help us as Christians with many different theological views to transcend our brotherly disagreements.

A Further Study

One of the outstanding lecturers I had been privileged to study under in the seventies was Robert Davidson, Professor of Old Testament at Glasgow University. In the winter of 1988 I was having coffee with him at the University restaurant when I was surprised to know how keenly interested he was in the ongoing Israeli/Palestinian conflict. I was even more surprised to learn that he had read my recently published booklet and was largely impressed by it. To use his words, "Your point of argument was very much needing to be said." He was particularly interested in my argument vis-a-vis the conditionality of the Old Testament covenant. God's covenant with ancient Israel was no blank cheque. In the course of our conversation he suggested that it might be a good idea if I would consider addressing this subject fully in a Master of Theology Degree. And that was precisely what happened.

In the autumn of 1989 I began my M.Th. Dissertation under the title 'Israel, Covenant and Land in the Old Testament'. I had not long been under his supervision when he was called to the Moderatorship of the General Assembly of the Church of Scotland and Professor Robert Carroll was appointed as my supervisor. I consider myself fortunate to have been under his supervision, for he was a tough critic and a very helpful guide to the most invaluable sources dealing with the historical origin, definition, and significance of the covenant in ancient Israel and normative Judaism today.

In addressing this subject three things became clear:

1 Ancient Israel was more of a heterogeneous than a homogeneous people. The formation of the people of Israel as it is organized at the time of the Judges was the result of a much more complex process than mere linear descent from the twelve patriarchs. The formation of the people of Israel rested entirely upon actual solidarity of a conglomeration of tribes and peoples at certain point in time i.e. after the arrival in Canaan. The consciousness of their solidarity was translated into the simple terms of linear descent and thus blood link. The question is, what really constituted Israel? Not race, not language and not even government. The only bond that unified all these miscellaneous groups was the worship of Yahweh: Yahweh is the God of Israel, Israel is the people of Yahweh.[5]

2 The Old Testament concept of the covenant was not as simple as I had thought. I came to discover a number of different opinions among Biblical scholars regarding the Old Testament concept of the covenant. The most interesting of them was that of Julius Wellhausen. In 1885 he argued that Israel's covenant was a late Biblical concept arising from the legalising tendencies of the Deuteronomistic

---

[5] Robert H. Pfeiffer, *Religion in the Old Testament*, Adam & Charles Black, London, 196, pp. 49f.; for a full study on this subject see Giovanni Garbini, History & Ideology in Ancient Israel, SCM Press 1988.

school. Originally, the Torah of Yahweh fell under the category of divine aid, especially in doing justice, of divine guidance in the solution of difficult questions. But later it came to be understood "as incorporating the demands on the fulfilment of which God's attitude towards Israel entirely depended. In this way arose, from ideas which easily suggested it, but yet as an entirely new thing, the substance of the notion of covenant or treaty." He finally points out that "the Babylonian exile no doubt helped, as the Assyrian exile had previously done, to familiarise the Jewish mind with the idea that the covenant depended on conditions, and might possibly be dissolved."[6]

This view was later championed by Lothar Perlitt (1969), Ernst Kutsch (1973) and lately E.W. Nicholson (1986). As proponents of Wellhausen's view, they strongly defended the late Deuteronomistic nature and meaning of the Hebrew concept of 'berith' (covenant). This covenant stood as a characterization of Israel's relationship with God. But this relationship was no more than one of a unilateral obligation imposed by Yahweh and accepted by Israel.

For them the entire Deuteronomistic concept of the covenant is one of a conditional agreement between Yahweh and Israel. Failure to stick to the terms of this covenant would inevitably lead to serious retribution and even separation. Judaism has always rested upon the Deuteronomistic concept of the covenant, which was understood as being conditional in character. However, the Deuteronomistic literature in the Old Testament consists of the book of Deuteronomy, including what is known as the Deuteronomistic history which consists of the books of Joshua, Judges, 1 and 2 Samuel, 1 and 2 Kings. The message of the book of Deuteronomy is 'this is the way Yahweh made the covenant with Israel'. The message in the Deuteronomistic history is 'this is what happened to Israel when she failed to keep that covenant'.

3　I was particularly astounded by the discovery of the origin of the divine ownership of land, which was deeply rooted in henotheism. Until the post-exilic period, the concept of monotheism, i.e. that the God of Israel is the only God of the universe, had not yet been accepted in ancient Israel. In common with all her henotheistic

[6] Julius Wellhausen, *Prolegomena to the History of Israel*, Edinburgh: Adam & Charles Black, 1884, pp. 417f.

neighbouring nations, ancient Israel acknowledged that Yahweh her God was supreme, but admitted there were other gods. To give but a few examples:

(a) When Gideon destroyed the altar of Baal the townspeople recommended that he should be put to death for such a sacrilege (Judges 6:28-32). The Israelites who had settled in Oprah had begun to worship Baal instead of Yahweh. These Israelites were now worshipping one of the gods of their newfound lands, accepting by their practice that different gods had their own territory.

(b) When Na'aman, the Syrian commander, recovered from his leprosy he asked to take home two mules' burden of earth from the land of Israel (2 Kings 5.1ff.), clearly the idea being that a god could not be worshipped outside his own territory.

(c) When David was forced to flee the country, he complained that he would no longer be able to worship the God of Israel but would have to worship other gods, ". . . *they have driven me today from my share in the heritage of the Lord, saying, 'Go, serve other gods'.*"[7]

Now, just as each nation was believed to have its own god, each god was believed to have his own nation and his own territory. In a world of territorial deities, the territory was usually a gift of the god to his own nation, and Yahweh, the God of Israel, was no exception.[8] The book of Judges tells us that Jephthah sent a message to the king of Ammon with the following words: "*Will you not possess what Chemosh your god gives you to possess?*"[9] Obviously, even Jephthah recognized that, just like Yahweh in relation to Israel and the land, there was another god elsewhere who had the authority over his people and his land. But there is a difference in this respect between ancient Israel and other nations. This difference is summed up in the words of Louis Rabinowitz: "With regard to all other nations, their right appears unconditional. With regards to the Jewish people, it is conditional, depending upon the moral standards which they maintain."[10]

---

[7] 1 Sam. 26:19. See also Solomon Zeitlin, *Studies in the Early History of Judaism*, KTAV Publishing House, Inc. (New York, 1975), Vol. 3, pp. 3-7.

[8] See Lev. 25:23; Ps. 85:1; Isa. 14:2; Jer. 2:7; Hos. 9:3; Joel 2:18.

[9] Judg. 11:24. Curiously, Chemosh was the god of the Moabites, not the Ammonites, whose chief god was called Milcom, (or Molech – 1 Kgs. 11:5,7).

[10] Louis Rabinowitz, 'Conditional Right to the Land', Jerusalem Post, April 28, 1977.

We finally come to what are known as *'the Songs of the Servant'* in the book of Isaiah.[11] It is outside the scope of this paper to deal in detail with this particular subject. Suffice it to say that *'the Songs of the Servant'* leave the reader with the strong impression of a sublime personality (if the term personality is allowed). That personality, which the Targum equates with the Messiah (and was later perceived by the Church as Jesus Christ),[12] transcends Israel herself, her nationalism and her territory. Indeed, even her old covenant is replaced by a new and eternal one.[13]

On April 1991 I submitted my Dissertation to the Faculty of Divinity of Glasgow University, and on July of that year I graduated with the degree of Master of Theology (MTh). It was a very joyful occasion, and I could only wish that Betty had been there to share my joy of that achievement. In a sense, it was an achievement which was realized despite extraordinarily tough and painful circumstances. Hemmed round with dilemmas, tripped up with doubts and frustrated by loneliness I simply refused to be discouraged. When everything seemed to be falling apart, I calmly decided that a sense of duty must remain. Again and again it has simply been that sense of duty which has kept men on their feet. One would not be wide of the mark to add that 'a sense of duty' is one of God's demands.[14]

---

[11] Isa. 42:1-4; 49:1-6; 50:4-11; 52:13 – 53:12.

[12] See L. Gillet, *Communion in the Messiah: Studies in the Relationship Between Judaism and Christianity* (Lutterworth Press 1942), pp. 94f.; W. Manson, *Jesus the Messiah*, Hodder & Stoughton, London 1943, pp. 168ff.

[13] Heb. 8:13.

[14] Lk. 17.10.

Chapter 21

A MEMORABLE CULMINATION

"Then Samuel took a stone and set it between Mizpah
and Shen and called the name of it Ebenezer, saying,
'Hitherto hath the Lord helped us'."

(1 Samuel 7:12)

Shortly after my graduation, St Andrews Parish church of Fauldhouse decided that it was high time to sell the old manse and the land on which it stood, and build a modern one. About the end of June 1992 a brand-new modern manse was built, and by early July I moved into it. After seven years residence in a creaky and draughty old Victorian manse, I was now living in a splendidly modern and comfortable house. I could not help reminding myself that the good Lord had surely rewarded my long patient endurance with a modern and highly delightful one. As a result, I had resolved that only my time of retirement would see me leave that lovely manse. However, I seemed to have forgotten the maxim which says, 'Man proposes but God disposes'.

Some months later I had been going through a brief difficulty (which may be common to any minister), when an old friend of mine phoned me from Prestwick. He informed me that the Parish Church of John Knox in Stewarton was vacant. He told me that this Church, which is within the bounds of the Presbytery of Irvine and Kilmarnock, was thoroughly evangelical and charismatically inclined. The credit for that goes to the Revd George Campbell who had brought it to that spiritual level. Moreover, from the annals of the Church of Scotland one would know how associated this church was with what was historically known in mid-19th century as *'The Stewarton Case'*.[1]

When I heard this piece of news I was on my eighth year as minister of Fauldhouse St Andrews Parish church. Needless to say

---

[1] John Cunningham, *Church History of Scotland* (James Thin, Edinburgh 1882), Vol. 2, pp. 523f. Also Thomas Cassels, *History of John Knox Church, Stewarton*, 1925.

there were friendly voices that described the above-mentioned vacancy as a golden opportunity and urged me to apply for it at my earliest possible convenience. I talked to some of my colleagues about this matter and they were positive and encouraging. I also talked to the Revd P.G. Thomson, under whom I had served my probationary period. As one who knew well all the churches within the bounds of the Presbytery of Irvine and Kilmarnock, he had everything good to say about John Knox Parish Church in Stewarton. One of his last words to me was, "That church seems to be cut out for you, Sam!"

His words were prophetic. But it was the last thing that would have crossed my mind when he said that. At that moment in time I found myself on the horns of a dilemma.

A Crucial Decision

There is a sense in which a change of a clergyman from one charge to another can be a helpful and most refreshing move. In my case, however, a move from my Parish church was not something that had even crossed my mind. There were two reasons for that. First, with Betty's death I seem to have gone through what may be called a psychological paralysis. Without Betty I simply had neither the desire nor the will to move anywhere else. Second, during my eight years as Parish minister in Fauldhouse, a remarkable bond of love and amity had developed between me and most of my congregation. Being alone I considered my Parish church family as my own family. I could be forgiven for thinking that of all congregations within the bounds, mine was the best one!

A few years after Betty's death, the task of keeping my house clean and tidy had become too much for me. Consequently, when it became known that I needed some help two ladies from my congregation responded – Mrs Janice Ramsay and Mrs May Henderson. They decided to take care of the manse one day a week. Janice could do one week and May the following week. I was profoundly touched and grateful to these ladies for their willingness to help me. What they did served only to enhance my endearment for my congregation.

Sadly, shortly afterwards May was diagnosed with terminal cancer of the lungs and decided to withdraw. A couple of months later she passed away. After May had withdrawn owing to her grave illness, Janice told me that she would be happy to take care of the manse once a week on her own. I could not help feeling a combined sense of appreciation and embarrassment. Here was a lady who was doing all this for nothing. She had from the outset strongly refused any payment for the work she was doing for me. She had determined that her work, as she put it, "would be a gift to the Lord". According to her, my teaching ministry had done much to consolidate and enrich her spiritual life. But, as far I was concerned taking people's practical kindness for granted was not my trade mark. I soon found ways in which I could be kind enough to reward her kindness which by far had surpassed mine.

"Gratitude," said J.B. Massieu, "is the memory of the heart." As long as I live I shall remain eternally indebted to Janice for the care and the help she had given me. Indeed, I shall always remember and appreciate the remarkable value of her true worth. Her profound faith in the Lord and her unfaltering reliability I had seldom seen in others. Because of these and other noble qualities and characteristics I found myself secure and in good hands. Moreover, if I ever needed to seek her mind about one thing or another, I was sure to get a good opinion or a sound advice.

Now, being on the horns of a dilemma as to whether or not I should apply for the vacant charge of Stewarton John Knox, I had no choice but to pray hard for divine guidance. I found myself pulled in two directions: On the one hand, I had been quite happily settled in my Fauldhouse Parish church for almost eight years. I had also been enjoying the comfort of my recently built new manse. To crown it all, Janice had thus far been my God-given helper the like of whom would be rare among mortals. How could I possibly leave my church family after having been a father figure to them for a reasonably long time?

On the other hand, I had heard a great deal of wonderful things about Stewarton: John Knox Parish church. Its profound evangelical life and its outgoing evangelistic activities had an irresistible appeal for me as one belonging to the evangelical wing of the Church of Scotland. After all, I wondered if perhaps the time had come when a refreshing move to another Parish church might be just what the Lord wanted. I prayed a lot about this matter, and there were times when I felt somehow disposed to the idea of applying for that vacant charge.

But a lingering doubt remained. So, I wanted to seek Janice's mind on this matter. As a fine Christian and elder of the Church, I very much knew and appreciated the value of her honest opinion. I even went a little further and decided that whatever her answer might be I shall take it as an instruction from the Lord. Having listened carefully to all that I told her about Stewarton: John Knox, her simple answer was, "Go for it". She also added that "should the Lord call you to that Church and you still need my help, then as long as I am able, I shall gladly travel to Stewarton once a week to work for you."

I was overwhelmed both by her positive answer regarding this charge and by the gracious offer of her continued help. Looking back, her words had eliminated any reluctance I might have had, and I took that as a signal from God that I should go ahead and apply for that charge. True, God does speak to us directly from His word, but it is also true that He sometimes speak to us through individuals. He did exactly that as I was struggling to reach a crucial decision.

A Step of Faith

About the end of January 1993 I sent my application together with my CV to the Vacancy Committee of Stewarton: John Knox parish church. Two or three weeks later I received a call from the Vacancy Convener to say that the whole Vacancy wished to come and hear me on Sunday the 28th February, and afterwards meet with me.

I remember how extremely cold that Sunday morning was. And with wide spread ice covering the roads to Fauldhouse, I was quite worried the Vacancy might cancel their planned visit. I was soon relieved to learn of the Committee's arrival. The roads must have been well gritted the night before or very early that morning. As I stood that Sunday morning before the Vacancy Committee who were scattered here there among the congregation, I felt an enormous sense of courage and peace in my heart. Regardless of the outcome, I was prayerfully mindful throughout that service that I was there essentially to commend Christ and glorify Him and not to sell myself. Needless to say the consciousness of God's presence was so real in the service that Sunday morning. I took for my sermon our Lord's letter to the Church of Laodicea (Rev. 3:14-22) and spoke passionately of its immense relevance for our church today. As a result a good number in the congregation were touched, including the Vacancy Committee, as I learned afterwards.

After the morning service the meeting with the Vacancy members took place in the manse, and was opened with prayer. I was pleasantly surprised to see young people among them. The atmosphere of our meeting was very relaxed and cheerful. It is outside the scope of this paper to describe in detail the issues that we discussed. Suffice it to say that our discussion did not take the form of a negotiated business agreement based on what they liked and what I liked. It was rather a discussion between two who were of kindred spirit – I was of the evangelical wing of the Church and so was the congregation that the Vacancy represented.

Throughout our discussion it was abundantly clear as to the theological line and the evangelical character of the person they were looking for. However, their warm compliment about the message I preached without notes and from the heart was most gratifying. The entire interview took the form of a hearty spiritual discussion on the importance of the propagation of the gospel, the move of the Holy Spirit in the Church and the absolute necessity of evangelism. These things, I told them, have always been the theme and purpose of my ministry.

At the end, someone asked this question: "What is the one thing that you prize most in your ministerial life and work?" My answer was simple, "Preaching, teaching, visiting, counselling and youth work are among the many things which I prize in my ministry. But the one thing I also prize most is the unremitting support and prayer of my congregation. A ministry which is wrapped around in prayer has every chance of being an effective ministry". At this point I was asked to close with the benediction. This was the most joyful and uplifting Vacancy interview I had ever had in my ministerial career.

When the Vacancy Committee had left, I determined not to let my mind engage in a post-mortem session about the meeting, or waste my time anxiously wondering if Stewarton: John Knox would call me to be their minister. Instead, I decided to attend to my ministerial duties as usual and leave the rest to God. I had faith to believe that my application for the vacant charge of that parish church was a rightly-guided step. There is a sense in which faith is the art of holding on to things which your reason has once accepted against all odds.

On Friday the 12th March I was invited to preach at Stewarton: John Knox parish church on Sunday the 18th April as sole nominee. It is extremely hard to describe how immensely delighted I was with that invitation. And for a few days that invitation was for me a subject of reflection that my application for that charge was indeed a rightly guided step. It was the outcome of a simple step of faith.

A God-Chosen Place

It is no exaggeration to say that from the moment I stepped into Stewarton: John Knox on Sunday the 18th April as sole nominee I knew in my own heart that it was the place of God's perfect choice for me. That morning my sermon was based on Luke 24:15, *"While they (the two Emmaus bound disciples) were talking and discussing together, Jesus himself drew near and went with them."* It was generally felt that God's present in the service that morning was unique. When the service was over I was escorted to the vestry to wait for the outcome of the vote. After a while I was informed that the congregation had overwhelmingly voted me as their new minister. A couple of weeks later the Presbytery of Irvine and Kilmarnock scheduled my induction service to Stewarton: John Knox. It was to take place on June the 24th 1993.

On June the 20th I took my last service at St Andrews Fauldhouse. For me, that service was a very sad occasion full of memories, among them the painful memory of Betty's death in April the 28th 1986, just ten months after my induction on July 3rd 1985. There was also the sadness of having to say good bye to my congregation most of whom had been exceptionally kind to me and faithfully supportive of my ministry throughout the last eight years. A deep sense of sadness also seemed to pervade the entire congregation that morning.

It is not easy for a congregation to lose their minister after a long time. After all, I am credibly informed that I had been the longest serving minister in that church since its foundation in mid-19th century. Also, the thought of moving into a new situation and residing among an entirely different people was naturally in the back of my mind and seemed to make me feel slightly uneasy. But the very thought of Janice's willingness to come weekly and take care of the manse was most comforting and reassuring. As a matter of fact, when I moved into the new manse in Stewarton on Monday June 21st, both Janice and her husband James of happy memory, came and stayed with me for three days. During those three days they organized my Stewarton manse in a most remarkable manner, for which I am most grateful to them.

As scheduled by the Presbytery my induction took place on Thursday June 24th. It was a moving occasion. In addition to the John Knox congregation, members from neighbouring churches were there. The induction service was also graced by the presence of many friends, some of whom I had not seen for a long time. Last but not least, a delegation from my former congregation of Fauldhouse kindly travelled all the way to Stewarton to attend my induction. It was also a loving gesture to convey their final farewell. I was deeply touched.

The induction was followed by a splendid reception during which a number of people gave speeches welcoming me as their new minister. Some of those speeches were quite humorous. A speaker told a story of a church-goer who said, "Our Vicar's sermons always have a happy ending. The moment they've ended everyone feels happy!"[2]

At first, I could hardly stop laughing. But on reflection I wondered what any congregation expect from their minister on Sunday. A touch of humour in any sermon can certainly be a refreshing ingredient to the theme of the sermon. The trouble occurs when a speaker drifts into foggy intellectual areas where his congregation cannot follow him. It is true to say that a preacher must get at his congregation much more deeply through their hearts and their emotions than through their minds and their intellects. It is obvious that this is just one of the marks that are missing in so much of modern preaching and modern theology. There is nothing worse than listening to a sermon or a theological lecture and suddenly finding a mist before your eyes. It was Radhakrishna, the great Indian thinker, who once said, probably to a group of Christian from the west: "Your theologians seem to me like men who are talking in their sleep". Of course, people can hardly make out what one is saying when he is talking in his sleep.

At this point I remembered what J.S. Whale once said. He talked about running around the burning bush taking photographs from suitable angles instead of taking off our shoes from our feet because the place whereon we stand is holy ground. He talked of theologians (and no doubt preachers) who put their pipes in their mouths and stick their feet up on the mantelpiece and talk about theories of the atonement instead of bowing down before the wounds of Christ. I realized at that moment that if I were to follow this line, then I will be unworthy of this God-chosen place.

---

[2] Years later I discovered that joke in Phil Mason's *Christian Crackers*: *Church Chuckles*, p. 70.

Making Room for God

Usually when the induction and the reception are over, there follows what is often known as the honeymoon period. It is that period in which the new minister is doted upon in a manner that is short of glorification. I have heard it said that in his first year the congregation idolize him, in his second year they dislike him, but in his third year they begin to understand him. So, his honeymoon period eventually comes to an end and he gets down to brass tacks.

Personally, I had not been aware of going through these three stages in this particular charge. In fact, I can only describe my entire thirteen years ministry in Stewarton: John Knox as an uninterrupted honeymoon period. The memory of John Knox parish church and its lovely congregation will remain indelibly stamped upon my heart and mind for the rest of my life.

With the induction and reception behind me, I indeed got down to brass tacks. Being aware that so far the church had had no evening or mid-week services, I decided first to propose to my Session of elders the possibility of starting Sunday evening services. I was aware that in addition to the statutory Sunday morning worship, the idea of starting evening services might not be favourable to the Session. After all, evening services were becoming extremely rare in the country at large, and where such services exist the attendance is most often quite small. To my delight the Session approved.

Then, I thought I would go a step further and suggest mid-week services, which would be held every Wednesday evening and would take the form of Bible study and prayer fellowship. I also recommended a 'covered dish' meeting (an American imported idea) on the last Wednesday of every two months. Couples or individuals would bring cooked meals to share with our invited guests. Afterwards a guest speaker (in most cases a minister), would share his personal testimony. He would simply tell us how he came to know the Lord and how he was called to the ministry. I was greatly heartened when the elders gave me their unequivocal approval.

The mid-week services continued steadfastly throughout my entire thirteen years ministry in Stewarton: John Knox. A good number of books from the Old and New Testaments were dealt with. I began each book with a clear and comprehensive introduction. For me, it was important to follow the remarkable advice of F.J.A. Hort. In his introduction to his unfinished commentary on 1 Peter he wrote: "To understand a book rightly, we want to know who wrote it, for what readers it was written, for what purposes, and under what circumstances."

The longest study I conducted was on the Gospel according to St John. It lasted well over two years, and which eventually turned into a book and was published shortly after my retirement in 2006 under the title *JESUS AS JOHN SAW HIM*. Preparing for mid-week Bible studies was by no means an easy task, but it was something which I enormously valued. Indeed, it was part of the 'brass tacks' which I thoroughly enjoyed. I have always been aware that a successful ministry requires hard work. There is the Roman maxim which says, '*Per ardua ad astra*' i.e. the way to the stars is always steep. "The gods," said Hesiod, "have ordained sweat as the price of all things precious."

My predecessor, the Revd George Campbell of blessed memory, had remarkably built that church to the level of an ardent evangelical and charismatically inclined congregation. As his successor, I simply entered into his labour.[3] He had been a source of great encouragement to me throughout my ministry. Later on when the Presbytery appointed me as his Pastor my life was abundantly enriched by his godly fellowship. I was also greatly impressed by his deep humility. On one occasion I informed him that I started doing something at the end of some Sunday morning services which was foreign to the Church of Scotland. From the look on his face I could tell he had an idea what it was. After all, his family were members of my Church and they must have told him. Nevertheless, he wanted to know what it was. "Since its foundation in 1841," I said, "I seem to be the first minister to introduce the *altar-call* in John Knox Parish Church. This is done at least once a month during the last hymn of the morning service."

He did not seem surprised at what I said, which indicated that he was already informed. "To my great surprise," I added, "the congregation's reaction was spontaneously positive as they saw needy individuals members coming forward to seek a prayer or a blessing by the laying on of my hands." George's most remarkable response was: "During my ministry at John Knox I had been reluctant to introduce a few things, and probably the *altar-call* was one of them." Then, he said to me with a broad smile, "Well, Sam,

---

[3] Jn. 4:38.

I'm gratified that you've taken the congregation a little further along the spiritual path!" I was profoundly touched and was able to learn something from his profound humility. It made me realise that the smaller we are the more room there is for God.

A Rewarding Trick

One never knows what would happen when he (or she) sets out on a journey. In the Old Testament there is a vivid story that proves that. It is found in 1 Samuel 9. As a young man, Saul set out with a servant to look for his father's donkeys which had strayed away. At the end of the journey he found, not the donkeys, but a kingdom; for before he returned home, the prophet Samuel had anointed him as king of Israel. Here was a young man who set out to look for his father's donkeys, and he found a crown. It must have been an exuberantly happy experience for him. In the case of each one of us the unforeseen and thrilling find can be something completely different.

During the few weeks after my induction into John Knox Parish Church, I spent at least the first part of each day walking the streets and meeting the Stewarton people. Apart from a couple who thought I was an Italian priest, the rest of the people knew who I was. Some greeted me with a nod and smile, but other did not hesitate to stop and talk to me. In either way the people's warm welcome and good wishes to me as John Knox's new minister was most gratifying.

One day I was happily walking up a street when I saw a tiny little boy strenuously trying to ring a doorbell of a house, but his little finger could not reach it. "Could I help you?" I said with a smile. The little boy was startled as he quickly turned and looked at me with his finger in his mouth. He was not unaware I had been nearby watching his fruitless struggle. "Do you want me to ring the bell for you?" I asked him. He nodded his little head vigorously in agreement. I stepped forward and rang the doorbell; and no sooner had I done that than he shouted, "Now, let's run!" Then he bolted into the distance as fast as his little legs could carry him. I stood there utterly dumfounded and completely embarrassed. I certainly could not run to catch him. After all, what would people think of a clergyman running down the street after a wee kid!?

As I looked round for a few seconds to see if anyone had just been watching the tragic comedy a lady opened the door. Before I could apologize and explain to her what exactly happened she joyfully yelled, "Oh, our new parish minister!" Then she rushed in to tell her family of what she thought was my intended visit! "Please do come in," she said as she returned with her husband and a young daughter. "We are greatly honoured by your ministerial visit, sir . . ." The family seemed very happy to see me.

Now, the way I had just been tricked followed by getting a warm welcome from a family I had never meant to visit, seemed mind boggling. However, as we chatted over a cup of tea, it transpired that the family were part of my flock but none of them had darkened the door of the church for a very long time. They told me that in their living memory I was the first minister to grace their home with a visit. They assured me that a lack of a ministerial visit was no excuse for being absent from church. Finally, they solemnly promised to return to church and never lapse again. Time proved that they were absolutely true to their word.

A few days later I saw the little 'speedy Gonzales' with his mother at the local Safeway! As soon as he saw me walking towards him, he hid behind her. "Hello, my wee pal," said I smiling tolerantly on the little guy. Pushing him in front of her, his mother snapped out, "Come on, don't be so shy and say hello back to the minister!" In spite of that he remained quiet and could not look me in the eyes.

"Do you know our wee Alex?" she curiously asked me with a smile. "Oh, I most certainly do!" I replied. Possibly being a school chaplain, the mother assumed I might have known him at one of my recent school services. Had I told her how I first got to know him, he would have been in deep trouble! "I just don't know what's wrong with him this time," she said. "He is normally such a good, happy and helpful wee boy." And like a shot back came my response: "He is indeed an exceptionally good and very helpful wee kid! Please take very good care of him."

As he walked away with his mother he turned and looked back at me with what appeared like a little smile. It might have been a way of saying thank you for not taking the lid off! In the silence of my own heart I regarded him as a lovable but a slightly mischievous little boy. Yet, he was a God-send. Had it not been for his trick, that family might never have been restored to Church. I still remember that incident not with a sense of embarrassment, but with an unwearied sense of amusement. I shall always regard the trick which he had played on me as a most rewarding trick!

The Core of the Problem

My trips to the USA, which began in 1976 have continued to the present day. The bond of love and spiritual relationship with a good number of my fellow American Christians have been the motivating factor in my long flight to the USA once or even twice a year. There have been times when the idea of skipping a year or two seemed advisable. But my good friends across the big pond will have none of it. After all, they have always covered my plane fares and provided me with their warm hospitality.

Moreover, a fair number of churches and assemblies always counted on my yearly ministerial visits to their congregations. At home, however, some of my friends and colleagues still consider me quite fortunate to be a frequent visitor to the USA. Yet, all good things come to an end, as the saying goes. There may come a time when, for one reason or another, I shall no longer visit the USA. But for the time being the long standing love of my good American Christian friends and my good state of health will not allow me to stop. On the whole, my trips to American have always been most enjoyable – except one.

On Monday September 10th 2001 I flew from Glasgow, Scotland, to Dulles airport, Washington DC. Waiting for me in the airport were Freeman Meadow and David Burkholder, faithful friends and men of profound spiritual calibre and sincere love. They drove me to a Motel near Elkton, Virginia, that evening and promised to pick me up for breakfast in the morning about 9.00 a.m.

Next day (Tuesday September the 11th) I got up about 8.00 a.m. and put on the TV for the News. Then I stood at the mirror both shaving and watching the CNN News from the TV behind me. At first, what I saw did not look like News. For me, it was unlike the CNN to show Hollywood films of apocalyptic proportion at that hour of the morning. Yet, the sight of planes flying into high buildings suggested that this was not a film, but something horrible was actually taking place somewhere in the world. Until now the sound of the TV had been low, but when I raised the volume a little higher and sat down to watch what was really happening, I was overwhelmingly appalled and terrified.

The horror that I was now witnessing on the TV has come to be known as the 9/11 attack, or rather attacks, on the USA by an Islamic terrorist group 'al-Qaeda'. They were a series of four coordinated attacks. Four passenger airliners were hijacked by 19 al-Qaeda terrorists most of them were Saudi nationals. Two of the planes, American Airlines Flight 11 and United Airlines Flight 175, were crashed into the north and south towers of the world Trade Centre in New York. Within an hour both towers, known as the twin towers, collapsed. A third plane, American Airlines Flight 77, was crashed into the Pentagon, causing a partial collapse in its western side. The fourth plane, United Airlines Flight 93, initially was steered towards Washington DC. This one crashed into a field near Shanksville, Pennsylvania, after its passengers tried to overcome the hijackers. In total, the attacks claimed about three thousand lives. The country was so traumatised that for almost a week no plane was allowed to occupy its airspace.

I was eternally grateful to my dear and long-time friends, Larry & Darlene Dickerson, who managed to find me someone to drive me to Charlotte NC, where I was scheduled to speak. That one was none other than my good friend Charles Queen, the Session Clerk of the evangelical Presbyterian church of Elkton. The entire world was shocked by such an appalling crime. For Bin Laden, the head of al-Qaeda, that crime was a religious duty and a noble service to God. It was a 'Jihad'.

Before 9/11 Bin Laden had been calling on the USA to remove its military bases from Saudi Arabia. Meanwhile, many Muslims were outraged at the permanent presence of Americans, British and French military personnel there. Although the USA was not engaged in a war with any Arab or Muslim country, the continued presence of its troops in the sacred land of Arabia was the basic motive behind the September 11th terrorist attacks. Moreover, Bin Laden and all devout Muslims were aware of the prophet Muhammad's dying order banning "the permanent presence of infidels in Arabia".[4] In fact, the USA and other European personnel were in Arabia at the request of the Saudi government and could leave only if ordered by the same

---

[4] Ahmad Ibn Hanbal, *al-Musnad* (Cairo 1995), Vol.18, No. 26230; see also Ibn Qaiyim al-Jawziyah, *Ahkam Ahl al-Dhimmah* (Beirut 1994), Vol. 1. p.176ff.

government. Al-Qaeda and most Muslims knew that very well. The blame should really have been laid at the Saudi government's door step, and that was not forthcoming. So then, Bin Laden's notion of the permanent presence of infidels in Arabia was designed either to expose the arrogance of the West or to create a pretext for launching a 'jihad' against it, which was exactly what happened. But the Jihadists like the Qaeda (or Isis and Nosra today) need no pretext for launching attacks against infidels. In Islam the 'Jihad' is an axiomatic article of faith and it is to continue until the end of time. To deny it constitutes apostasy. How did it all begin?

The prophet Muhammad embarked on spreading his message in Mecca, his birth place, around 610 A.D. His twelve years preaching in Mecca did not win him many converts. During that period he (and his followers) suffered a great deal of hardship from the Meccan people. In the face of their bitter opposition and rejection of his mission, his message was one of conciliation, tolerance and gentleness. The following passage is typical of this Meccan period:

> Invite (all) to the Way of thy Lord with wisdom and
> beautiful preaching; and argue with them in ways that are
> best and most gracious: For thy Lord knoweth best who
> have strayed from His path and who receive guidance. [5]

Shortly after his migration (i.e. *Hijrah*) to Medina in 622 AD, things began to change. No longer in a weak position as in Mecca, Muhammad was fortified by an increasing number of converts, so that in a short time he became the ruler and statesman of Medina. His position of power at this stage created a shift from peace and forbearance to permitting the believers to take up arms and fight in self-defence for the first time. And with the following verse, as Muslim scholars assert, the previous stage of peace and conciliation was abrogated:

> To those against whom war is made, permission is given
> (to fight), because they are wronged; – and verily, God is
> Most powerful for their aid."[6]

The third stage was marked by making the 'jihad' a binding duty on every Muslim, but only in the event of the enemy's military aggression. In this case strict limits must not be transgressed:

---

[5] Surah al-Nahl [16]:125.

[6] Surah al-Hajj [22]:39; See also al-Qurtubi, *al-Jami' Li Ahkam al-Qur'an al-Karim* (Cairo date?) Vol. 7, p. 4460.

Fight in the cause of God those who fight you, but do
not transgress limits; for God loveth not transgressors" [7]

The fourth and last stage was when the *'jihad'* became a binding duty against all unbelievers regardless whether they were the aggressors or not.

> *Fight those who believe not in God nor the last day, nor*
> *hold that forbidden which hath been forbidden by God*
> *and His apostle, nor acknowledge the religion of truth,*
> *(even if they are) of the people of the book, until they pay*
> *the jizya with willing submission and feel themselves*
> *subdued."* [8]

The *'jihad'* has now become not only a defensive war but more so an offensive war. This was evidently the basis for the early Islamic conquests which began with the prophet Muhammad in the 7th century. Within a short period after his death, the Muslims conquered a vast territory stretching from the borders of China and India, the Middle East, North Africa, Sicily and the Iberian Peninsula to the Pyrenees.

Most – if not all – of those conquests were historically conducted in a ruthless manner. In the early Islamic conquests of North Africa the Berbers apostatised from Islam time after time. According to Ibn Khaldun, they revolted against their Muslim conquerors twelve times and were put down with the utmost cruelty. Islam became firmly established among them only during the governorship of Musa Ibn Nusayr in the end of 7th century and the beginning of 8th century.[9]

However, such wars of expansion were only advanced by the devotion of the faithful to the concept of *'jihad'* as stated in the above-mentioned text.[10] And this is precisely what Isis, and Nosra and other

---

[7] Surah al-Baqarah [2]:190.

[8] Surah al-Taubah [9]:29; *'jizya'* is a poll tax i.e. which is a form of protection money. It was imposed only on 'the people of the book' i.e. Jews and Christians in the event of refusing to convert to Islam. However, if they refuse to pay the *'jizya'* they are put to death. Polytheists have only one of two choices – conversion or death. The recent treatment of the Yazidis by Isis in Iraq is a good example.

[9] Ibn Khaldun, *Kitab al-'Ibar wa Diwan al-Mubtada' was al-Khabar* (Beirut 1992), Vol. 1, p. 174; See also the English translation by F Rosenthal, *Muqaddimah Ibn Khaldun*, p. 333.

[10] For more detail see Ibn al-Qayyim al-Jawziyah, *Zad al-Mi'ad fi Huda Khayr al-'Ibad* (Cairo date?), Vol. 3, p.143.

Islamists are doing in Syrian and Iraq today. Unsurprisingly, a good number of Sunni Muslims consider the 'jihad' as the sixth pillar of Islam. At any rate, the 'jihad' in Islam remains an axiomatic article of faith. But in the light of the weakness of the Muslim world today, Islamic jurisprudence regards the 'jihad' as somehow postponed but by no means cancelled or abrogated.

The question is why do most Muslims still hold on tenaciously to the notion of 'jihad' in the 21ˢᵗ century? The answer is simply because it is an article of faith. Such a belief is certainly not consonant with human right, international law or with modernity as whole. In the tenth or eleventh century of our era the gate of 'ijtihad' was closed, as al-Ghazali declared.[11] It remains closed to this day. Finally, it is worth noting that historically monotheistic faiths like Judaism and Christianity have gone through what is known as 'reformation', but Islam has not yet had that experience. It has remained unchangeably the same, and that has arguably been the core of its problem.

A Token of Appreciation

The year 1998 had marked my very enjoyable fifth year ministry at John Knox Parish church. As I previously stated, my honeymoon period here had not ended on my first or second year after my induction. Indeed, I can honestly describe my entire thirteen years ministry in this church as an uninterrupted honeymoon period. I had simply revelled in the love and support of my congregation.

On a summer day of 1998 I had been in church browsing as before at the photos of all the previous ministers, beginning with the Revd James Cleland (1830–1839) to the late Revd George Campbell (1971–1992). As I looked carefully at their names and academic qualifications, I realised that none of them had a doctorate. As I turned to walk away, an unexpected idea sparked off in my mind. Might it not be a good idea if I were to do a PhD in honour of my good church? As I mulled over the idea during the next couple of weeks I became convinced that that would be something I should be very happy to dedicate to my church.

---

[11] Robert R. Reilly, *The Closing of the Muslim Mind* (Wilmington, Delaware 2011), pp. 119ff. *'Ijtihad'* means the exercise of independent reasoning unshackled by case law or past precedent. Also see, Ayaan Hirsi Ali, *Heretic: Why Islam Needs A Reformation Now* (Harper Collins Publishers USA 2015).

I was sure my congregation would be very pleased. Moreover, I made sure that my endeavour must be devoid of any sense of personal pride whatsoever. I was mindful of C.S. Lewis' brilliant words, ". . . the pleasure lies not in what you are but in the fact that you have pleased someone you wanted to please. The trouble begins when you pass from thinking, 'I have pleased him; all is well', to thinking, 'What a fine person I must be to have done it'. The more you delight in yourself . . . the worse you are becoming." However, apart from confiding in the Presbytery Clerk and two or three other close friends, I kept this matter in complete secrecy.

As an ex-Islamic student I have always been interested in the subject of apostasy in Islam, and particularly its widely known legislation of death penalty against apostates. After much consideration I resolved to make a research study into this subject for a PhD at Glasgow University. On my visit to Mona Siddiqui, Professor of Islamic Studies at the University, I received every encouragement from her to begin as soon as it is convenient. Shortly after registration in the spring of 1999 I began my research work with Professor Siddiqui as my supervisor. I remain eternally grateful for her advice and wise supervision during the whole period of my research work.

Briefly, my thesis focused almost entirely upon the issue of apostasy and punishment in Islam. My careful study examination of the Qur'anic verses on apostasy does not indicate any that clearly teach death penalty for apostasy. What is clear however is that apostasy is punishable not in this world but only in the hereafter. Evidently, there were apostates in the prophet Muhammad's own time, but he is never reported to have executed or punished any of them.

This research work has led to the discovery that the idea of death penalty for apostasy belongs entirely to the domain of tradition ('Hadith').[12] It is from here that some Muslim commentators have attempted to smuggle the death penalty idea into certain Qur'anic texts. Attention, therefore, is focused on the tradition 'Hadith' and its authenticity as a whole, and in particular on the authenticity of only two 'Hadiths' on apostasy and punishment. In the next and final step it is carefully demonstrated, by textual and mostly a historical-critical approach that these two traditions ('Hadiths') are themselves of doubtful authenticity and provenance. They are later accretions.

---

[12] Report of the words and deeds of the prophet and other early Muslims; considered the second authoritative source of revelation.

Indeed, they are most likely the product of Ikrima (d. 725 AD) and al-Awza'i (d. 774 AD). The signs therefore are that these traditions are of late Umayyad and early Abbasid provenance, and are deeply rooted in the politics (or theo-politics) of these two periods.

Enormous effort was expended to address this research study (a *desideratum*). At first, the obstacle to achieving this aim seemed insurmountable when it transpired that our Glasgow University library has little in terms of Arabic and Islamic literature. This called for a number of trips to Egypt to purchase the necessary material for this particular study. Secondly, the absence of any publication on this topic meant a great deal of reading and, had I not been a fast reader of the Arabic text, the realisation of this work would have been nigh impossible.

In the spring of 2002 I completed my research thesis under the title 'THE DEVELOPMENT OF APOSTASY AND PUNISHMENT LAW IN ISLAM *11 AH / 632 AD – 157 AH / 774 AD*', and it was duly submitted to the Faculty of Divinity of Glasgow University. A couple of weeks later the Faculty decided on the date of what is known as the '*viva*'.[13] The oral exam (the *viva*) was scheduled to take place at the Faculty of Divinity on Friday 22nd March 2002 at 2.00 p.m. The panel of examiners consisted of Professor David Thomas of Birmingham University as the external examiner; Allister Hunter, Professor of Old Testament of Glasgow University as the internal examiner; Dr Joseph Houston lecturer of Philosophy as chairman; and last but not least Professor Mona Siddiqui my supervisor.

The oral examination took nearly two hours after which I was asked to leave to be recalled a short time later. When I was recalled, Dr Houston as chairman congratulated me on the success of my research thesis, and so did the members of the panel. Then, Professor Thomas, the external examiner, pointed out that before the graduation in June there were a few sentences in two paragraphs, which he marked out, that needed to be toned down. That was done within a week under the supervision of Professor Hunter, and I was ready for my graduation in three months' time.

On Easter day March 31, 2002 the good news was announced from the pulpit by John Baxter, one of my excellent elders. After the warm

---

[13] This is a Latin phrase meaning literally "*with living voice*", but most often translated "*by word of mouth*". It is a term used as a reference to an '*oral exam*'.

congratulations on behalf of the congregation for the award of the PhD by Glasgow University, he pointed out that "this was specifically done by our minister in honour of John Knox Parish Church in Stewarton. The history of this Church has now marked him as its first PhD minister since its inception in 1841. And as a congregation, we feel enormously proud and deeply grateful for the honour he has brought to our church." The joyful surprise of the congregation that morning following John's announcement quickly burst into a warm standing ovation. I was profoundly touched by such a remarkable expression of love.

The great and memorable day of my PhD graduation took place on Wednesday July 10, 2002. It was indeed a grand achievement. Yet, it is an achievement which I never designed to use for my own personal benefit, but rather for the benefit of my own Church. After all, I had only four more years left with my congregation before my retirement. It was therefore a sincere token of my love for and appreciation of my congregation.

Staying as I Am!

It is true that everything in this world is subject to change and humans are no exception. *'Change and decay in all around I see'* says the hymn. "Wow, you haven't changed, man!" exclaimed an old friend who had not seen me for twenty seven years. "What keeps you so young and fresh?" he laughingly asked. After that a couple were amazed when I told them that next year I shall be 75. When they next asked what my name was I replied, "Peter Pan!"

Age is quite an undefinable thing. It really has very little to do with the date on one's birth certificate. The fact is that some people are hardly ever young, whilst others are hardly ever old. An ancient proverb says, 'whom the gods love, die young'. This does not suggest that those whom the gods love are taken away from this world in their early years. It simply means that if the gods love a person, no matter what age he is, and even if he goes beyond the three score years and ten, he still has the gift of essential youth.

However, age has never been a cause of worry to me, and in my interaction with all sort of people I noticed that for some people age can be a worrying factor. I observed that men and women particularly differ in their attitude to age. Men, for example, do not mind being asked about their age, and some might even tell you how old they are without being asked. But when they reach seventy and upward they would likely prefer not to talk about their age. On the other hand, ladies would prefer not to talk about their age, and some would even take exception if they are asked how old they are. But when they become octogenarians they will proudly tell you their precise date of birth!

Age has so far not wearied me, hence the reason perhaps why it has not worried me either! Some might relate it all to the genes. Apart from my mother who died in her early twenties, most members of my family lived to a very old age. For example, my maternal grandmother who died in later 1960s recalled in some detail the time when slaves were being sold in the market-square of our home town. My maternal grandfather, figures in the town's municipal record of 1880 as a young constable.[14] It is perhaps a mistake to associate longevity or short life with the genes.

On April 15, 2006 I retired from my charge in Stewarton. After a great evening farewell party organised by my good congregation, I drove to my new home in Kilmarnock. As I entered the house, the lingering joy of a couple of hours earlier seemed to change into a slightly sombre mood. The thought suddenly struck me that as from that moment I had no church or congregation or a pulpit to preach from. Sadly, I did not even have a family to rally around me and inspire me with the hope that when one journey ends another begins. There were no children to pat me on the back and say, "You've done well, Dad, and we are proud of you!"

Unfortunately, my middle aged daughter and son who currently live in England are seldom in touch with me. In the silence of my new house that evening I was somehow stunned for the first time to realize that in 1966 I arrived alone in this country to begin a new life, and now four decades later I began my retired life alone. In between life had been quite strange, full of ups and downs, failures and successes, sorrows and joys, battles and victories . . .

These and much more are the stuff of life from which no human can escape. In my case, whether during my university days or during my ministry I made sure that only a few people knew about some of these things in my life. But all the time I was confident in that text which says, *"Give all your worries and cares to God, for He cares about*

---

[14] Mustapha Bouchara, *Immigrations et Protections au Maroc 1863–1894* (Imprimaie Royale – Rabat 1987), Vol. 2, pp. 684f.

what happens to you".[15] Moreover, at my bed time I have always been careful to close the door on all the problems and worries of the day before I fall asleep.

Since my retirement in 2006, I have been careful to remain as busy and as active as I possibly can. In a retirement there can be a great deal of unhappiness, and most of it has its source in boredom. In this situation it is easy also to become a prisoner, or even a victim, of unhealthy thoughts. Therefore, I decided that if I spend most of my retired time dreaming of tomorrow and regretting yesterday, I will not find a great deal of time left for doing anything today.

It is said that time is so valuable that God gives only a moment of it at once, and He gives that moment but once in all eternity. Moreover, the thing which keeps a man healthy and sound and the thing which keeps him really alive is *interest*. My interest has always been reading and writing, walking, travelling to the USA for lecturing and preaching. I have pursued these things tirelessly right to the present day.

Lately, however, I have been a frequent visitor to my original native country of Morocco, and specifically to the historic cities of Marrakech and Essaouira. My interest has particularly been excited by the enormous transformation of this country since I left it in the summer of 1963. Thanks to King Muhammad VI and the current government of Pre-minister Ben-Kiran the country is experiencing an unprecedented period of freedom and stability whilst most of the Arab and Muslim world is in turmoil. Consequently, Morocco, its wonderful king, and its remarkable people have constantly been in my thoughts and prayers.

So then, between birth and death there is an interval. It is called 'life'. Through all circumstances I have enjoyed that interval and I still do. After retirement one may still have a fair time to live, then comes the time when he goes the way of all flesh. A Christian should not worry about that. "Take care of your life," said George Whitfield, "and God will take care of your death."

In truth, I have no fear of death. I simply believe in the death of fear. "*Whoever lives and believes in me*", Jesus said, "*will never die.*" And in St Paul's words, "*The last enemy that will be destroyed is death.*"[16] This point, among other things, has kept me confident and staying as I am.

---

[15] 1 Pet. 5:7 NLT.

[16] Jn. 11:26; 1 Cor. 15:26.

The Immutability of God

By God's immutability, theologically speaking, I mean that He cannot be changed by anything from without Himself, and that He will not change from any principle within Himself. As to His essence, His will, and His states of existence, He is the same from eternity to eternity. Thus, He is immutable in Himself.[17] In the words of St James, *"With Him there is no variableness, neither shadow of turning."*[18]

He changes things but remains unchangeable. In everything past, present and future He has the last word. On the other hand, we mortals are subject to the ravages of years, which for many will inevitably have their last word. This sounds pessimistic. Such pessimism will eventually pale into insignificance if we focus on the eternity of Christ, the author and finisher of our faith. He is *"the same yesterday, today and forever"*.[19]

The Christ of Yesterday

The text may best be understood in the context of the preceding verse. Here the Hebrew congregation are told to remember their leaders, their message and godly conduct and endeavour to imitate them. They have left this scene of time, but Christ is timeless. Learning from people of the past can be an incentive. But the greatest incentive of all is the unchanging Christ. The Psalmist prayed: *"A thousand years to you are like one day."*[20] Not long ago we entered a new millennium. To God a millennium is no more than a day to us. Yet, the events God initiated or established in a millennium are inextricably linked to those of the next, and the events of the next millennium will merely be an extension of the one before it. In all this we can see the indelible mark of God's active purpose in this world's history generally, and in the Church in particular. Spurgeon once wrote: "Christ is the great central fact in the world's history; to Him everything looks forwards or backward." In this way we are able to appreciate the meaning of 'the Christ of yesterday'.

The Christ of Today

This alone dispels any sense of pessimism and puts to flight all delusions. Human nature, yes, even common sense, admits that *'in the*

---

[17] A.A. Hodge, *Outline of Theology* (Paternoster Row, London 1886), p. 113.
[18] Jas. 1:17.
[19] Heb. 13:8.
[20] Ps. 90:4 (GNB).

midst of life we are in death'. In Christ the reverse is true. Calvary was a region of death that seemed to be saturated with God's absence. Hence Jesus cried, *"My God, my God, why have you forsaken me?"*[21] Yet, in the midst of death there was life. *"Today you will be with me in Paradise,"* Jesus said to one of His fellow sufferers.[22] The word *'today'* holds out the promise and the opportunity of hope instead of doom and gloom. Such a promise and opportunity are quite often underlined by that word *'today'*.[23]

> I've shut the door on yesterday
> And thrown the key away
> Tomorrow holds no fear for me
> Since I have found to-day.[24]

Step by step with Christ the crooked places will be made straight and doors will open up before us. I, among many others, can most decidedly rejoice because we have absolute confidence in **'the Christ of today'**.

The Christ of Forever

Not much ink has been spilt on the term *'forever'*. Scholars have tended to shy away from saying much about it. Any attempt on my part would make me look like the preacher who, instead of saying, "I want to expound this text," said, "I want to confound this text!"

Over the triple doorway of the Cathedral of Milan there are three inscriptions spanning the splendid arches. Over one is carved a beautiful wreath, ***"All that pleases is but for a moment"***. Over the other is sculptured a cross, and these are the words beneath: ***"All that troubles is but for a moment"***. But underneath the great central entrance in the main aisle is the inscription, ***"That only is important which is eternal"***. "All things flow, nothing abides," said Heraclitus. The days of our years also swiftly come and go. A good many of them are forgotten and good many of them remain unforgotten. It is vitally important not to forget that ***"Jesus Christ is the same yesterday, today and forever"***.[25]

---

[21] Mt. 27:46.

[22] Lk. 23:43.

[23] Lk. 19:5; Heb.3:7,13,15.

[24] Vivian Y. Laramore.

[25] Heb. 13:8.